Women Journalists at Ground Zero

Women Journalists at Ground Zero

Covering Crisis

Judith Sylvester
and
Suzanne Huffman

ROWMAN & LITTLEFIELD PUBLISHERS, INC.
Lanham • Boulder • New York • Oxford

ROWMAN & LITTLEFIELD PUBLISHERS, INC.

Published in the United States of America
by Rowman & Littlefield Publishers, Inc.
A Member of the Rowman & Littlefield Publishing Group
4720 Boston Way, Lanham, Maryland 20706
www.rowmanlittlefield.com

PO Box 317, Oxford, OX2 9RU, United Kingdom

British Library Cataloguing in Publication Information Available

Library of Congress Cataloging-in-Publication Data Available

ISBN 0-7425-1943-0 (cloth : alk. paper)
ISBN 0-7425-1944-9 (pbk. : alk. paper)

Printed in the United States of America

♾ ™ The paper used in this publication meets the minimum requirements of American National Standard for Information Sciences—Permanence of Paper for Printed Library Materials, ANSI/NISO Z39.48-1992.

From Judith Sylvester:
To those who rush in when others rush out.

From Suzanne Huffman:
To all whose voices have been silenced.

Contents

Preface   ix

Acknowledgments   xi

Part I: The Attacks

1   The Time Line of Events on September 11   3

Part II: The Women Journalists at Ground Zero

2   Kerry Nolan, WNYC Radio, New York City   11

3   Beth Fertig, WNYC Radio, New York City   17

4   Amy Eddings, WNYC Radio, New York City   23

5   Rehema Ellis, NBC News, New York City   29

6   Rose Arce, CNN, New York City   41

7   Judy Woodruff, CNN, Washington, D.C.   51

8   Susan Sachs, *New York Times*, New York City   59

9   Suzanne Plunkett, Associated Press, New York City   65

10 Amy Sancetta, Associated Press, New York City   73

11 Gulnara Samoilova, Associated Press, New York City   81

12 Beth A. Keiser, Associated Press, New York City   89

13 Madge Stager, Associated Press, New York City   99

14 Mika Brzezinski, CBS News, New York City   109

15   Susan Harrigan, *Newsday,* New York City   115

16   Charlotte Hall, *Newsday,* Long Island, New York   125

17   Cynthia McFadden, ABC News, New York City   129

18   Ann Compton, ABC News, White House Press Corps,
     Sarasota, Florida   135

19   Lesli Foster, WUSA-TV, Washington, D.C.   141

20   Elizabeth Cohen, CNN, Atlanta, Georgia   147

21   Miriam Falco, CNN, Atlanta, Georgia   151

22   Gabrielle DeRose, KDKA-TV, Pittsburgh, Pennsylvania   159

23   Emily Longnecker, WTAJ-TV, Altoona, Pennsylvania   163

24   Elizabeth McNeil, *People* Magazine, New York City   169

25   Fannie Weinstein, *People* Magazine, New York City   173

Part III: Conclusion

26   Coming to Conclusions   179

Appendix A   Biographies   187

Appendix B   Dart Center for Journalism and Trauma   195

Index   201

About the Authors   207

Art Credits   209

Preface

A history of the twentieth century in the United States can be told through the images seared into the collective consciousness of its citizens by the mass media. Those images were captured by newspaper, magazine, and newsreel photographers and later by television film and video crews and tower cams. They were described in words by the writers and reporters who were eyewitnesses.

Those unforgettable images include the explosion of the *Hindenburg* zeppelin on May 6, 1937; the Japanese bombing of Pearl Harbor in Hawaii on December 7, 1941; the D-Day invasion of the Normandy coast of France on June 6, 1944; and the U.S. atomic bombing of Hiroshima, Japan, on August 6, 1945.

Those images include the November 22, 1963, motorcade assassination of President John F. Kennedy in Dallas, Texas, the days of shock and national mourning that followed, and the poignancy of then-toddler John F. Kennedy Jr. saluting the funeral cortege of his father.

They include happy times, such as when the nation celebrated the end of World War II with the image of a sailor kissing a nurse in New York's Times Square on August 15, 1945; U.S. astronaut Neil Armstrong stepping out onto the surface of the moon on July 20, 1969; and the tall ships armada sailing into New York harbor on July 4, 1976, marking the nation's bicentennial. They include such televised rituals as the Macy's Thanksgiving Day Parade, the Super Bowl, and the Olympics.

But so many of the collectively remembered images are tragic ones: the 1979 taking of American hostages in Iran; the 1986 explosion at launch of the Space Shuttle *Challenger* with teacher-astronaut Christa McAuliffe and six other astronauts on board; the 1995 truck bombing of the Murrah Federal Building in Oklahoma City, Oklahoma; and the school shootings in Jonesboro, Arkansas, in 1998, and in Littleton, Colorado, in 1999, among others.

Now what is forever etched into the collective consciousness of all U.S. citizens in the twenty-first century is the awful image of One World Trade Center on fire in New York City after it was deliberately rammed by a hijacked commercial jet. While we were focusing on that horrific television image and struggling to comprehend it, a second hijacked commercial jetliner rammed into Two World Trade Center. Before the morning was over, both 110-story World Trade Center towers had collapsed, taking thousands of workers, visitors, firefighters, and police officers to their deaths before our eyes. In the chaos of that September morning, a third commercial jetliner dove into the Pentagon outside Washington, D.C., and a fourth nose-dived into a rural Pennsylvania field.

That awful day was Tuesday, September 11, 2001. These are the stories of twenty-four women who were called on to cover this story at Ground Zero. By Ground Zero, we broadly mean the site of the World Trade Center towers in New York City; the command post, hospitals, and triage centers that were close by; the site of the Pentagon outside Washington, D.C.; other threatened sites in the nation's capital; and the field in rural Pennsylvania where the fourth airliner went down. These journalists worked for television networks and local stations, for national radio networks, for the wire services, and for major national and daily newspapers and magazines. Every one of these women was called on to do extraordinary work on September 11, 2001, and the days immediately following. These are their stories based on personal interviews, televised interviews, and the coverage itself.

While we realize we have not told the story of every woman who covered this story, we have made a concerted effort to interview a representative sample of them.

Acknowledgments

We wish to thank our editor, Brenda Hadenfeldt, and Suzanne's colleague Phil Seib, who introduced us to her; Judith's dean, John M. Hamilton, and associate dean, Ralph Izard, for their advice and support; Suzanne's faculty colleagues and students at Texas Christian University; Judith's faculty colleagues and students at Louisiana State University, especially Ryan Goudelocke, our research assistant; the publicists and news directors and others who introduced us to these women and helped us secure photographs; and our family members, who were helpful and patient.

I

THE ATTACKS

1

The Time Line of Events on September 11

UNITED STATES OF AMERICA

September 11, 2001, Eastern Daylight Savings Time. (Some of the following times are approximate.)

8:00 A.M., Boston, Massachusetts: American Airlines Flight 11 lifts off from Logan International Airport. The Boeing 767-200, loaded with twenty thousand gallons of jet fuel for a transcontinental flight, is bound for Los Angeles with eighty-one passengers and eleven crew members on board. The plane heads west, over the Adirondacks, before taking a sudden hundred-degree left-hand turn to the south and barreling down along the Hudson River toward the heart of New York City. In the cabin, a flight attendant makes a telephone call to the American Airlines Operations Center warning that a hijacking is in progress.

8:14 A.M., Boston, Massachusetts: United Airlines Flight 175 takes off from Logan International Airport. The Boeing 767-200, carrying more than ten thousand gallons of jet fuel for a transcontinental flight, is bound for Los Angeles with fifty-six passengers and nine crew members on board. When it passes the Massachusetts-Connecticut border, it makes a thirty-degree turn to the south, and then an even sharper turn, and bears down on Manhattan. A passenger makes a cell phone call to his father, saying the plane is hijacked and is going down.

8:21 A.M., suburban northern Virginia: American Airlines Flight 77 departs from Washington-Dulles International Airport, twenty-six miles west of downtown Washington, D.C. The Boeing 757-200, loaded with thousands of gallons of jet fuel for a transcontinental flight, is bound for Los Angeles with fifty-eight

3

passengers and six crew members on board. It heads west but does two very unusual things. Over Kentucky it begins a 180-degree turn and heads back to Washington. Then the plane's transponder is turned off. Barbara Olson, a television commentator traveling on Flight 77, manages to reach her husband, Solicitor General Theodore Olson, by cell phone and tells him that there are hijackers on board armed with knives and a box cutter.

8:42 A.M., Newark, New Jersey: United Airlines Flight 93 departs from Newark International Airport. The Boeing 757-200, loaded with eleven thousand gallons of jet fuel for a transcontinental flight, is bound for San Francisco with thirty-seven passengers and seven crew members on board. The plane is forty-one minutes late taking off because of the airport's heavy morning traffic; it misses its scheduled departure time of 8:01 A.M. As it passes south of Cleveland, Ohio, it takes a sudden, violent left turn and heads inexplicably back into western Pennsylvania. Air traffic controllers try to reach the crew via radio. There is no response. A passenger on United Flight 93 makes a cell phone call saying, "We are being hijacked." Another passenger, thirty-one-year-old Jeremy Glick, calls his wife on a cell phone and tells her that he is going to rush the hijackers. And thirty-two-year-old Todd Beamer asks an Airfone supervisor in Chicago to recite the Lord's Prayer with him. When they finish the prayer, Beamer asks the Airfone supervisor to stay on the line. Then she hears him say, "Let's roll!"

8:44 A.M. approximately: Officials at NORAD (North American Aerospace Defense Command), notified by the FAA (Federal Aviation Administration) that the two airliners from Boston have been hijacked, scramble two F-15 fighter jets from Otis Air National Guard Base in Cape Cod, Massachusetts.

8:46 A.M., New York City: American Airlines Flight 11, flying at over 400 m.p.h., slams into the north face of One World Trade Center, the north tower, 110 stories tall, and explodes in a fireball. Television and radio helicopters are in the air, as they normally are, covering weather and the rush-hour morning commute. CNN begins broadcasting live pictures of the World Trade Center within three minutes. People's first thoughts are that this is a terrible accident.

9:03 A.M., New York City: United Airlines Flight 175, flying at an extremely high speed for its low altitude, over 500 m.p.h., hits Two World Trade Center, the south tower, 110 stories tall, and explodes. CNN continues airing live pictures. A growing television audience is watching, stunned. People are now beginning to realize that what is happening is no accident.

Hundreds of news reporters, producers, writers, and photographers throughout New York City, who themselves have been watching TV, begin making their way from their apartments and homes and offices to the site of the World Trade Center complex in Lower Manhattan. By now, almost every TV camera in the city is trained on the Twin Towers.

Shortly after 9 A.M., Sarasota, Florida: President George W. Bush, seeking support for his education bill by visiting a class of second graders at Emma E. Booker

The south tower begins to collapse. Photo by Gulnara Samoilova

Elementary School, is notified of the increasing gravity of the situation in New York. He calls the plane crashes "an apparent attack on our country."

9:24 A.M.: NORAD officials, notified by the FAA that the flight from Dulles has been hijacked, scramble two F-16 fighter jets from Langley Air Force Base in Virginia.

9:32 A.M.: The New York Stock Exchange, located in Lower Manhattan near the World Trade Center, suspends trading and closes.

9:40 A.M.: The FAA orders the entire nationwide air traffic system shut down. All flights at U.S. airports are stopped. All nonmilitary planes are grounded, and all flights in the United States are canceled. Planes in the air are ordered to land immediately.

9:45 A.M., Arlington, Virginia: American Airlines Flight 77 dives into the west side of the Pentagon, where Army personnel are contacted. One of the building's five sides collapses in a fireball fed by jet fuel. Secretary of Defense Donald Rumsfeld is at work in the Pentagon. Vice President Dick Cheney and National Security Adviser Condoleezza Rice are at work in the White House. Speaker of the House Dennis Hastert and Senate Majority Leader Tom Daschle are on Capitol Hill; so is First Lady Laura Bush. Secretary of State Colin Powell is on a diplomatic trip in Lima, Peru. Federal Reserve Chairman Alan Greenspan is in a plane over the Atlantic en route from Switzerland to the United States.

9:55 A.M., Sarasota, Florida: Air Force One, carrying President Bush, takes off on a zigzag course to Barksdale Air Force Base, a secure military base outside Shreveport, Louisiana. An extra fighter escort is added. Thirteen members of the press corps are on board. In Washington, the White House and the U.S. Capitol are evacuated.

9:59 A.M., New York City: The south tower of the World Trade Center collapses in a plume of pulverized ash and debris, trapping hundreds of rescuers and thousands of workers in the building and endangering those on the streets.

By 10:00 A.M. all bridges and tunnels into New York City close. All financial markets in the United States close.

10:10 A.M., rural Somerset County, Pennsylvania: United Airlines Flight 93 crashes just north of the Somerset County Airport, eighty miles southeast of Pittsburgh. The plane dives nose-first at full speed, drilling a crater ten feet into the earth.

10:24 A.M.: The FAA reports that all inbound transatlantic flights are being diverted to Canada.

10:28 A.M., New York City: The north tower of the World Trade Center also collapses, trapping still more rescuers and thousands of workers in the building and further endangering those on the streets.

12:04 P.M., Los Angeles: Los Angeles International Airport, the original destination of three of the hijacked flights, is evacuated and closed.

12:15 P.M., San Francisco: San Francisco International Airport, the original destination of one of the hijacked flights, is evacuated and closed.

1:44 P.M.: President Bush leaves Barksdale Air Force Base for Nebraska's Offutt Air Force Base and an underground nuclear command center near Omaha, home to the U.S. Strategic Air Command. The navy dispatches aircraft carriers and guided missile destroyers to New York and Washington. Around the country, fighters, airborne radar planes, and refueling planes scramble. NORAD goes on its highest alert—Force Protection Condition DELTA. U.S. borders with Canada and Mexico close. President Bush will leave Offutt Air Force Base at 4:30 P.M. and return to Washington, D.C., where he will address the nation from the Oval Office at 8:30 P.M., vowing to track down and punish the terrorists responsible for the day's "evil acts of despicable terror."

Since 8:46 A.M., reporters throughout the United States have been scurrying to cover this most murderous terrorist attack in U.S. history. An ever-growing broadcast audience is watching these events unfold on television and radio. People throughout the country call relatives and friends and tell them to "turn on the TV." Cell phone lines are jammed. Major Internet servers report overloads as millions log on. Malls shut down. Schools and businesses close. High-rise landmarks—such as the Sears Tower in Chicago, the Space Needle in Seattle, and the Trans-America Pyramid in San Francisco—evacuate and close. Churches open for prayer services. Broadcast networks cease regular programming and begin round-the-clock, commercial-free coverage. As the story breaks, all the major TV news organizations decide to share video footage and satellite feeds, agreeing that it is more important to get information out than to compete this awful day.

Among those covering this story are women journalists who witness gruesome scenes, unrelenting dust and debris, and the heat of fires. *Newsday*'s Susan Harrigan remembers, "I got off the subway at Wall Street and walked into hell."

These are the personal stories of those journalists, the women at Ground Zero, and how they covered the events of September 11, 2001.

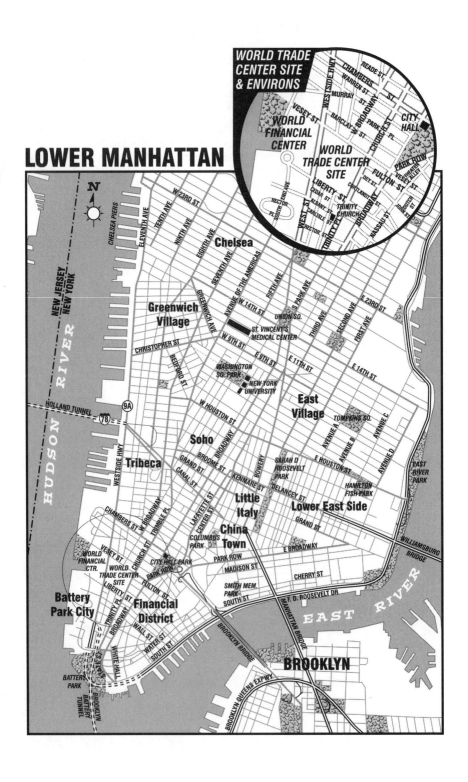

LOWER MANHATTAN

WORLD TRADE CENTER SITE & ENVIRONS

WORLD FINANCIAL CENTER

WORLD TRADE CENTER SITE

CITY HALL

PARK ROW

READE ST
CHAMBERS ST
WARREN ST
MURRAY ST
VESEY ST
BARCLAY ST
PARK PL
W. BROADWAY
WEST SIDE HWY
WEST ST
CHURCH ST
DEY ST
FULTON ST
VESEY ALLEY
VERMESER

LIBERTY ST
CEDAR ST
ALBANY ST
CARLISLE ST
RECTOR PL
SOUTH END AVE
RECTOR ST
CORTLANDT ST
TRINITY CHURCHYARD
BROADWAY
NASSAU ST
JOHN ST
MAIDEN

TRINITY PL

N

CHELSEA PIERS

NEW JERSEY
NEW YORK

HUDSON RIVER

HOLLAND TUNNEL

9A
78

WESTSIDE HWY

W 23RD ST
ELEVENTH AVE
TENTH AVE
NINTH AVE
EIGHTH AVE
SEVENTH AVE
AVENUE OF THE AMERICAS
FIFTH AVE
S. PARK AVE

Chelsea

Greenwich Village

GREENWICH AVE
CHRISTOPHER ST
BEDFORD ST

W 14TH ST
UNION SQ.
ST. VINCENT'S MEDICAL CENTER
W 9TH ST
E 9TH ST
E 11TH ST
E 14TH ST

THIRD AVE
SECOND AVE
FIRST AVE
E 23RD ST

WASHINGTON SQ. PARK
NEW YORK UNIVERSITY

W HOUSTON ST

East Village

TOMPKINS SQ.

AVENUE A
AVENUE B
AVENUE C
AVENUE D

Soho

Tribeca

BROADWAY
BROOME ST
GRAND ST
CANAL ST
KENMARE ST
BOWERY

SARAH D ROOSEVELT PARK

E HOUSTON ST

DELANCEY ST

HAMILTON FISH PARK

EAST RIVER PARK

Little Italy

China Town

Lower East Side

GRAND ST

LAFAYETTE ST
CENTER ST
CHAMBERS ST
W. BROADWAY
TRIMBLE PL

COLUMBUS PARK
CITY HALL PARK
PARK ROW
MADISON ST
CHERRY ST
E BROADWAY

WILLIAMSBURG BRIDGE

VESEY ST
WORLD FINANCIAL CTR.
WORLD TRADE CENTER SITE
LIBERTY ST
FULTON ST
CHURCH ST

SMITH MEM. PARK
SOUTH ST

F. D. ROOSEVELT DR

MANHATTAN BRIDGE

EAST RIVER

Battery Park City

Financial District

TRINITY PL
BROADWAY
WHITE HALL
WATER ST
SOUTH ST
WALL ST
WATER ST

BROOKLYN BRIDGE

BROOKLYN

BATTERY PARK

BROOKLYN BATTERY TUNNEL

BROOKLYN QUEENS EXPWY

II

THE WOMEN JOURNALISTS AT GROUND ZERO

2

Kerry Nolan, WNYC Radio, New York City

Kerry Nolan began the morning of September 11 as she did most weekday mornings, packing her son off to school and letting the dog out in the yard to run. As the local host for the weekend *All Things Considered* and *Weekend Edition Saturday* and *Sunday* for WNYC, she normally spends weekday mornings at her home in Atlantic Highlands, New Jersey, directly across the Sandy Hook Bay from the Twin Towers. Her son had just left the house when the phone rang. The call was from a producer at the Canadian Broadcast Company (CBC) in Toronto for whom she had done some freelance work. "Are you watching CNN?" he asked. Kerry responded, "No. Should I be?" His answer was, "Well, you might want to put on the TV because you're going live to Canada in about five minutes." She quickly turned on CNN to see the first tower smoldering. She put a sixty-second spot together and went on the air live at nine o'clock.

"At that point I called NPR (National Public Radio) to see if they needed something from me because I had a feeling that everyone at WNYC was either scrambling to get out of the building or to get to the site. I had some distance and was more available," she said.

She then called NPR in Washington, D.C. "NPR said they were going to put me on the air with Bob Edwards, host of *Morning Edition,* in about ten minutes and to find out what I could." She repeatedly tried to call WNYC's newsroom located in the Municipal Building four blocks away from the World Trade Center, but she couldn't get through. Kerry finally made connections with a news producer. "I just asked, 'Where do you want me to go, and what do you want me to do? I'm on my way into the city.'"

But before she could make a move, the second plane hit the tower. "I'm watching this plane on television, talking to my producer. Apparently the impact and explo-

11

Kerry Nolan

sion shook our building. All I heard on the other end of the phone was 'Oh, my God! Oh, my God!' Then the phone line went dead," Kerry remembers.

She called NPR back to tell them what she knew. "They said they were going to put me on the air live with Bob Edwards. 'He'll ask you questions. Just tell him what you've seen. Tell him what you've heard.'"

She reported, "We don't know if this is a terrorist attack. We can make assumptions that it is either that or that something has gone horribly wrong with the air traffic control system." She described the smoke and flames she could observe from her own front door. She reported that the FBI was investigating a possible hijacking. She also said that firefighters likely would be unable to put out a fire so high up, probably at about the eighty-fifth floor. "This is going to be a long, hard day for people in New York," she concluded.

From there she said, "It just became a race to see how much information we could get, how quickly we could get it, and then disseminate it."

Kerry didn't make it into the city that day. "Since I couldn't get in, my job became covering the people who had escaped. Commuter ferries and local fishing vessels were pressed into service and brought people into the harbor in my home-town. A triage unit had been set up right down the street from me, and I was talking to people and watching them come off these boats just covered in ash and shell-shocked."

The people arriving were first seen by medical personnel, and if it was determined that they didn't need further treatment, they were then taken to a tent where they were essentially hosed down because "nobody knew what this ash contained. Every-one assumed it was asbestos." She covered these events the rest of the day and into the night.

The morning of September 12 brought some relaxation in travel restrictions, and Kerry was able to take a train to Newark and then another train to upper Manhattan. The subways were running. "The city was remarkably normal from midtown north. If you didn't know something had happened, you would think it was a Sunday just because there was no traffic. I was able to get around fairly easily. I was real surprised at that." Later in the week she was able to take a ferry service between the foot of Wall Street and her home. She said she wasn't hassled and was allowed to walk where she wanted because she had press credentials.

Kerry reunited with her newsroom colleagues, and they all "hit the streets." Armed with a notebook, a minidisk recorder, and a cell phone, Kerry spent the next two days going back and forth to various hospitals. "It was very chilling when you heard medical people say, 'We were ready . . . we had the triage unit set up . . . we waited . . . and *nobody* came.' That was their moment of truth. Ordering more body bags was what they were going to have to do. These people who were trained to save lives could do nothing.

"That was the saddest thing to me—to be at the hospitals and just watch them have all this stuff set up in the street ready to take people in and nobody came," Kerry said. "I think they only pulled five survivors out after the towers fell."

Sadly, the failure of some of those inside the building to grasp the enormity of the impact resulted in fewer people getting out. "There were people who were told everything's fine; go back to your desks. And a lot of people did that," Kerry said. "The fact that planes hit at roughly the eightieth to eighty-fifth floors meant there were twenty floors above that were never going to get out. That would be Windows on the World and Cantor Fitzgerald, Aon Corporation, and all the other companies on the top floors of the towers. People on the fifteenth floor thought, 'We've lost the top half of the building, but we're okay.' *Nobody* anticipated those buildings coming down."

Then the story direction began to change. "Once we realized that the first wave of horror was over, it then became 'How is the city responding? How is the city reacting—in different communities, the medical community, the arts community, the religious community?'" The WNYC reporters fanned out to get those stories.

"I was chasing down stories that were surfacing. There were so many false leads," she said. "There was at one point a report that under the rubble they had found an SUV with six firefighters inside alive." There was confusion as to which hospital the firefighters had been taken. "I went to Bellevue Medical Center, and everyone there who was in some position of authority confirmed everything—yes, this is what we are waiting for. I went to a news conference where the CEO of the hospital said they had been put on alert. He went into a very medical description of why you couldn't just yank these men out of the vehicle and bring them to the hospital and how this was going to take a long time." Kerry reported the story on the air for WNYC and NPR, using her cell phone. The whole thing was a hoax.

This story is but one illustration of the confusion and misinformation surrounding coverage in those first days. "There were so many people speaking for the city— for the police and the fire department. They hadn't quite coordinated any kind of pressroom yet. The mayor's Office of Emergency Management had been at No. 7 World Trade Center, and that building collapsed. So, it was a matter of finding a place where the press could get information. Those first two days we really didn't have a place like that. There were just so many wild goose chases," she said.

Kerry had never been through anything like this before. She admitted that she was afraid initially when it became obvious that a terrorist attack had occurred so close to home. "All the fear went, and I was able to focus when I heard that all the airports had been shut down and the air space secured. I thought, 'OK, nobody can come overhead and get me now. That's cool.'"

She said that was when she had to choose what to do next. "I had to go in and tell some stories and just record it," she decided. "For some reason you have this idea that nothing will happen to you because you're observing it. You're reporting on it. Of course, nothing is going to happen to you. Don't even think about that. You have this idea that there is a bubble of safety around you. Otherwise you wouldn't do it.

"This was an extraordinary moment. I hope I never go through anything like it again. I'm not a war correspondent. I'm not Christiane Amanpour [a CNN war correspondent], as much as I wish I were. The thing that just amazed me the most is that our news team just hit the streets and came back with amazing, amazing work. I am so proud to be working with these people and so proud that I work at WNYC. I've never before been involved in anything like this. It made me very, very glad that I do what I do," Kerry said.

Working was difficult in the aftermath as well. "The air smelled horrible. It was very acrid, like burning wires. We're all convinced we will have lung cancer in ten years," she said.

Kerry was at the New York Stock Exchange the day Wall Street reopened. The air was still very thick. She had to wear a surgical mask—although she said it didn't make much difference—and her eyes stung. She noted with irony that even though the air was "thick enough to cut with a knife," she saw several people walking past her on their way to work smoking. "I thought, 'Why bother? Breathe deep.' Here were these thin women in their Chanel suits going back into the Stock Exchange, sucking on their cigarettes. It was so bizarre. It was the first thing we could laugh at."

All the WNYC reporters spent the next several days in a state of high emotional and physical activity. "As a reporter you get this perverse adrenaline. When something horrible happens, you just go into high gear. You look at each other and just go, 'Isn't this amazing? Isn't this incredible?' Everybody was high on adrenaline for days," she said.

But there was the inevitable letdown after the first days had passed. WNYC had trauma counselors available on the Sunday following the attacks. However, Kerry said she and some of the others were feeling like it was too soon to process it. "Don't ask me to process this yet. If I have to sit down quietly and think about it, I'm not going back out. It was disturbing for a lot of people to have to acknowledge all of it." Although she noted that it was useful in some respects for some people, "For me it was way too early to start thinking about it." But she did have her moment a couple of days after September 11 when she returned home for the first time. "When I got home, my husband handed me a glass of wine, and I went out and sat on the front porch and just cried my eyes out. It was the first time I had done it. I think I'm not alone in that. Once you had a chance to catch your breath, just the enormity of it overwhelms you. It's huger than you can imagine. On a clear day, I can look out my front door and see Lower Manhattan. I still look at it and go, 'Oh, my God. They're gone. They're just *gone*.' I still can't wrap my mind around this."

The first night that Kerry managed to get into the city, she stayed at her sister and brother-in-law's apartment in Greenwich Village. "All we did all night was just watch the footage over and over again for every possible angle. People took pictures. We couldn't understand it. There was one piece of news footage that showed the second plane going into the building, and it was like slipping a letter in an envelope. How the hell did they do that? We still can't get over it." She thinks it will be a long, long time before this generation of New Yorkers recovers.

Kerry was extremely proud of the work her newsroom team produced. In fact, she had high praise for broadcast coverage in general. "TV did as well as it has ever done," she said. "CNN works well with raw footage. Peter Jennings was so terrific, cool and calm. He gave the facts."

She has returned to Ground Zero several times since the attacks. "The place is almost a tourist attraction," she said. "It was pretty macabre for the first few days after people were allowed down. The wreckage is so huge. The scale of this thing is just amazing. It really is hallowed ground. What the rescue workers have seen and what they continue to excavate have got to do enormous [psychological] damage."

Then, like most of the New York media, WNYC had to deal with the anthrax threat. The mail service was suspended as management tried to find the best way to screen incoming mail. "Personally, I'm not that afraid. I don't get much mail at work," Kerry laughed.

Although she didn't worry much about WNYC being a target, she acknowledged that reporters could be placed in jeopardy just doing their jobs. "New York governor George Pataki announced that spores had been found in his New York City office. We send reporters and interns over there all the time to pick up news releases and tapes, so it has touched us in some respects," Kerry said. "Reporters who have been there may have to be tested."

She said getting on the subway still gives her a twinge because New Yorkers have realized how vulnerable the subway system could be to attack. But that doesn't stop her. Some of her shock has given way to a more tangible emotion: anger. "All of us are just really angry. We feel very protective toward New York. It became very clear that we are all so in love with this place. There's nothing else like it on the planet. In the history of human civilization there has never been a city like New York—not Rome, not Athens, not Alexandria. How *dare* they do this to our city!"

3

Beth Fertig, WNYC Radio, New York City

September 11 was primary election day in New York. WNYC reporter Beth Fertig was sleeping late in her Greenwich Village apartment, because she expected to be out most of the night covering the candidates. At 9 A.M. a frantic phone call from her acting news director, Kevin Beasley, woke her up. He said, "A plane has crashed into the World Trade Center. You have to get here right away. I'm going to need you to find the mayor or the police commissioner."

"I was completely taken by surprise. I had no idea what he was talking about," Beth said. "A few weeks earlier somebody had tried to parachute onto the Statue of Liberty, so I thought, 'Oh, it's just another crank who did something stupid and bumped into the World Trade Center.' I didn't know it was a real plane."

She turned on her radio and remembers hearing Mark Hilan, WNYC's morning anchor, saying that a plane had struck the World Trade Center and that they didn't know what was going on. "But I still wasn't paying attention to how serious it was," she said. "I jumped into the shower. My boyfriend called and said 'Turn on CNN. You've got to see this.'"

She turned it on and saw the Twin Towers burning. "But I still was not processing it. I thought, 'OK, I'll go cover this, and then I'll go cover the election.'" She was still so far from understanding the magnitude of the situation that she dressed in a suit and sensible shoes, debating whether she should vote before or after she covered "this little fire."

As she was preparing to leave her Greenwich Village apartment, she heard Mark interviewing an eyewitness in the studio. "I remember thinking, 'That's really weird. I don't recognize that voice.'" She said the man turned out to be someone who had seen the attack from his window. Then she heard Mark say that he might have to leave the studio.

She ran downstairs and outside where she had a perfect view of the World Trade

Beth Fertig

Center. "I saw all these people in the street, staring. I looked south, and the Twin Towers were clearly visible to me with holes in them and burning—these big, black holes in each tower and flames shooting out. It was a perfect, blue-sky day, and the towers were perfectly illuminated by the sun—sparkling, silver towers with these holes in them and with flames jumping out. It was the most striking image. I didn't think it was real. I was looking at it like a surrealist painting. Then I realized, 'Oh, my God, this is *real!*' I could smell the smoke. Everybody's out in the street. It felt very weird." She realized in that instant that she was witnessing a huge tragedy.

With her bag of equipment, Beth ran to her train station on Bleeker Street. She was approximately one and a half miles and three stops from WNYC's studio in the Municipal Building, near city hall, and six blocks from the World Trade Center.

Beth was incredibly nervous and was still trying to process what was happening. She needed some sense of normalcy—something to distract her. "I thought, 'OK, I'll put on my mascara on the train. I'll just get to the studio and do what I need to do.'" Everyone on the train was behaving calmly, seemingly unaware of what was going on at the towers. But when she arrived at her stop, the air was thick with smoke. She saw "little bits of stuff" floating around her. That was when she realized she was not going to vote—that she was, in fact, facing a horrible day.

"Everyone was crowding around city hall. I ran up to our newsroom, and no one was there. The whole place had been evacuated except that Mark Hilan, [local] host of *Morning Edition*, was on the air. And a couple of our managers were here, and they were saying the building had been evacuated. So I ran downstairs again, and there were a few people from work standing outside the building." The people she met were from programming, none of whom knew whether any reporters had made it to the scene. None of their cell phones were working, and long lines were forming at the pay phones.

Since she was assigned to find the mayor or the police commissioner, she ran over to One Police Plaza, which was right behind WNYC's building. The building had been evacuated, and no one was allowed in. She ran to city hall, only to be told that that building also had been evacuated. The police told her that the mayor had gone to the World Trade Center to his bunker, called the Emergency Command Center, in Seven World Trade Center, next to the Twin Towers. "I'm thinking, 'He wouldn't be crazy enough to go to his bunker if the towers are burning, would he?'" The police insisted he was gone but told her that she hadn't heard it from them.

"So I ran back across the street to my little cluster of people from work, and I saw the program director, Dean Cappello. I said, 'Dean, I'm just going to go. I don't know what's going on, but I'm just going to go.'" He told her not to do anything crazy.

"I go running down the street, and I'm pushing through this crowd of thousands of people standing in the middle of Park Place alongside City Hall Park just staring at the towers burning. I heard from a news truck parked along the street that the Pentagon was hit. By this time, I'd figured out that it was terrorism, but I didn't know it was beyond New York."

She remembered pushing through the crowd and looking up at the southern tower, which she said "looked like a candle melting." She noticed that the building was getting a little shorter because the flames were eating it away.

She made it to the southern edge of City Hall Park's traffic circle, two blocks north and one block east of the World Trade Center complex. The buildings were looming above her. She was looking up at the towers when she was stopped by a female police officer, who told her, "I can't let you get any closer. We're telling people to turn away."

Beth showed the police officer her press pass and her microphone. "I'm like all indignant and shouting, 'I've got to get there. The mayor is there. I've *got* to get there! I've *got* to cover this!'" Unmoved, the officer said, "I can't let you go. I'm doing this to protect your life. We don't know what is going to happen next."

As if on cue, the first tower came down. "I hear this huge rumbling noise like an elevated train above my head. I'm staring at this in disbelief. I just held my microphone out to get the sound of it and, after a few seconds, started narrating what I'm seeing. 'The building is falling, people are running, there's smoke . . .'—whatever was happening, I just started narrating. Then, I realized, 'Oh, my God, everybody is running.'" Beth decided to run, too.

But she didn't know where to go, because she didn't know which way the building was falling. "It just descended like a timed implosion—like when they are deliberately bringing a building down. It was the strangest thing to see. It was coming down so perfectly that in one part of my brain I was thinking, 'They got everyone out, and they're bringing the building down because they have to.'"

Thick, brown smoke was pouring out and rushing east toward her. "The wind was blowing, and also the canyons of Lower Manhattan were sucking it. I didn't know where the stuff was blowing, so I knew I'd better run."

For the first time Beth thought her life was in danger. "Previously, we were in this suspended state of disbelief, just watching it," she said. She ran north alongside City Hall Park. "People were running like in a disaster movie. This one man was completely inarticulate. He was just shouting, 'Oh, my God.' He couldn't even speak, he was so upset. I kept trying to get him to talk to me, but he was just unable to speak." Then she thought she didn't really have the time to speak to anyone; she'd better keep running. "I was bumping into emergency vehicles, dodging police who were telling everybody to go north, to go east."

She found a fellow reporter, Marianne McCune, outside WNYC's building. "All I remember was hugging her and saying, 'Don't go there. I just came back. I saw it all.'" The two women started walking away from the towers, hugging and crying. "It must have been a really strange sight because here are these two reporters holding their microphones and just crying."

Then both women realized they had a job to do. "Marianne calmed me down and told me to turn on my tape recorder and just narrate what I saw again." They started walking toward Foley Square, just north of their office building, where all the courthouses and the federal building are located. They tried to call the station. Although Beth's cell phone wasn't working, miraculously Marianne's was. "She got through to Mark Hilan, who threw me on the air. I started saying, 'I saw it all. This is what I saw.' And I played some of my tape. I put my headphone up near the phone and tried to play the tape." Then Marianne starting pulling witnesses to the phone. She found a man who had witnessed everything, including people falling from the building. He described what he saw while the building was still burning.

"We stood there together doing this and helping each other because we were both so freaked out. We were really helping each other get through this and coming up with ideas. What do we do as reporters?"

While they were on the air, the second building collapsed. "Mark had us on the air, and I was saying, 'What's that sound?' and Marianne was saying, 'The building is coming down.' Right before it came down, he asked me to describe what I was seeing. I said, 'I can't see the first building. It's come down apparently. But the second building is getting shorter.' In retrospect, it made sense what I was seeing. We did that for a while, and then we went to interview other witnesses. We interviewed five fire marshals. We interviewed some office workers who fled the eighty-third floor.

"It was a really strange experience because you don't want to be traumatizing people more, but we wanted to get their stories on the air."

Another woman, who was comforting two women who had fled the Port Authority, told them they should talk to these reporters, because if their names were on the air, their families would know that they were all right. "So, we did that for a while. When we lost cell phone power, we went into the Department of Health building where we noticed they were setting up a triage center on the ground floor with doctors and nurses helping people who were mildly injured. The woman who ran the press office let us use her office so that we could get back on the air and tell Mark and NPR what was happening." After a while, they decided Marianne would stay downtown and continue doing interviews. They had stopped all public transportation. The Health Department told her where the mayor was, so she walked about forty blocks to find the mayor at his new makeshift command center, where he was beginning to give press conferences. Beth worked through the night. She did a feature that NPR ran of her tape and Marianne's tape, just recounting the experience of being at Ground Zero.

When Beth finally could head for home at 4:30 A.M. on the 12th, she couldn't take a taxi, so she had to walk from 14th Street, about a mile to her home. "That was the worst experience of my life. I was walking home alone in the dark, looking toward the Twin Towers. They were gone. It was just the saddest thing in the world."

4

Amy Eddings, WNYC Radio, New York City

WNYC Radio reporter Amy Eddings was assigned to cover Alan Hevesi, a Democratic candidate for mayor, on September 11, primary election day in New York, as he campaigned with the head of the New York teachers' union. Amy showed up for a scheduled campaign stop in Brooklyn Heights, near one of its busiest subway stations. Along with her heavy recording equipment, she was carrying a pair of her fiancé's shoes to take to a shoeshine shop near the World Trade Center. Her wedding to WNYC anchor Mark Hilan was scheduled for September 15.

"I was also carrying my cell phone and its charger," she said. "The battery was dead. I was planning on charging it up during the day in order to use it that night from Hevesi's election night headquarters."

Hevesi was late. He hopped out of his car and announced to everyone that a plane had hit the Trade Center. Amy said her feeling was that it must have been a small prop plane, a little Cessna. She ruefully thought that someone else would have to cover it, since she was following Hevesi. "Brooklyn Heights is a mostly residential neighborhood, right across the East River from Lower Manhattan, with a great view of the Twin Towers," she said. "Where I was, tall buildings obscured the view. But suddenly over Hevesi's shoulder I could see a white cloud of debris forming in the sky. I pointed to it, and Hevesi and others muttered, 'Oh, my God!' This was a bigger story than I imagined."

Amy's pager went off. It was her newsroom, asking her to go to the scene. She hopped onto the subway. "I was very lucky; I got on one before they shut the system down. I got to Fulton Street about three or four blocks east of the World Trade Center. I started walking west toward the towers." She could sense panic. "People were running. There were loud voices."

She knew only about the first plane, but by the time she exited the subway the second plane had hit and both towers were smoking. "I did not know what to

Amy Eddings

expect. I didn't know what I was looking for. I steeled myself to see blood and guts. I didn't see anything like I thought I was going to see," she said.

People were clustered on the sidewalk and in the streets, watching the towers, but Amy did not see scores of injured people. Lots of people were streaming out of the towers. Several were crying and visibly upset. She saw one man lying on the street, unconscious, with a gash on his forehead. Blood was running toward the gutter, and Amy stepped over it. She asked the paramedics who were tending him whether he had been hurt by falling debris. A bystander said, "No, it was by all the people!"

"I kept looking for big parts of the planes," Amy recalled. "Instead, I saw lots of shoes, nuts and bolts, headphones, a book bag." She kept looking for the plane and someone official to interpret what was going on. It dawned on her that none of the firefighters and emergency medical technicians knew any more than she did. The people who did know were walking past her, leaving the scene. "I starting interviewing people, asking, 'What did you see? What do you know?'"

Three men told her they saw at least ten people jump from the towers. "And they hit the ground, and there was a loud explosion," one man said. "I was in a conference room in Four World Trade Center, and I couldn't believe my eyes. At first I thought they were, like, stuffed animals or something. But then I saw them waving their hands—ladies, men." Another man said cars parked along Liberty Street were exploding. One man told her he had run down seventy-three flights of stairs in the south tower. "We saw lights flicker, and then a ton of debris came over the side, and then smoke . . . and then the smell of aviation fuel." He was soaking wet with sweat. Another man thought only one plane had plowed through both buildings. Two women said they came from the thirty-sixth floor of the south tower, the second one hit. "Our lights flickered, and then there was flying debris, and then the building shook," one said. "Everyone said, 'Bomb!' so we just ran."

As Amy stood there looking up at the north tower, she could see the mark of the

wing where it had sliced into the building. She w[as]
the firefighters going to get the fire out?"

She walked to a nearby pay phone across the st[ree]-
ter, with a clear view of the north faces of both to[wers]
was out," she said. "I thought I could describe the
cally standing at the bottom looking up at the bui[lding]
her newsroom, but no one answered. The buildin[g]
the World Trade Center complex, was being evacu[ated.]

She called the National Public Radio news desk
9:30 A.M. She was asked what new information she had and was asked to describe the scene. "I saw the building burning and a huge, gaping hole. People were leaving. Papers were fluttering in the air. The plane had completely disappeared into the building." Amy was in the process of being patched through to the news program *Morning Edition* to go on the air when a plainclothes police officer flashed a badge at her and asked her to relinquish the pay phone. She flashed her press credentials and said as firmly as she could, "I'm filing a story." But he was "a big brass guy" who ordered her to "get off the phone right now" for "security" reasons. She reluctantly yielded the phone.

Amy spent the next ten minutes going from corner to corner trying to find a pay phone. She was moving farther north. She ran into a shoeshine store and offered a man twenty dollars to use his phone. But his cell phone battery had died because of others who had made the same request. She couldn't find another cell phone or pay phone. "I was running out of options. I was about six blocks away from WNYC. My instinct was to get this on the air . . . just get what you have on the air."

She decided to run back into the WNYC Municipal Building, schlepping her equipment and her fiancé's wedding shoes. "Waves of people were coming out of the building. A security officer told me the building was being evacuated, and I couldn't go in." At that moment, Laura Walker, president and CEO of WNYC, appeared and told the guard Amy was coming with her, back to the station's offices. There, they joined Mitch Heskell, vice president of finance, and her fiancé, Mark, who had slipped back upstairs, despite the evacuation order, and had continued broadcasting. "We stared at each other and asked, 'Now what?'"

They debated. "We knew this was a big story, and we should be covering it," Amy says. "But there were rumors being broadcast of more planes in the air—I had even heard a detective on the street, near the towers, telling people to get out of the area because another plane was headed our way—and we didn't know if our building was safe." The consensus was that WNYC listeners and NPR in Washington needed their help to get the complete story. They decided to stay in the studio and keep broadcasting. Walker was able to prevent their evacuation.

Amy said it was inconceivable to everyone that the towers would fall. "No one, we knew, had factored in the effect of all that jet fuel and the size of the planes." The WNYC building shook and she heard a rumble, but she said it didn't immediately register that a tower was collapsing. "I was numb. It was really hard to break

nial. It was a good thing because it helped me keep working." The
what had happened didn't hit her until two days later, when she had a
watch video images of the collapse.

y forced herself back into the usual newsroom routine, making calls and tak-
g care of administrative duties. Other WNYC reporters were able to get through
and were going on the air. There were decisions to make. When she was pulling
sound bites from her tape, she ran across the one from the man describing bodies
falling. "It was pretty graphic," Amy said. "I could cut it so it was less graphic. But
we decided we wanted to paint an accurate picture of what was going on. We used
it in its entirety. As time went on and the story developed, as it shifted into a different stage about the rescue efforts, rather than the attacks themselves, we no longer
used that cut. Our coverage changed, accordingly."

When the north tower collapsed, its antenna was destroyed. So was WNYC's FM
signal, along with the signals of several local television and radio stations. WNYC
was able to continue broadcasting on its AM frequency, through a telephone line
linking the station to its AM transmitter in New Jersey. They were able to stay on
the air from the studio until about 6 P.M. After that, Mark Hilan handed over the
reins to WNYC broadcasters who were now based at NPR's New York Bureau
office, about forty blocks uptown from WNYC's evacuated building. But Amy and
Mark didn't want to leave the studios. "We slept in the green room overnight."

The next morning, Amy headed for Ground Zero. "Ash was on the ground. The
scene was quiet and hushed in terms of the absence of people, but noisy with Verizon
and Con Edison crews trying to get phone and electricity service into the area, laying
new cable and getting water and phone service restored. The air smelled terrible.
Lots of pieces of paper were on the ground."

Her goal was to get into Ground Zero using her press credentials, but the police
barricades made the attempt frustrating. She knew some reporters were sneaking in,
but she didn't think that was the course she should take at the time. But she now
wishes she had been more persistent. "I really didn't know how to cover it. I went
around prominently wearing my press pass. It didn't dawn on me that I needed to
be more aggressive, that I needed to sneak past the police and the National Guard.
My own sense of playing by the rules played a role. I think about it a lot," she said.

There are no rules, however, for some of the situations reporters encountered in
covering the attacks on America. One of the greatest dilemmas was using information that could not be confirmed. Concerned about getting as close to the action as
she could, Amy ran into a man who described himself to her as a firefighter. "A lot
of water service around the area was shut off. He had opened a fire hydrant with a
long wrench and was filling a cooler with water. He told me he was getting it for
his wife and child. Their apartment was nearby. He gave a moving story. He said
he was off duty September 11. He said several from his engine company didn't come
back. He broke into tears and said, 'I hope they're all right.'" The man identified
his engine company and spoke in detail about being recalled to duty and assembling

at a battalion. But the man wouldn't give Amy his name. She couldn't be sure he really was a firefighter or confirm the losses to his company. "I used it, but I was walking on very thin ground. I couldn't believe that anyone would fake a story or capitalize on this situation, and yet that has happened." She said that he provided enough details and used enough "fireman-speak" that she believed him. "It was tricky. Would I have liked to have had his name, and did I learn more about being persistent? Yes."

About a week later, when the operation was still termed a "rescue," Amy was with two other radio reporters from other stations, waiting beyond the barricades around Ground Zero for a rescue worker shift change. They were grabbing workers as they were coming out to get quotes for what she termed "morale stories." "An American Red Cross volunteer said, 'I can't vouch for this, but some have said they heard tapping from victims still trapped beneath the debris.'" The only verification they could get was another secondhand report. One of the other reporters put it on the air. Amy decided not to go with it. "The other reporter said it is the media's responsibility to keep people's hopes up. I disagree."

Amy said she had problems with Mayor Rudolph Giuliani continuing to refer to a "rescue and recovery" operation as long as two to three weeks later. She covered a town hall meeting in Lower Manhattan, on October 3, when people who lived in the World Trade Center vicinity were to receive information about when they could return to their homes. She asked one of the press officers in emergency management why they were still characterizing the work as a rescue. He told me, 'If you had friends or family in that rubble, you would want it to be rescue, too.'" Although reporters knew it was increasingly unlikely that survivors would be found, some underground areas still had not been reached. They had to consider the possibility that people could still be there with access to food and water. Sadly, no one was found alive.

Amy was grateful that her station provided a debriefing for reporters, newscasters, and producers with American Red Cross officials. "I wouldn't have done anything on my own," she said. "You think, 'You're not the victim; the victims were in the buildings, so buck up and get on with it.'"

About the session, Amy said, "We were all trying to digest it or make sense of it, regardless of whether we knew anyone in the buildings. We all told our stories. Everyone said they wished they could have done more."

Some reporters had to deal with being unable to do anything because they had been at home preparing for the long election night coverage. They couldn't get in to the city. Amy understood the frustration they felt. "I would have been enormously frustrated. I was grateful to have something to do. The work has been helpful in making sense of the events." She said that getting back into the office, seeing people she knew, and establishing a routine was comforting. Talking about it made her feel better.

Still, Amy experienced what she calls a "curious form of survivor's guilt," causing her to relive those days over and over and ask herself questions with no answers.

"How could I have stayed down there longer? What if I'd gone left instead of right? Were there more people I could have interviewed if only I'd stayed near the towers longer? It's woulda, shoulda, coulda." Her self-struggles come down to whether she could have reported more, reported better, or helped more people. She thinks now that she wasn't able to get into Ground Zero because "I walked up to barricades with my press credentials and asked the police officers nicely if I could go through!"

Amy said she learned from her experience. "Two months later, I covered the crash of American Airlines Flight 587, in the Belle Harbor neighborhood of Queens. I sneaked past checkpoints by hiding in the back of a van filled with volunteer fire-fighters, and I got within a block of the crash site by ducking under police barricades when officers weren't looking and cutting through people's backyards."

In spite of her second-guessing about her World Trade Center coverage, Amy believes that WNYC staff members ended up being exactly where they needed to be. "Several of my colleagues were outside, interviewing survivors and rescue work-ers, while we were inside the station, assisting the anchor." As a team, they were able to cover the story and keep their station on the air in spite of extremely difficult conditions. No reporters were injured. "It really worked out fine," she said.

Everything worked out except her wedding. Work and the inability of family members to fly in for the event resulted in a postponement. And there was another small problem. The reception was to be held in the officers' club at the Fort Hamil-ton Army Base in Brooklyn. But Amy got a call from the club's catering director. "She told me, 'Everything's canceled for the weekend. The FBI is here, and the catering staff is feeding them.' No civilians were going to be allowed on base for some time." The two were married in January 2002.

5

Rehema Ellis, NBC News, New York City

Nearing the end of her vacation, NBC correspondent Rehema Ellis planned to spend the day just enjoying New York City, an opportunity that she says is "more uncommon than people imagine." The nature of her job does not afford her many opportunities "to go to plays or enjoy the park." But the pager resting on her dresser began to beep shortly after 9 A.M. on September 11. The last day of Rehema's vacation turned into the longest working day of her career.

"I placed a call to the office and found out why I was being paged. They told me to turn on the television," she said. "I was as horrified as anybody else. I actually didn't think that this was real. I had a sense of disbelief," she said. "I thought I'd go down and cover a story about a plane crashing into the top of the World Trade Center, that I'd work all night and do something for the *Today* show the next morning, and then I'd go off to another story the next day. That's what I thought initially because the first report I heard on the air indicated a small plane had crashed."

She looked out the window of her high-rise apartment on the Upper East Side and saw a thick cloud of smoke coming from downtown. "I saw all this smoking and knew something was terribly wrong, in addition to the television pictures confirming it for me. I wasn't dressed to go to work, but I got ready in very short order, and I rushed out the door."

Rehema caught a cab and went racing down FDR Drive. "The cab driver was so upset, he could hardly drive. I asked him to keep the radio on. Quite honestly, I wanted to get him out of the driver's seat and drive the cab myself. He was so upset he was not being the usual, aggressive cab driver. But he did manage to pull himself together, and I got downtown," she said.

She made her way to an NBC live satellite truck located about ten blocks from Ground Zero. "People were running away, and I was running toward Ground Zero. It was a strange feeling. I've been a reporter for a long time, and often people are

Chapter 5

Rehema Ellis

leaving a place as I'm going to it. But this was different. New York is a city of ten million people, and it was as if all of them were in the street. Everyone was in a state of confusion with this look of 'What do we do and where do we go?' There was just a blank look of disbelief on their faces."

Initially, she was frustrated as she tried to locate the crew. Her cell phone was not working, and the pay phones she encountered were either not working or had long lines of people stretched before them. She was allowed into a closed Victoria's Secret lingerie shop to use the phone. She called her office, the New York bureau, and asked where she could find the crew. After that, she was out of contact with people at the bureau for a couple of hours. "I was told to go to the area and hook up with the crew, but nobody from the desk said to get to the heart of what was the World Trade Center."

When the first tower came down, Rehema was walking alone, still trying to make her way to the live shot location. "It was not a good feeling to be alone because people were running and crying. It was strange because I was afraid, too, but I also thought I had a crew closer than I was at that point, and I had to get to them. And once the dust settled to a degree, I just kept making my way to my crew. To tell you the truth, I just didn't think. If I'd given everything a whole lot of thought, I might have turned around and run in the other direction, too. But I didn't. I just kept thinking that I had to get to where the crew is. I didn't have a sense of the magnitude of what had happened. It was a day when everything was upside down—my own sense of what was going on was upside down."

By the time Rehema reached the satellite truck, the second plane had hit. "The air was raining debris. Paper was flying in the air, coming down, with edges burned and jagged, like a pirate treasure map. All over the street, I could see just corners of pages that were torn off. It was raining paper and dust. Even before I got right into the middle of the disaster, it was already covering everything on me—my hair, my face, my purse, everything. It was just that heavy, even ten blocks away."

The MSNBC crew was already on the air from the site, and no NBC producer was there. There was only one cameraman, and he was operating the live shot. "I took a moment to try to figure out what was going on and what I could possibly do. The telephone line that was operating in the satellite truck was in use to get a live shot up and going. I went up to a Con Edison truck and asked the technician if he had any kind of mask." He didn't, but he offered her a red rag that he promised her was clean. "I tied it around my neck and used it as a mask to protect my face from the dust. It was difficult to breathe. I'm slightly asthmatic and allergic to dust, so I knew I had to cover up. I knew there was no point in me being one of those brave souls saying this isn't so bad. *It was bad.*"

While she was trying to decide what to do without a crew, she spotted a producer, Mary Beth Toole, who had been shopping downtown near the World Trade Center when the first plane hit. Mary Beth had felt the earth quake. She had immediately phoned in to the New York bureau to find out what was happening. When the building was tumbling, she luckily had rushed inside a store and watched in horror as the black cloud of dust rolled past the door. A short while later she made her way to the satellite truck that was parked at the corner of Chambers and West Broadway. When Rehema met her, she had an NBC News DVD camera that she had taken out of the satellite truck.

"When I saw Mary Beth, I just knew we had to do more than we could do from where we were standing," Rehema said. "We were not in communication with anyone at the bureau. No producers, no directors, no executive producers—nobody. I looked at her and asked her if she was willing to go further in. She looked at me and said, 'Yes.' I said, 'Well, let's go. Let's see if we can make our way in.' That's what we did."

Rehema said that there was so much chaos at that point that the police weren't fully organized yet to stop people from going in. "That just wasn't the objective at that hour of the day—ten o'clock. The thinking was, 'No fool is going to go in here anyway.' Nobody stopped us. We literally inched our way into Ground Zero, taking pictures, talking to people," she said. She started doing stand-ups, talking into the camera about what they were seeing.

They stopped at a hospital, and then they went on to city hall, which is located three or four blocks from Ground Zero. That's where they ran into resistance from the police. "The police at city hall were telling us we could not go any farther. We were only three or four blocks from Ground Zero. Because they were protecting city hall, the police were all around that area."

She turned to her left and saw that in this usually congested section of Manhattan, there was no traffic, no cars. "I saw a bridge, and I was totally, totally disoriented. I've lived in New York for seven years. I've been down to city hall numerous times. I've been over this bridge more times than I care to count. I didn't know where I was, even though I knew where I was. That doesn't make any sense, but there are a lot of things about that day that don't make sense. I asked the policeman who was standing there, 'What bridge is that?' He told me, 'It's the Brooklyn Bridge.' My jaw dropped because I *know* the Brooklyn Bridge, and I couldn't believe that I didn't recognize it."

Rehema said there was debris floating in the air, and the few people she could see were all on foot heading away from Lower Manhattan. She likened the scene to what it must be like for people to return to their neighborhood after a tornado has ripped it apart and nothing is recognizable. "We walked toward the Brooklyn Bridge, and we saw a sea of people walking across the bridge—not on the sidewalks but in the road where vehicles are supposed to be." She had to go up on the bridge to get a picture of this mass exodus of thousands and thousands of people. "We talked to some people, to get their reaction about what was happening and to find out how they had escaped. I opened up my story that night showing that shot of the Brooklyn Bridge and of people leaving because it was one of the most stunning things for me and other New Yorkers to see."

Although the police told them they could go no farther, the women decided that they had to get closer. "We climbed off the bridge onto a grassy knoll where there were no officers, jumped over a fence, and worked our way up the backside by the Wall Street area. By being willing to step into places we wouldn't advise others to go, we managed to make our way around the police. We got to a staging area where there were dozens and dozens of firefighters. We saw very few police officers there because the fire captains and chiefs were controlling everything."

Rehema asked a firefighter to explain what was in the two-inch thick dust and ash all around them. He told her he thought it was pulverized concrete. "At that moment when he said that to me, it clicked in my mind that if concrete was smashed into dust, what in the world had happened to the people?"

At this point, Rehema and Mary Beth were playing "beat the clock," because they knew they had to gather as much information and get as many pictures as they could and then get back to the satellite truck. "The whole point was to get on the air and show people what we had. We went to the hospital because we wanted to see if any injured people were there. The hospital, only blocks from Ground Zero, has the only emergency room in the Wall Street area. They had set up a cafeteria as a triage area. There were wall-to-wall people." She said they had heard some incredible stories about how people had gotten out of the towers. "Some had walked down several flights of stairs. A man in his sixties had climbed down seventy flights. All he could think about was his wife, children, and grandchildren, he said, and that he *had* to live for them. He told me it put strength in his legs, and it propelled him down the stairs.

"A man in his thirties who works on Wall Street was caught right in front of the World Trade Center when it started to crumble. He ran for his life and remarkably escaped with just a few scratches. He had an EKG and MRI to be sure that he didn't have anything clouding his lungs. It was one story like that, one after another," she said.

They took pictures of cars that had been demolished and trucks that had been crushed. Rehema was struck by the empty newsstands and fruit stands along the way, because she said New York merchants just don't leave their merchandise unattended. "There were carts and merchandise all over the street. People had just run away and left everything behind. Shoes were all in the street—did they come from people who literally ran out of their shoes, or . . . ?" She didn't complete that thought.

She could describe in detail the debris that had rained from the sky. "We saw glass, sticks, paper—the things that come out of office buildings that was all in the street. We just made our way along, taking pictures of everything we could, and we only had *one* tape for the DVD."

They would quickly rewind the tape, find the point of the sound bite they wanted, and erased everything else. A two-and-a-half-minute interview with a hospital administrator became a twenty-second sound bite. "We created a story, editing along the way, in the camera. Together, we consulted with one another about what was good, about what we should do, and what we should keep and what we should erase." Those decisions were difficult, because Rehema and Mary Beth couldn't anticipate what else might happen that day.

Rehema found a telephone booth to call the bureau to see when she might get on the air. She immediately was put on the air with Tom Brokaw for a telephone report. "I told him I was about four blocks from Ground Zero, but I have since gone back to that telephone booth where I did my report, and I was actually only about a block and a half away. This was another indication of how disoriented I was by the fact that the landscape had changed. The familiar New York skyline had changed, but at ground level it had changed, too. It was unrecognizable to me."

Rehema didn't do an on-camera live shot until later that night. She and Mary Beth fed their videotape in so they could do a report for *Nightly News* with Tom Brokaw, a special edition that went from 6:30 until 8 p.m. Her story, "Video Diary," aired during that block. "We put that together in about fifty-five minutes, which is not a lot of time in television. We fed in our material, and then I sat down and wrote the lead-in. I tried to do it from my point of view, telling a story throughout. I did several live stand-ups in this report, saying, 'I'm here; I'm talking with this guy; I'm looking at this'—that kind of thing. I didn't have a lot of narration that I had to write when I got back to the satellite truck because I'd been editing so much in the camera, but I still had to think of the sequence in which I wanted to place the picture and narration."

She was in contact with a producer in Burbank, California, who received the pictures they had shot. Because her computer wasn't working and she didn't have cell phone access, Rehema told the producer what she wanted for the piece over the phone. She then sat back nervously as she waited for the piece to be edited and then aired. "I was very pleased with the final product, but I had a lot of anxiety about it," she said.

Rehema worked nonstop from nine that morning until eight that night. She had no food and very little water all day. She had gotten one bottle of water from the hospital she had visited earlier that day.

"I was really tired, so for that hour that I waiting for my report to air, I just sat down. And I tried not to worry. My report then aired after 8 P.M., and I realized at that point that there was much more to the story than what I could tell on the safe side of the barricade. By now, the police had set up a much more defined perimeter around Ground Zero. That is where everybody was doing their live shots. I still had not gone on live, with the exception of that telephone report."

Ground Zero was now dark. There was no power except for searchlights and TV crew lights. Rehema knew she didn't want to go back there alone. She turned to Mary Beth and then to two NBC crew members, Buba Adschiew, a producer, and William (Bill) Angelucci, a cameraman.

"Buba and Bill had both gone down into Ground Zero and gotten pictures that nobody else got. The material was powerfully disturbing. They went up inside Building Five three hours after the towers collapsed. A firefighter didn't stop them, so they went in. I decided I needed something more than what was at the perimeter. We needed to see what was behind the barricades. And that is what we went after. Once darkness fell, the four of us looked at each other, and it was a collective idea that we go back. We decided we would team up and do this."

Police told the crew they were crazy to even think of going in and to go away. "We turned around, and we walked down the street out of their view and quickly turned a corner until we got to another police officer, who also told us to get out of there. We turned around again like we were going through a maze. We just roped our way around the police officers because they did not want us in there. They weren't ready yet for the world to see what it looked like right down in there," Rehema said.

But the crew made it in, walking through ankle-deep water. Firefighters were hosing down everything because of the fire. "So there is water, and metal, and wood, and it is all in the street. You don't know what you're stepping on. You don't know whom you are stepping on. We were walking through water trying to get to the front of what was left of World Trade Center No. 1, No. 2, No. 5, No. 7, and the rest of it. We did make our way through there, by finding a way to get past the police barricades. When they told us we couldn't go, we just found another way in."

Although Rehema still was using the red cloth she had gotten from the firefighter and a paper painter's mask, she said it was still very, very hard to breathe, and it was *hot.* "September is still summertime. That day was a very hot day in New York, and so the heat, combined with the dust and pulverized cement that was in the air and floating all around, made it very difficult to maneuver our way through there. We were moving as quickly as we could, sweating and covered in dust. It was uncomfortable, but we didn't think about those things."

When they reached a staging area for firefighters across from Trinity Church— one street from Ground Zero—they learned that a Port Authority worker had been rescued. "They didn't know his condition, but they were just so excited that they had gotten somebody out alive. When we got right down there in what had been World Trade Center No. 1 and No. 2, we heard another Port Authority worker had been brought out alive. So, that was *two* people. I did a stand-up right on top of the rubble in front of World Trade Center No. 1 and said it is almost unbelievable to imagine that anybody could survive when you look around and see what has happened to the metal, the concrete, and the steel. I was elated that two people survived, but I felt sad because I didn't know that there could be hope for anyone else coming out alive."

Rehema was dismayed when she saw the burned-out shells of WTC buildings Seven and Five. "We were just thirty feet from the building that would come tumbling down the next day. One of the reasons that police didn't want anybody in that area was because everyone suspected that the foundation of all the buildings in the area had been compromised by the crash and subsequent collapse of the two towers. We just refused to think about it. We didn't know if another building would come down. We knew it was dangerous, and we knew that police were trying to keep us out because they were doing what they could to protect us. When the building came down the next day, the group of people I worked with all got together and said, 'Wow, but for the grace of God . . . who knows?'"

In spite of the personal risks they were taking, Rehema and her colleagues believed they had to tell this story. "At a moment like that, your adrenaline just overwhelms you. This is what we do. I think that's why my colleagues and I were so determined that no could not be the answer. We had to let people see what it looked like down there. Daytime video was one thing, but nighttime video was altogether something else."

Rehema and the crew had a "pretty sobering moment" as they watched the firefighters work. "They were going up in long lines, raking through the piles of rubble, sometimes on hands and knees. The look on their faces was of hopelessness and sadness. They didn't want to leave anybody behind; they didn't want to leave their brothers. They were determined they weren't leaving until they had done everything they could possibly do. There was so much sadness. I saw what they saw, and it was hard to have hope.

"We were looking very carefully where we stepped that night and the next day. We walked gingerly through the debris, and we were looking around to see if anything was going to fall on us. We weren't just racing through there like mice in the dark. We were watching what we were doing. We were careful, but this experience didn't frighten me away from anything," she said.

Rehema said there was no need to discuss whether to show any of the images they were recording that night. "The concrete had been pulverized. What was the chance that we were going to see anything human? I didn't. Body parts have been recovered from Ground Zero, but that night it was hard to see. It was dark and so much was covered by twisted metal, and steel, and glass, and water that you couldn't see a lot."

However, later on, she did have to consider whether to use the term *body parts* on the air, when in the course of an interview a source told her rescue workers were finding them. "I paused for a minute to think. Do I want to say that on the air when there are people who were watching who may have loved ones in the building?

What would I think if my sister or brother were in that building, and I heard somebody telling me they are finding body parts? I thought about it. As it turned out, I never had to use that bit of sound. All my stuff was just live. They just wanted me to talk. But in the days that have followed, people have become more capable of being able to hear the phrase *body parts*. Some of the sting has been taken out of it for the general public, but not for the individual relatives who lost loved ones. I don't think the sting goes away for them."

Rehema did her last live shot at about 1:30 A.M. on September 12. She then worked on a story for the *Today* show, so she didn't stop to rest until about 3 A.M. At that point, she and a producer climbed into an SUV, where she rested for a short time. Rehema considered going home for a few hours until she learned that police had closed off the area. If she left, she might not be able to get back in. "I was the only NBC reporter left there at the time, and I was hesitant to leave. What if they get really ugly about this and push all of us back or just say the people who are down there now are the only ones who are going to work? NBC might not have a reporter on the scene, so I said, 'I'm not going to leave.'"

Rehema got a bagel, some toast, and a carton of orange juice from a small diner that remained open to offer sandwiches to rescue workers. A neighborhood tavern across the street from the diner provided a bathroom. One of the producers slept on a sofa in the tavern, while Rehema and another producer sat in the SUV. "I closed my eyes for twenty minutes, but I never slept. I was too worried and too nervous to sleep. I was feeling so much anxiety, and it was hard to breathe. That morning when I opened my eyes, I was thinking about all I'd seen, all the lives lost. It was very difficult to sleep. I was better when my eyes were open. I didn't like what I saw when my eyes were closed."

City workers started sweeping the streets and watering them down, which helped to settle the dust. At about 4:30, Rehema went to a nearby garage, where the attendant had let her use the bathroom earlier. Although she thought the story was more important than how she or any television reporter looked on the air, Rehema wanted the audience to focus on what she was saying rather than on how she looked. "I washed my face in a sink to get the dust off. I tried to brush some of the dust out of my hair, but I didn't spend a lot of time on it. There was no place to shower, and I didn't have clean clothes anyway. I tried to put on some makeup so as not to look *so* bad on television the next day."

Rehema still had no cell phone service, but the garage man's landline was still working. Rehema used his phone to call in her reports on September 12. "When we got up the next day, I felt it was important to go back down to Ground Zero. So I got the crew and went back. We had to work around the police again, and by now they were much more organized. Sergeants in their white shirts were there ready to arrest reporters like me and take our police passes away. I managed to get down there and do one standup in front of World Trade Center No. 1 before I got thrown out."

Rehema doubts that the reporting done about September 11, no matter how excellent, could have actually conveyed the full scope of the horror of the attacks. "We were struck by what we saw when we got there that night. And we were emotionally unprepared, and despite all the high-tech equipment we had, it seemed the story was so much bigger. It was so overwhelming," she said.

"I do know that the world understands what happened here. And everyone is heartbroken. But it is something when you actually go into the belly of the beast. You see what is there, and it's not your imagination, and you're not in a dark theater looking up at a screen at the manifestation of someone else's imagination. This is horror personified. It's difficult to swallow. It's difficult to look at. And as grim as the pictures are, they still do not fully capture the scope and scale of this tragedy. But the pictures we were able to put on the air—and that I tried my best to talk around—were only possible because I work with a tremendously brave group of people."

The pressure on Rehema and her crew was enormous that night. "When we got back from standing in front of what was left of the World Trade Center, we had a matter of minutes to feed our tape in, and then they were saying, 'Rehema, get in front of the camera.' I had seconds, maybe *three minutes,* to think about what in the world I wanted to say. I had no monitor to see what pictures were being shown. I don't know what the audience was seeing while I was talking. I have a sense of it because I was there, but being able to be specific in talking about the pictures, I couldn't see any of it. The best television is when you can actually narrate to the pictures. I was a little bit frustrated that I couldn't do it that way. What was more important than for me to be able to see it was for people at home to be able to see it, to see how dark and desolate it was. That was a place that used to be just so alive. And now it was dead."

Rehema stayed at Ground Zero from about 10 A.M. on September 11 until 9 P.M. on September 12, but she continued to cover the aftermath of the attacks. In the days following the attacks, she was among the reporters who were beset by family members of victims. "I was in front of the Service Center where people were coming to describe relatives and bringing in strands of hair. I stood on that corner for several days and was showered with pictures of people they loved caught in the most wonderful moments of life: from marriages to birthdays, to high school graduations, to parties, to vacations. These were the high points of what life is all about. These were pictures put on a poster to say, 'This is who I love. This is who I'm looking for. See how alive he or she is? How can I imagine them now gone in a flash? You cannot expect me to accept that in an instant, because only a short while ago they were as alive as they are, and as beautiful as they are, in this wonderful photograph.' It is just inconceivable for human beings to turn their emotions like that from life to death when a catastrophe like that happens."

Rehema found the spontaneous yet collective action of people posting photographs of their loved ones incredible. "I've never been in anything like that in my life. I've been doing television for almost twenty years. I'm often out on the street, and people run behind you and say silly things. This was not like that. This was not people who were looking for fifteen seconds of fame. This was an opportunity for desperate people to reach out and to ask anyone who might have seen their loved one, to please let them know. It was desperate because the chances were slim to none that anyone would find someone that way. But the desire to hope and to hold onto someone whom you love is so strong and so powerful that it made thousands of people who would never ever think about doing something like that do it. These were people from all walks of life—every color, every race, every religion, every economic background, from the folks who had made lots of money on Wall Street and their relatives to those who were serving them coffee in Windows on the World. Everybody turned out to try to do whatever they could do to find somebody whom they loved. It was extraordinary."

Although NBC provided counseling to help employees cope with the trauma the attacks caused, Rehema preferred to turn to her family for support. "I am blessed in that I have a wonderful family and wonderful friends, and I have cried my tears with them. All of us that day and in the days that have passed cried a lot. Our country lost a lot of people that day. I don't feel weak by telling you that I felt it. It was heartfelt for me. In the days that followed September 11, I went to memorial services, funerals, and talked with numerous families. It is beyond my ability as a reporter and a human being to listen to people who are remembering someone they lost in a flash like that and not to feel it in my heart, too."

The reaction her family had to her reports gave her a sense of purpose. "My eight-year-old nephew and ten-year-old niece were watching as I was on the air. They were so upset because they could see their mother and father were upset. But my eight-year-old nephew and his ten-year-old sister turned to their mom and said, "It is going to be OK because Auntie Rehema is there. And if she is there, it's got to be OK.' Somehow my reporting made it possible for my nephew and niece to sleep that night. If I was able to do that for my own family, I hope by extension in some small way I might have been able to do that for other people as well. The grownups knew it wasn't all right and that I couldn't make it better. But at least we could tell people as much as we possibly could about what had gone on and what we could see."

Well into 2002, Rehema continued to cover stories related to 9/11 because "that's the news." She has struggled with her inability to get away from the reality of sadness that surrounds New Yorkers every day. "Unlike reporters from California, Atlanta, or Chicago who can get removed from the story, here in New York it is hard to separate yourself from it. There is a sense in New York that 'it ain't over.' Three hundred forty-one firefighters were killed. There are funerals every day—many at St. Patrick's Cathedral just a block away from Rockefeller Center [where the NBC studios are located]. The bagpipes wailed daily. I could hear them from my office. It's a story that you can't step away from here."

One of her stories, "City of Funerals," focused on the fact that there was one funeral after another, after another, after another. She also reported about why mental health workers needed some mental health counseling themselves. Unlike any other trauma they had assisted people in overcoming before, they, too, had been traumatized by what happened on September 11. "This was an event that touched the nation. It wasn't a typical plane crash because, for one thing, most people don't see the plane go down. And if they do, they seldom know someone who knew someone who was on the plane. This was different. We watched it go down. And over, and over, and over again we watched the towers crumble. So each person in this city and in this country has a collective sense of grief. Mental health workers are not immune to that. So when they are trying to counsel someone, they are saying to themselves, 'I'm feeling pretty bad, too.' We did a story about how they were talking to each other and trying to help each other get past the difficulty of day-to-day things they have to go through being with the firefighters and the recovery workers. It's a 24/7 operation down there that hasn't stopped since September 11."

Rehema also reported on the anthrax threat to NBC. One of Tom Brokaw's assistants was exposed when she opened an envelope containing anthrax spores. This occurred about fifty yards from Rehema's office. However, she had not been in the building for two or three weeks and was not exposed. "I was very concerned for my colleagues who had been in the building. I was also concerned because this was a learning experience for everyone, especially health officials. I knew from the information I was getting that the people we were counting on—meaning the Centers for Disease Control and health officials—didn't know what the hell was going on. That made me nervous. I have to admit that after the word came out on Friday, I had to work that Saturday and Sunday across the street in the *Today* show area because the floor where my office is located was shut down. I came to work that Saturday morning with a lump in my throat. I was feeling anxious about things that had happened. But as strange as it may seem, I was actually glad to go to work because working takes your mind off being nervous. You don't have time to be nervous; you just have to do the job. As I went through the course of the day and gathered information about the anthrax that had hit NBC, it made me feel better because I realized everyone was doing the very best they could. They were getting on top of this whole story. NBC was very good in terms of stepping up to the plate and saying, 'This is very serious, and we will take the security procedures necessary to protect you and the public from who knows what.'"

Andrew Lack, president and chief operating officer of NBC, provided hourly updates to let employees know what was going on and how the situation was being addressed. "Anybody who had any questions could pick up the phone and call Andy. He was very open and very good at sharing what he knew and providing as much assistance as possible to every employee in this company. It made me feel good," Rehema said.

Rehema acknowledges that September 11 has made a difference in the way news is covered, but she doesn't know whether the effect will be long lasting. "Since September 11, I think the people in the business I'm in—television, radio, newspapers, magazines—have done an outstanding job in terms of educating the public about who are the people who have different views from our own. Where are they? What are those views? I think it's been a magnificent job. If people across the country don't know where Afghanistan is now, it's because they don't want to know, not because no one has told them."

Rehema has been changed by the events of September 11. "I've always cherished my family. I didn't think I could love them any more, but I do. In terms of my career, it has made me ever more thoughtful, ever more determined, and ever more resolute to be the best possible journalist I can be. One of the things I hope will happen in my career is that there will be more times that people will see my work and think that there is some value in what I do and the way I do it. Exactly what it is going to mean for me, I don't know. I just hope I have an opportunity to keep telling stories."

She said the lesson for reporters on September 11 is that they have to go and get the story they want to tell and not wait for someone else to hand it to them. "You have to go get it even when people tell you they don't want you to get it, but you have to respect some forces or situations that could really put you in a terrible fix."

In recent days, Rehema has looked at some of the videotaped coverage from September 11. "I felt so inadequate that day because I thought that as a medium there was no way television could transmit to people the enormous scope and the scale of what had happened at the World Trade Center. That day, it was hard to comprehend how we would be able to put this devastating picture in a box and frame it in a twenty-one-inch screen or thirty-one-inch screen. I didn't know how we could do it. I stood in the middle of it all and thought, 'Oh, my God, how will people ever understand the depth of what has happened down here?' And yet we did it. Clearly people are struck and in awe of the events of September 11 and what we showed them on television. The fact that people are drawn to Ground Zero is proof of that. They want to see it all for themselves.

"Looking at some of the coverage brings back sad memories, but it also reminds me of the power of this story and the overwhelming impact that it has on this city, this country, this planet," said Rehema. "There are so many aspects of what occurred, so many facets of how people were affected: first and foremost the victims who lost their lives, their families who now struggle to live on without them, and then the people who attempted to rescue them and then put their own lives in harm's way. There was even the impact on the reporters themselves, and it goes on and on and on. Each layer of this story is, to me, fascinating. The storytelling and the tellers—yet another layer of this tragedy. People will look back one day and ask, 'How did they do that?'"

6

Rose Arce, CNN, New York City

In some ways, Rose Arce was uniquely qualified to cover the events of September 11. As a WCBS-TV reporter, she had covered the World Trade Center bombing on February 26, 1993. She had shared a Pulitzer Prize with colleagues for a subway crash story she had covered for New York's *Newsday*. She covered plane crashes and other disasters there.

Rose, a CNN producer, just wanted to spend a few minutes enjoying a beautiful, sunny day in New York City before running over to her local polling center to cast her vote in the primary mayoral race. "I was going to vote and then cover the election. I was told I would be working a late shift," she said. But first she went to get coffee at a deli across the street. "It was a really beautiful day, just a gorgeous day. Usually by September 11 it's gray already." After she got her coffee, she heard on NPR that something had happened at the World Trade Center. "It sounded ominous. I immediately flipped on my cell phone and called the office. I said, 'I heard about the World Trade Center. Where do you want me to go, because I'm going to start running downtown.' Whoever answered the phone said, 'Just go, go, go and call us when you get there.'"

Rose lives near Horatio and Washington, which makes a straight line down to the Trade Center. "I started running south, and people were just standing in the street, looking up. I got about two blocks and could see the building on fire." An African American woman, whom Rose said she would never forget, came by in a black Lexus. Rose knocked on her window and flashed the press ID hanging around her neck. "I said, 'Hey, I'm with CNN. Please give me a ride downtown.' I jumped in her car, and she took me down a few blocks from the Trade Center," she said.

Her cell phone had stopped working, so she ducked into a deli to use the phone to call CNN. Then she started running farther south, with a swarm of people coming at her. "It was like a weird movie. People were running in business suits, all with cell phones trying to talk as they were running. I was running against the traffic. My intention was to get inside the north tower, because that is what I had done in 1993.

Chapter 6

Rose Arce

Then there was this hum, like when the subway is passing underneath me, except that it was in the air."

As she was being pummeled by people running past her, she saw a little girl nearby who was screaming, "Daddy, Daddy! They are doing it on purpose!" First, there was a loud sound, and then a plane came out of nowhere and "just slammed into the building." She still had her cell phone in her hand and was frantically trying to dial CNN. But she just kept getting a busy signal.

She ran across the street to an apartment building where a woman was standing. "Do you live here?" Rose asked her. "She said her husband Jim was on the top floor, so I ran up the stairs and knocked on his door." She told him she was from CNN and that she had seen his wife downstairs and wanted to come into his apartment. "He said, 'Yeah, yeah, yeah, come in,'" she said. "People were unbelievably helpful that day. Everyone was like 'The world is going to end—what do I care if you come into my apartment?'" Jim turned out to be a photographer who takes children's pictures. "I've seen him a few times," Rose said. "He's a real sweetheart."

Rose described the apartment as "a construction site, because they were redoing the floors." Several other people were coming in and out of the apartment, but they were a blur to Rose. "We turned on the television set. Jim had one of those carry-around phones and the battery was dying, so I had to keep running to the back room where I couldn't see and put it on speaker phone so I could call in to CNN to give them reports of what I was seeing."

As CNN showed live pictures of the towers smoking in the distance, Rose described what she was witnessing. She could either stay where she had a phone or try to get closer to the scene. "I was frantic to get inside the building. I was only two or three blocks away. But I couldn't because my phone wasn't working. So I stayed at this guy's phone. When I finally got through to Atlanta, they were so panicked. They would suddenly throw me on air again with the anchor. I kept stretching the phone cord and saying, 'You won't believe what I'm looking at.'"

Normally, anchors would be asking questions. But not this time. "There were no questions," Rose said. "I would just keep talking, and there was silence on the other end. It was like they couldn't believe what I was saying."

Rose had a two-way pager with her that she rarely used, because it wasn't very reliable. But suddenly it started going off. "People were paging me, and they were saying, 'Are you OK?' 'Have you heard anything?' 'Do you know about the building?'"

In between her phone calls to CNN to get on the air, she called her cell phone. "I was hoping it would ring. I didn't know if something was wrong with it or the tower. I could get into my voice mailbox, but I couldn't get the phone to work. I just kept thinking that if I could get my phone to work, I could go downtown."

The best she could do was retrieve agonizing phone messages from friends. Some of them had friends or family members who might be in one of the towers. One was perhaps in a meeting on the nineteenth floor. She was able to call back only one friend. "I told her that it looked really bad. I didn't know what to tell her. I didn't know if people were going to get out of there."

Rose said when she heard these messages, she became even more focused on her duties. "I had this overwhelming feeling of 'Oh, this is what I do for a living.' It's this weird thing. You do what you do every day, but sometimes you lose touch with what the value of it is or why it is you do it. All I could keep thinking was, 'My God, all these people are listening to me on television, and I'm the only news they have.'"

At that point, Rose walked outside to view the buildings. "You could see this enormous hole in the tower. It was like this big thing had been ripped in it. There were sirens and noise. There was a stampede of people going in one direction and occasionally a rescue team going in the other direction. Looking up, I could see into the building. It was far away, but I could see shadows of people behind the glass. They were waving."

Rose returned to the apartment where Jim loaned her his DVD camera. She used its magnification to get a closer look. "It was clear people were starting to break the glass. Sprinkles of glass were coming by. One by one I saw hands coming out the window. Then I saw things being waved. It looked like people's shirts."

Rose and Jim began to speculate about how these people were going to get out. Was there something that was going to catch them? What are they doing? "We couldn't accept the fact that there was nobody to save them. We could see that the fire was getting closer and closer. It was above them, below them. We could see the building was stressing."

Then the most horrific scene Rose had ever witnessed began. "All of a sudden one person came to the window, and it looked like he was helping people jump. One by one they started jumping. Then, from a variety of windows, a bunch of people started jumping. They were flailing against the wind as they fell down. Some of them were holding hands."

When people started jumping, Jim screamed. His wife and daughter were standing in the back of the apartment. His wife said, "Jim, be quiet. Be quiet." Rose told him, "You guys should go. I'm going to stay." They went down to the basement, and Rose was alone.

The building again commanded her attention. "At some point as people were jumping there was this buckling. The building was crumbling. From far away, it looks like an explosion, but it collapsed almost like a deck of cards. These huge pieces just came raining down, puncturing the roof of each of the buildings around it. There was a swell, almost like a mushroom cloud, of debris just tumbled over the buildings in front of me that came pouring out toward the building where I was standing."

Rose started backing up into the center of the apartment as debris started hitting the window. "It was a strange, surreal moment because all I could think was, 'Is it going to break the glass? Is this building going to collapse?' And yet at the same time I was thinking, 'There is nothing I can do; there is absolutely nothing I can do.'"

Still connected to Atlanta, she screamed into the phone and then just hung up. "Suddenly, it went from being this beautiful sunny day with the deafening noise of sirens and people to just silence and black, almost like it was nighttime. It was so quiet. I walked up to the window and tried to see if the phone would work again. It did. I looked down, and the street was absolutely empty. It reminded me of ten years ago when there was a blizzard here and there was lots of snow on the ground. The city was so paralyzed, you didn't see cars. This was the same thing. There was this snow on the ground. Snow falling, and it was totally dark. And there was absolutely nobody. The sirens had stopped. And there was nothing in the air except this tremendous debris cloud."

Rose's pager started going off again: "Are you OK? Are you OK?" Messages were coming through asking if she had seen various coworkers and friends. "It was very freaky. There was a time period when I started thinking, 'I hope this person is OK. What about that person? Am I going to be OK?' The whole thing was almost not real. On the one hand, I felt very upset. But on the other hand, I was overwhelmed with this sense of mission. That sense of mission almost made it feel like it wasn't real because I was so focused on the job."

Rose looked down at the street. It was still totally empty. She was on the phone, when suddenly she saw someone: a firefighter running up the street carrying the body of another firefighter. "That was the first time I was genuinely afraid because I thought the rescue workers were running away. I have covered New York City firefighters for fifteen years. They run from *nothing*. I thought if a firefighter is running away, everybody down there is dead, and it is really, really dangerous."

Rose decided she had to get out of the building, which she admits in retrospect might not have been the best decision. She walked outside. "Once you got out on the street, you couldn't see anything." But she decided to try to find a CNN cameraman. "I ended up running east, and I stopped at pay phones along the way to call in. It was amazing that the pay phones were still working. My eyes were really burning, and I was coughing really hard at that point."

When she found the cameraman, they kept walking. The second tower collapsed at some point along her walk, but she doesn't remember it. "We found a firefighter. His pants had all burned off. He was standing there, quietly staring downtown. I'll never forget that he kept saying, 'I've got to get back down there. I've got to get back down there.' He had been with his ladder company, and they had been crushed in the debris. He dove underneath his truck and survived. He kept telling me that all the guys on his truck were dead. He had run away to escape the debris. But he was frantic to get back in. The two or three police left down there kept telling everyone to run, to run north. The fireman kept saying, 'I can't run away. I've got to go back. There's got to be people down there.'"

Rose said that everybody coming from the area was saying that everyone was dead. "There was just no rescue operation. There was nothing but fire and smoke. The debris was awful—little pieces of everything you can imagine in a building. If you just took people and desks and computers and drywall and porcelain and just put it through a shredder, it would all come back out as little, tiny pieces. People's business cards, sticky pads, glasses, photos on their desks, all charred and chopped up. And the closer you got, blood. It was just awful."

Rose and her cameraman, carrying a BetaCam, kept trying to get closer. "Although people think of the World Trade Center as two tall buildings, it is really a complex, with several big buildings that don't look big compared to the Twin Towers. Those buildings were completely on fire, crushed, and in danger of collapsing. We got very close to those. At that point, I think I was more in a state of shock than I realized until much afterward. Once or twice my cameraman grabbed me and said, 'Hey, Rose, we've got to get out.' I was standing there trying to work. And things were not looking good around us."

Television news is driven by the technology, but Rose says they weren't focused on that. "At that point, I gathered that we had a lot of material that other people didn't have. Swirling in my head was, 'How do we get the tape back?' 'What do they know?' 'What's missing here?' When I called the office, there was incredible activity there, but I felt so disconnected from it. They didn't even know where to start with this stuff. One of the beautiful things about CNN is that they are very good at covering disasters and breaking news, and there's a certain calm to it all. But that day, the thing you kept hearing was, 'Give us more! Give us more! Tell us everything you know!' There was an unending stream of things that needed to be gathered. Questions that needed to be answered."

In her quest for a good view of the scene, Rose went onto the balcony of a man who had been celebrating his son's first birthday. His terrace overlooked the Twin Towers. "We talked about it for a while as he held his little boy. It was just so odd. It was like being at Pearl Harbor—just a weird feeling. We were watching the buildings burning, and the Twin Towers were gone. I asked him how he was going to explain this to his son." They projected thirty years into the future when he would tell people that during his first birthday party, terrorists attacked New York.

Rose went back to the office, bringing back tape. She did a story about what she had seen. After midnight when she finished, she asked for a cameraman and went back down to Ground Zero. "We went to a huge parking lot that was next to the north tower. It was very chaotic that first day because they were hoping they were going to rescue someone. They were still waiting to get back in because the fire and debris were so enormous that they couldn't get access to the building. There was very little security. There were firefighters and police who were trying to shut off streets, but there was such pandemonium that we just walked right through it," she said.

They crossed Chambers Street, a street that cuts east to west in Manhattan. "There was an armada of firefighters, military, police officers, emergency medical service workers, Red Cross, Federal Emergency Management Agency, just a convoy of trucks from all over the country. I saw firefighters and wondered, 'How could you be from a state that far away?' It was amazing. It was absolutely a war zone."

She saw bodies being taken uptown, trucks full of debris, and people who had been injured in the rescue operation. There also was truck after truck containing water, food, and supplies. "We maneuvered through it all and got to a parking lot and went through a fence. Inside were crushed, burning cars. We wove through those cars in the construction lot and got out the other end. We were standing at Two World Trade Center."

There was a makeshift morgue in the American Express Building where they were squirting saline solution into the eyes of the firefighters. "Two World Trade Center was about eight stories high and was completely engulfed in flames. There were fire trucks crushed like tuna cans all over the place. There was a mudflow of stuff from all the water. We were sloshing through this mud. For the first time, about one o'clock in the morning, rescue workers were coming into that area. I thought, 'Oh, God. This thing has been burning since this morning, and this is the first access they have had, which means that anybody who might have survived the collapse had been there without any hope of being pulled out because there was just no way in,'" she said.

A school across the street housed another morgue. "Everybody was absolutely silent. I had never seen a situation where there were that many people, not talking. There were two big spotlights that were trained on the water hoses."

Rose got separated from her cameraman, leaving her alone to trip through the mud. She became covered in the muck and scratched from shards embedded in it. She was really angry that her cameraman was gone. But she was able to use her cell phone to call the office to try to locate him. "Finally I emerged into an area where there was a floodlight. That was the first time I got a real look at the area and what was actually in all this mud. I was essentially walking in mud mixed with blood mixed with body parts mixed with debris and water. It was just awful. There was this overwhelming stench of burning metal."

Rose wore a mask, but she was "coughing like crazy" as she walked around. She had coughing problems for several weeks after. She also damaged her eyes from sandy debris. "I couldn't wear contacts for a while, and my vision got weaker." She knows that some of the elements she inhaled, possibly asbestos, could be dangerous to her future health. "I think all that stuff is very real, but from where I sit now, there is nothing I can do about it. It's not that I don't worry about it, but I don't gain anything by worrying about it."

Rose didn't go home until about 4 or 5 A.M. for a quick nap. Going home was "really creepy," she said. "My building was pretty much empty. I changed clothes. I went back in and worked for a few more hours, about fourteen. By then everyone from Atlanta had come up, so my office was pretty much a battle zone, too. Everybody was freaked out but doing an amazing job. People were very calm and very focused, which really helped me."

Rose said that a lot of grief counselors were at the office, but she didn't talk with any of them. She did see her own therapist. "Really, I think the thing that helped me the most was spending time with friends. It was nice to see them and talk to them. I could see that everybody was there, and we could talk about what we were going to do next," she said. "I think we have on one level or another sought help. What we sought more was time away from it, which has been very hard to come by."

She also is aware that "many little things that day" kept her from getting killed. She knows that if her cell phone had been working, she would be dead. "I wanted to get into the building. Who in the hell knew it was going to collapse? I wanted to be there. I wanted to get as close as I could and get as much information as I could. That's what I do," she said. "I've covered breaking news my entire career. My strength has been in not panicking and keeping my wits about me, being able to gather information and be aggressive, clearheaded, and able to balance the danger to myself and others with the need to get information. I've done all that before, but what it all comes down to is that sometimes it's just dumb luck."

Rose thinks her previous experience with disasters did help her get through this one. "It does help you because there are certain things that you learn over time. One of those things is how rescue operations work. You get a sense after a while of when law enforcement is doing something for your own good—and you should be very respectful and heed them—and when law enforcement is simply trying to impede you from getting information. There are things you learn along the way, like what's most important. In TV, pictures are what are most important. But because I've done this for a while now, I knew the most important thing was to call, because I knew we weren't going to be getting the pictures immediately, at least nothing close by. Those things prepare you for the journalistic aspect of this."

But, she added, "Nothing prepares you for the horror of watching people die. I think at the point where you don't find that unusual or stressful, you've really got a problem. The residue of this has been much more profound than anything I've ever covered. The effect psychologically on me and on the people around me has been much greater.

"Really, the real issue for me for the first month and a half or so was every loud noise, every low-flying plane, the constant sirens were very stressful. There were a lot of sirens because the police were just in a panic with this rescue operation. Every time they went a few blocks, they would turn their siren on. I would hear it, and I would panic. I would think immediately, 'Is this it? Is this the next thing? Should we all run?' Your body stiffens with the next development."

Rose covered the next disaster in New York, the crash of American Airlines Flight 587 on November 12, 2001, in Queens. "The first thing I thought was the crash was completely unrelated. I was thinking everybody should calm down. With the anthrax and everything, it was time for sanity to set in."

Her CNN office had to deal with the anthrax threat. "We had our mailroom shut down. We have fire drills and an emergency procedure guide. We have a whole plan. I'm one of the captains to get people out of here. We're very much in ready mode, and that heightens both the fear and the sense of security at the same time," she said.

Rose also believes that journalists had to deal with a special kind of fear. "We get every bomb scare, every weird tip," she said. "Every one of these things is like, 'Oh, my, here we go. Maybe today.' We hear 'anthrax,' and we don't know where, we don't know who, we don't know how bad. By the time most of the public finds out about it, they are getting a very filtered version of events. It's like at one o'clock they found anthrax, but by five o'clock it's just a spore and nobody was hurt. We suffer the five hours of 'Is everybody we know at NBC going to be hurt or maybe dead?' So, in that sense, I think we live with a great deal more tension."

In regard to showing anguished friends and family members searching for lost loved ones, Rose said, "The problem was that we didn't know. A lot of families are angry now that they spent so much time searching, but it's because the authorities told them to keep searching. I suspected from the moment the building collapsed that most of the people left in the building had died. However, you don't know that. Who am I to tell someone, 'No, don't look for your mother's body'?"

She pointed out that people were looking for more than survivors. "People were looking for any information they could get about how their relatives died. They had a need to know. Who was my mom sitting next to? Was she scared when she died? Did she feel pain? To some people those details are really important. You have this strange balancing act that you do with the viewers out there. There are a lot of things people don't want to see on TV that frankly represent what is really happening. People have to be presented with the truth, however ugly that may be. I think the same debate goes on about how many obituaries will you do. Well, how many obituaries are too many for thousands of dead people? Two? Five? I think you have to give people a real representation of the grief and anguish that this caused, because decisions are made based on people's sense of the enormity of the event. Political decisions are made. Personal decisions are made. It would be a disservice to what really happened to diminish the enormity of it or to exaggerate it."

Although Rose's job did not include making decisions about what would and would not go on the air, she said there were many points along the way when CNN reporters were told what they could and couldn't show. "Decisions were made to limit certain things. I was extremely impressed in general with how restrained the media were about a lot of this stuff. I expected the worst, and I do think that people had valid complaints about the media as a whole and what they've shown. But I think that by and large the media were remarkably responsible. We didn't show the people jumping from the windows on live TV for hours and hours. We didn't show the plane hitting the building two months after the event over and over again. We could have."

7

Judy Woodruff, CNN, Washington, D.C.

With three children in school, CNN anchor Judy Woodruff normally spends her early mornings getting everyone organized and out the door. Then she focuses on getting herself ready to leave for the CNN studio in Washington, D.C., around 9 A.M., arriving in time for a morning staff conference call. On September 11, she deliberately had not turned on either her television or radio, because she was plowing through the morning newspaper editorials, as she does almost every day.

"I went out to get in my car, just after nine o'clock, and they were reporting about the first plane hitting the Trade Center," Judy recalled. "I immediately tried to call my researcher, who was trying to call me at the same time. Finally, we reached each other. She told me then about the second plane, which was just happening. I was headed into CNN, so, of course, I drove even faster."

Her next call was to Sid Bedingfield, then the executive vice president and general manager of CNN/U.S., in Atlanta. "I told him that I was rushing in and would be there in about fifteen to twenty minutes." She drove in listening to the news, arriving about 9:30 A.M.

"While I was in makeup, there were rumors and reports about more planes that were missing, and there was fear they were being hijacked. There was concern that one was going to crash somewhere near the Capitol. Of course, our bureau in Washington is just a few blocks from the Capitol, so there was obvious concern about that. We are on the eleventh floor, about as high as it is possible to be in Washington because of height restrictions (no building can be higher than the Washington Monument)," she said. "There was a lot of discussion about that, and it was shortly after that that I had come back to my office when we got confirmation that the Pentagon had been hit."

The Pentagon is located in Virginia, across the river from the CNN studio, so the staff there was too far away to hear the explosion or to be in physical danger

Chapter 7

Judy Woodruff

themselves. But Judy acknowledged that she felt the greatest fear in those moments before the plane reached Washington. "The only time I felt momentarily afraid was that morning. I visualized the fact that our building is near the Capitol and that we're located close to the top of the building. I was thinking, 'What if, what if?' But I don't think I've been physically afraid since then." The plane hit the Pentagon just after 9:30 A.M.

Judy spent about fifteen minutes in makeup and then stood in the control room waiting for a signal to go on the air. At 10:15 A.M. she began anchoring CNN's coverage. She was on the air when they heard about the Pennsylvania crash at about 10:30 A.M.

Judy went on the set armed with lots of notepaper and pens. She listened very carefully to everything she was hearing. "I was looking at as many pictures as I could, trying to absorb it. And, of course, you can't possibly absorb the horrific events that were taking place. You just try to soak in as much of it as you can," she said. "I tried to do my job, which is to report what is going on, to tell what we know, and to explain when we don't know something, and not to go further out on the limb than what we had. But this is a situation where the story didn't need much help from anchors. The pictures were so powerful and so horrible that there really were limits to anything we could add."

Walter Isaacson, chairman and CEO of the CNN News Group, and Sid Beding-field were in the Atlanta control room directing all the traffic. "There were a lot of voices. At some points it was almost a cacophony," Judy said. "There were voices in Atlanta. There were voices in New York, people who were closer to the action up there who were talking to the reporters and producers on the scene. We had producers and reporters in Washington and then at the Pennsylvania location. The president was in Florida, so we had people who were traveling with President Bush calling in and reporting from his press plane. It was an extraordinary juggling act, frankly."

The September 11 coverage was tilted toward the events in New York, even after the Pentagon was hit. Judy said there are a couple of reasons why New York got the lion's share. "One was the sheer number of people who perished in the Twin Towers. That had a lot to do with the coverage and also the graphic images of two very tall buildings collapsing, the planes flying into them. We didn't have that picture at the Pentagon. We just had the aftermath," she said.

There were fewer deaths at the Pentagon—189 people lost their lives, sixty-four of them were on the airplane. "The Pentagon proved to be, if not invincible, far less damaged than anybody would have expected," Judy said. "That is a very strong-looking building. It looks like a fortress. While nothing is completely invincible, it obviously withstood a lot of the impact. But, having said that, sure, the psychic damage, I think, was huge for the Pentagon because it is the symbol of American military might. The terrorists were obviously going after three great symbols: the Twin Towers of commerce, which represents one cornerstone of American power in the world, our military might, and our government. Everyone I know now believes they were headed for the Capitol. But, thank God, they didn't make it."

Judy said it is impossible to prepare for news events like those of September 11, but experience is invaluable. "On the one hand, it's impossible because there has never been anything like this, the worst attack ever on the United States, on our homeland. On the other hand, I have been reporting since 1970, so I do have over thirty years of experience, and that counts for something," she said.

Woodruff has experienced a lot. She was on the scene the day President Ronald Reagan was shot. She has traveled overseas with presidents and covered Washington for twenty-four years. "So I have extensive experience," she said, "and that helps me keep my wits about me and helps me stay composed. But, clearly, on the inside I'm like everybody else. I was horrified by what was going on, and I know that I reflected that in some of my comments that day. I was quite open at times to talk about what we were seeing and how horrible that was. But you can't just sit there and break down on camera."

Perhaps this event, more than any other, united anchors and audience. Judy believes the viewers took comfort in seeing anchors and reporters express the same horror and shock that they were feeling. The audience also didn't mind some displays of emotion from normally collected anchors and reporters.

"People have told me since then that the anchors that day were in some way comforting to them as they tried to deal with it. Some people were watching alone at home or in an office or with a group of people and our demeanor apparently had quite an affect on some people," she said. "I did break down a few times. Not that first day, but in the days after as we interviewed people who had lost loved ones in the Trade Center or at the Pentagon. Those were the hardest for me.

"The first day was just shock—seeing the buildings coming down, not knowing how many people were inside, knowing there had to be many people inside who couldn't have gotten out. You were stunned to the point of being speechless. But in the subsequent days it became a human tragedy as we saw family members of those who had lost loved ones, the wives and husbands, sisters and brothers, children and parents, boyfriends and girlfriends. That's when it became the painfully human story that it remains."

One of the most horrific images of the day was that of people jumping out of windows and falling to their deaths. "We actually didn't air very much of that. There was a lot that was left out. We were very careful about that," Judy said. "We did use it a couple of times, I was told, but I never saw it on our air."

However, through her involvement in the International Women's Media Foundation, Judy has grappled with the appropriateness of using such images to provide context. Women who participate in the organization are from different countries around the world that have fought terrorism in different ways. "A number of women journalists said they thought that the U.S. press should have shown pictures of people jumping because, in their words, 'You Americans need to know what you are up against.' I had never considered that point of view before. I had just rejected the idea of showing people jumping. But, as a result of hearing them, I would at least consider it."

People searching for missing coworkers, friends, and relatives presented other emotional images. Judy said she found the people who clustered around reporters on the street, giving out their phone numbers and asking for information, "very real" and a crucial part of the story of what was going on in New York at that time.

"To a large extent, you can't stop people from doing something like that. If a reporter is based near Ground Zero or at one of the hospitals reporting on family members coming, they were going to surround you. They were going to hold those phone numbers up," she said. "I don't think we went out of our way to put people waving those numbers in front of our cameras, but, on the other hand, I don't think we should have prevented it from happening."

Judy said reporters didn't have enough information in the first few days about the possibility of survivors to discourage people from coming forward. "Nobody really knew whether there were any survivors. It certainly didn't look like there could be many, but you didn't know. Who were any of us to tell these people to give up hope? That's just not our role. I think that would have been presumptuous for us to do that. The loved ones all have to come to that point themselves when they realize the loss is inevitable. They probably knew it, but they didn't want to believe it. I certainly would have had the same reaction they did."

For Judy, interviewing those who had lost someone in the attacks was the most difficult part of covering September 11 and its aftermath. "I lost my composure a number of times in the days after September 11. It was triggered in every instance by hearing someone who had lost a loved one. I think it's the mother in me. It was just very, very difficult," she said. She remembers in particular an interview that CNN reporter Elizabeth Cohen conducted. "She interviewed one man who was looking for his sister. It was just heartbreaking. She was tearing up, and I was tearing up. I couldn't help it, and I wasn't going to force myself to suppress my feelings. It was a human and natural reaction because the man was just completely broken down, but he wanted to talk. He wanted to talk about his sister. He was looking for her and hoping against hope."

Although reporters are often criticized for the insensitive way they handle people in times of personal crisis, Judy said sometimes people in crisis need to talk. "I think it depends on the person. For some people it is cathartic, and many people sought out our reporters and sought out our camera crews. They wanted to talk, and certainly, for obvious reasons, many people were holding pictures up because they did want to know, 'If you see this person, please . . .' And there were a lot of people who didn't find their way home in the immediate aftermath or who got out of the city and they couldn't get in touch with their families. Or there were some people who were just separated for the first day or two after it happened or even longer than that. There were people legitimately searching."

Most of the anchors and reporters covering this story had family members with whom they could not be in contact for several hours during the first day. Family members, children in particular, found this more difficult than the journalist who was totally absorbed in a story.

Judy's children were in school when she went on the air. "I just somehow took it for granted they were fine. They go to a school very close to our home. It's not downtown. I knew they might worry about me, but they could turn on the TV and see that I was OK," she said. "I did think momentarily that I would like to talk to them, but it was not practical. I was on the air until about 6:15 or 6:30 P.M. When I got home that night, we all hugged. The kids were just . . . everybody found it hard to speak about what had happened. They talked about how their school had dealt with it, how many children had been permitted to go home early. They had watched television news all day. There was one family at my middle child's school where the father was on the plane that went into the Pentagon."

While CNN staffers were still trying to cope with September 11, they were hit with the anthrax threat, which had an enormous impact on the nation's capital. "It's been enormously disruptive to the city and to the postal workers here. The U.S. Postal Service lost several postal workers in Washington, and there's been controversy over whether the government adequately notified postal workers that they were at risk. It's more than controversy—they clearly didn't," Judy said.

The situation led to congressional hearings. "They quickly gave workers in the Senate Office Building antibiotics, but they didn't do the same for the postal workers. There's a lingering resentment over that. So the city was very much affected by it," she said. "I know a lot of people who work on the Hill, who work at the Capitol on the Senate and House side, and those buildings were closed down. Capitol employees weren't dying, but there was great fear. There was a lot of anthrax in those letters, a lethal dose. So whoever sent all this is clearly trying to kill people."

The disruption was more than an inconvenience for Judy. "They found anthrax spores in my local post office, not too far from where I live. They think that's because of the Brentwood facility, a distribution center here in Washington," she said. "Yes, Washington was very much affected. Was it al Qaeda? The bin Laden terrorists? We don't know. Conventional wisdom now is that it was not—that it was probably a domestic source."

CNN's bureau was also affected. "Our mail completely shut down for a while. First of all, after the first attack at NBC, it wasn't long after that they swept our building looking for anthrax. They never found any, thank goodness. But we completely changed the way we process mail now. It all goes through a security screening process before we get any mail here. Security in the building itself was stepped up dramatically."

In spite of the anthrax threat, Judy was philosophical about the situation. "I thought, 'If the mail is contaminated we're going to find out, and then we're going to take antibiotics, and that's going to be it.' I wasn't concerned for my own safety. When I heard it was in my neighborhood post office, I was concerned because then I started thinking, 'Oh, my, is it going to get into the regular mail system and come into my house?' That did bother me a lot. My daughter (who's twelve) and I were talking about someone we knew moving to Washington. My daughter said, 'Why would they want to come to Washington? This isn't a safe city anymore.' But that's not my attitude. To me, even after all this the benefits still outweigh any hazard."

As the coverage gradually shifted to the war on terrorism in Afghanistan, decisions had to be made about whom to send. Were women reporters going to be as much of a factor in that coverage as they had been in the coverage of the attacks? "It was obvious from our standpoint that Christiane Amanpour would go, because she is our premier international correspondent," Judy said. "There have been a number of other women over there: Carol Lin is there for us in Pakistan; Rebecca McKinnon, who was the Beijing bureau chief and is now in Tokyo, was sent in."

Judy acknowledged, however, that CNN sent mostly men to be on the ground inside Afghanistan. "I think that has something to do with cultural and religious traditions. If it weren't for that, I don't think there would be much of a constraint. If you're a woman [reporter] in Afghanistan, you stick out like a sore thumb if you're not in a burka. By simply being there, you're considered offensive to a religion."

Journalists assigned to Afghanistan are in harm's way. "It's clearly more dangerous. Look at the journalists who died. I think two of them were women—both European, I think. They were right in there, in the middle of it," she said.

Judy has seen an enormous shift in attitudes toward women in the broadcast field, but she thinks it has taken place over many, many years. "Certainly from the time I got in during the 1970s as a reporter, it has changed dramatically. More than half the reporters in television news departments across the country are women. More than half the local anchor teams are women. The networks actually don't have as good a record. In the national broadcast networks, including CNN, women make up perhaps 30 percent of the on-air reporters. Even so, when you look at the stories in this country, there isn't much that women don't do."

CNN has offered counseling to staff members to deal with both the aftermath of September 11 and the anthrax threat. "It has been a very stressful environment," Judy said. "People have been asked to work much longer hours and many more days in the week, from five days to sometimes six or seven. Long days. And just to be processing all this and absorbing what's happened in addition to being at work so much and away from your families. It's a lot. People have clearly been stressed."

Judy knows that she herself is different. "I've certainly been changed. I think we've all been changed. I have a whole new appreciation for how vulnerable we are in the United States, which I didn't before. I have a whole new appreciation for being an American. My country is even more precious to me now than it was before. I hate to think that it took something like this for me to think that. Anybody else with any sensibility has been affected that way. The country to me is just more precious."

Looking back at her work, does Judy believe there is anything she would have done differently? "I'm sure there is," she admitted. "Every day I go home thinking I should have done a better job with an interview or written something better or said something better. But you can only do so much of that. This business of breaking news all the time—it just goes on and on and on."

8

Susan Sachs, *New York Times*, New York City

On the morning of September 11, *New York Times* correspondent Susan Sachs "was in the process of renting a car a couple of blocks from the *Times* office. Because it was city election day, my plan had been to go hang out around the Russian community in Brooklyn, where there had been some incidents. There were hot city council races going on, and there had been some confrontation in the Russian community." While waiting in line for the car, she overheard French tourists saying they would have to go north because a plane had crashed into the World Trade Center. "I stepped outside, but my cell phone didn't work, so I went to a phone booth and called the office about 9:30 A.M. I asked if it was a small plane and was told, 'No, it looked like a passenger plane.'"

By the time she got to the *Times* office, three eyewitnesses were already in the building. One lived in the vicinity of the World Trade Center, and two worked in nearby buildings. All three had snapped photographs in the area. Susan's first 9/11 assignment was to interview the three amateur photographers. "They had just come from downtown. They all were shell-shocked," she said. "One guy was an Asian American student who had been photographing people doing tai chi in the park. All he could talk about was people jumping from the building. He felt that he had intruded on something private by photographing people falling."

The woman in the group lived nearby and had gone up on her roof and focused her camera on the second tower. "She talked about what a beautiful day it was. She was struck by the contrast between the glorious day and the horror of the crash. While she had her camera lens focused on the second plane, she was thinking how beautiful the second plane looked with the sun shimmering on the wings. Her camera lens followed the plane into the tower."

Susan said the third person had a camera with him because it was his wedding anniversary. "He was the closest to the World Trade Center and was so shocked he could only talk about going out to dinner with his wife and not so much about what he had seen. All three had the feeling of being behind the lens and distant from the event. They had these very complicated reactions because they were looking at it with neutral eyes separate from their hearts."

After completing the interviews, Susan went down to the Metro desk. Editors and reporters were having difficulty getting to the office because many had come in from Brooklyn and other areas in New Jersey and New York served by trains, and so it took a bit longer than usual to organize the reporters who had not already gone to the site upon hearing the news in the morning. "I wasn't told to go down to Ground Zero but rather to go out into Manhattan and see what the city's reaction was. Right away—that is, about 10:30 A.M.—I went out and just began walking." Just outside the Times Building she saw a young woman with tears running down her face. "She was on 43rd Street, watching the wire service ticker in Times Square. Her boyfriend worked in the World Trade Center. She wanted to be a Broadway dancer and had just come from an audition. She was trying to call her boyfriend on her cell phone, but no one answered. She was asking, 'What should I do now? Where should I go?'"

Susan said the whole city was paralyzed. "Everything was very, very quiet. People were loaning cell phones to others. There was a tenderness to the way people treated one another. And there were long lines at pay phones, but people stood quietly, politely, waving ahead those who seemed most distressed. I went to Grand Central Station where there was a bomb scare. I just moved south, interviewing people along the way. When I got down to the lower part of midtown Manhattan or so, by late morning, one could see walking uphill from Lower Manhattan this continuous flow of people who looked like shocked refugees, covered with dust. They were a strangely quiet group of soot-covered people walking in lines up Lexington Avenue. They were carrying water bottles and gas masks that people had given them. It was a beautiful, brilliant blue day, and here were these very quiet, shocked people covered in gray, trudging along in a thick line of people."

Susan said the people made her think of refugees she had seen in northern Iraq, Jordan, and Kosovo. "It definitely reminded me of that. But it was more shocking because I saw these people walking through the canyons of New York City, everyone covered with ash. Close by was an inferno and tragedy. It was much more personal. The other places I have been I expected to see refugees. It wasn't something that happened suddenly. And when you see it overseas, you know there is a war."

Adding to the impact of the scene was the contrast of the beautiful fall day and the rest of the city that remained untouched. "These people were shell-shocked, trudging, determined. They were people whom you wouldn't rush to embrace because there was a certain dignity and privacy. That is what I saw when I saw these people coming up from Lower Manhattan. They had experienced something very private and very public at the same time," she said.

Early on, Susan thought of giving blood at Bellevue Hospital, in an attempt to get another view of the effects on the rest of the city. There she encountered another scene. "Hundreds of people were in line begging to get in, to do anything to help, from giving blood to carrying boxes. The hospital staff told everyone that they had all they needed. I couldn't get in to give blood, but I could get in as a reporter. There was a sense of fellowship and helping. People were desperate to do anything."

She walked as far as she could down 18th Street, then she realized she needed to get back to the office to write. She got back between 2 to 3 P.M. and began writing her story with fellow reporter Jim Dwyer. "I started to call people I knew who worked down there. I found one person who had wandered all day, walking from way uptown to downtown and back uptown, over a bridge to Queens, and finally hailing a bus to get back home. I found two other acquaintances—both Egyptian Americans—who had worked in the World Trade Center. One had managed to escape. The other couldn't believe his luck because he had been late coming to the office that day."

She said the scene in the Metro section was intense but not chaotic. "There was a determined energy there. I think what happened is that a number of reporters went down on their own to get as close as they could to the Trade Center. They weren't 'assigned' to go, they just went. They would call in. One of the Metro desk editors set up a special computer queue for everyone who called in to dictate or to submit information through the computer. The information was read and routed to reporters who needed it. It was very organized and the best way to get specific things to specific people. We started organizing the data in the afternoon. We had the general story, the Ground Zero story, the rest of New York, and the ripple-effect story."

Susan said that everyone was working under the assumption that no matter how many pages it took, they would tell the story of September 11. "There was a sense that this is the *New York Times* and this was an all-out effort. There was an effort to take this enormous body of information that had to be divided up. It was just 'Write your heart out,' basically. A lot of stuff didn't get into the paper. But I don't think there was a sense of rivalry or disappointment if your work didn't get in. There was a sense of being part of something and a sense of volunteerism. It didn't feel routine. The normal division between sections was not particularly important. That was reflected in the way editors were acting."

Much of the news that normally would be in the paper was thrown out, including ads. "This was something quite extraordinary," Susan said. "There was an acknowledgment that we would write everything we had. Everyone was doing something about this story. There was not even any question that what was happening in New York was *the* national story and *the* international story of the day. There was no other story."

In describing the content of the *Times* during the first week, Susan said that the attack on New York was given bigger play than the Pentagon attack. "There was something particular about the Trade Center that impacted more people than what happened at the Pentagon. It was just written as an event that superceded any other event. I think from the beginning, it was the magnitude of the potential loss of life; but as a reporter that day, there was a sense that the entire city had been affected. Everything was disrupted for millions of people. You saw and heard about small acts of kindness. There was a sense of everyone being engaged in some way. Perhaps the Pentagon was more isolated and not something that affected ordinary people the way this day affected New Yorkers. There wasn't a patch of ground that wasn't affected in some way. Everyone was engaged and involved in some way. Everyone knew someone who knew someone . . . the father of the girl who is a friend of your brother's.

"This was a sophisticated plan to attack America," Susan added. "There was a sense that ordinary people had been swept up in this. Entire companies of fire-fighters were missing. That really touched people, and that became clear early in the morning. We were trying to get a sense of the lay of the land from police and fire-fighters, and they were announcing very early they didn't know where entire compa-nies were. The major media being there made it more immediate. It didn't have the ripple effect in other communities that it did in New York."

Times editors also had to make decisions about how to cover the story visually. Graphics showed the number of building damaged, the landmarks, the things people were familiar with that were no longer there. Photographs were carefully selected to illustrate the events of the day. "During those first days, there was no sense that we had to impress on people that it was a horrible act. The editors had to pick a handful of still images that described what went on in New York, Washington—the personal and the political. The edition was published twenty hours later [after the attack]. It had to be the iconic images, with reporting and writing, to make the day what it was."

Until she left for Cairo on October 6, Susan continued to report on reactions. "The first week, I was out covering what happened. Either I was at Ground Zero, or I was compiling stories from reporters who were phoning in from Ground Zero. I generally covered the rescue effort based on other people's reporting and my own telephoning to companies that had crews at the scene. It was really a combination of my going out there and using information from people on the scene who were phoning in. Once in, reporters didn't want to leave, because the police were exercis-ing more restraint in who came in. I would occasionally go down and get as close as I could, so I had a sense of the scene. Everybody was covering something related to the attacks."

When asked whether she thought New York reporters sometimes became too per-sonally involved with the story, Susan responded, "No, not too personally involved in the story, but some other reporters lost sight of the need to let the people involved tell the story and not to be the story." She remembered one morning about four days into the event when she awoke to the complaints of a local television reporter doing a standup near Ground Zero. He was saying, "Well, it's not enough that the Twin Towers fell, but now it's cold and it's raining, and I don't have an umbrella, and it's cold out here."

For Susan this monologue was going too far. "The fact that this reporter was getting rained on had nothing to do with what other people were suffering. He had crossed a line by personalizing it to the point of making it banal. There is a line that is difficult to describe and impossible to teach. You try to channel someone's feeling into your writing and reporting. After a certain point in the business, you are so used to being a reporter and a translator that there is a line you don't cross into making yourself part of the story. A lot of reporters probably crossed that line in this story. There is something that kicks in when you try to transcribe what people are seeing and feeling. While you are doing the job, you retain a certain distance. That is automatic. Sometimes you think you can't do it; but, in fact, you can because you have something to do. You have a deadline, a job, a notebook, a pencil. You have to act, delve, and pull from people what they are seeing and what they are feeling. But you maintain a certain distance."

At the other end of the spectrum are the reporters who can't function in the face of tragedy. "Throughout my career, I've seen it happen to journalists. They are paralyzed by the magnitude of what they've seen," Susan said.

The *Times* provided food morning, noon, and night for several days and offered emotional support to staff members who needed it. "From the beginning they had emergency numbers to call if you were feeling vulnerable or shaken. They had group sessions for those who wanted to talk about it. They made counselors available who made a great effort to be there for anyone who was overwhelmed. I didn't feel it personally because I didn't know anyone who was killed. I knew people who survived. Everyone I knew in that area had some sort of miraculous story of survival. That was much better than not knowing their fate. I was touched, but not so personally as others were."

Susan said she didn't attend any of the support sessions, but she had her own way of coping. "Talking with other people at the paper was helpful. My parents called every day, which was unusual. Most evenings I was able to get out of work at 8 or 9 P.M. The first couple of nights I would come home at midnight and watch reruns of television news about the attacks until four in the morning. Then I realized this was a really unhealthy thing to do. So either I came home and tried to have a quiet dinner and then go to sleep, or I would go out to dinner with friends from the office to talk about our reactions. We were able to share that we were very much involved—not personally involved—but involved as in-depth witnesses. I had to make time for myself or spend time with colleagues." She said she and her friends would just try to imagine the effects of the attacks on New York, the economic effects, the impact of losing over three hundred firefighters.

However, once she left American soil in October, she had to deal with emotions she had not experienced on her previous trips to the Middle East. "There was definitely a sense of anti-Americanism. Yemen was the worst place. But that was my first time in that country. I had a sense of not knowing whom to trust. When you're in a place that is so foreign and some things seem familiar and some things don't, it is hard to know who is trustworthy."

As she traveled in Egypt, Yemen, Morocco, and Tunisia, Susan said she found the people "so many, many degrees removed from the event." She felt a disconnection even with Americans who were not in New York at the time of the attacks. People who blamed American policy in the Middle East for the attacks particularly irked her. That seemed to me a callous way to pass off what had been such a powerful event on individual people. "It was difficult for me to explain the impact that this event had on people's thinking and sense of security. If you weren't there, you couldn't get the full picture."

Susan said there are two aspects of the event that she will retain. "One is the shock of the attack itself, and the other is the sense of kindness, the sense of pulling together I witnessed. At the time, in the first week, it was as though everyone in the city couldn't do enough for others. People were walking around with bags of clothes and bags of food to give to someone."

But, once in the Middle East, she had difficulty trying to explain what happened in New York. "The intensity of the event—there was just no way to describe it to anyone who had not been in the country, or maybe not even to those who had not been in New York. Most people saw it as a television event."

Susan experienced some culture shock, which was unusual for her, when she encountered opinions about who had actually planned and carried out the attacks. "The entire five months I was there, I was hearing that the Mossad [an Israeli intelligence agency headquartered in Tel Aviv] did it, that the Jews did it, that the oil companies did it. The refusal to acknowledge that either an Arab or a Muslim could have done this left an impression on me."

Susan said she never felt that as a reporter she was in any particular danger while she was in the Middle East, although she was there when *Wall Street Journal* reporter Daniel Pearl was kidnapped and murdered. "In Yemen, there has long been a problem of kidnapping of foreigners. I was especially careful. I have a built-in warning signal generally."

She agreed that print journalists are in some ways more vulnerable than broadcast journalists, who generally have a crew with them when they cover a story. "A newspaper reporter is a much more solitary operator and thus more vulnerable. On the other hand, militants who want to make a point might find a high-profile television reporter worth capturing."

Susan acknowledged that there is such a thing as a reporter's "sixth sense" that perhaps kept reporters from being killed on September 11. "Something kicks in when you are a journalist. A warning bell goes off, but there is a sense that you have to be there to report it. You don't blindly rush in. It is not the same as being a firefighter or police officer. There is some sense that you have to get out. You have to live to tell the tale."

9

Suzanne Plunkett, Associated Press, New York City

It was Fashion Week in New York City. AP photographer Suzanne Plunkett had been up late the night of September 10 shooting a show. She planning to shoot the DKNY (Donna Karan) fashion show on the evening of September 11. "I was sleeping in when I got a page from the AP bureau. I couldn't get through when I tried to call them back. I turned on the television and saw the second plane go through. I realized what AP wanted, so I got all my camera equipment together and jumped on a train. I probably got the very last train because they kept stopping it. Finally, I got off at Fulton and Broadway, which is about a block from the north tower."

The AP supplies photographers with Nikon digital equipment. Suzanne had two Nikon cameras and three lenses with her that day. She also was packing her laptop computer. "I don't usually carry all that stuff, but I knew when I left the house that I might not be able to get back. I didn't know exactly what I was going into, so I brought everything. It's very heavy, but when your adrenaline is running, you don't notice."

Suzanne described the scene as "pandemonium" when she got off the train. "People were running and yelling. A woman was screaming, 'Don't go outside!' I couldn't find an open exit." On the way she had met up with her boyfriend, Doug, also a photographer, and together they tried to find a way out of the subway.

Once outside, Suzanne saw broken windows and glass on the street. "Although I normally don't do this, I set my cameras on auto when I was in the subway because I didn't know what the scene would be when I came outside. I heard someone yell, 'They're coming down, run for your lives!' I just started shooting because it happened about a minute after I came out of the subway, and I was rubbing my eyes from the bright sunlight. People were running and screaming. I turned around and took some pictures of what I saw: People were coming toward me, and a huge dust cloud was coming down. Then I turned around and started running."

Suzanne Plunkett with children in Kabul, Afghanistan

Separated from Doug in the chaos, Suzanne tried to outrun the fast-moving cloud, but then she realized she couldn't. "I took photographs of people as the cloud was passing. Then I realized I couldn't breathe. When I started running, I was thinking that the building would fall like a tree. I kept thinking that I'm not 110 stories away; I'm a block away. It was like a movie or a bad dream—I couldn't run fast enough. I felt sluggish because I had all my equipment with me. So I ducked into an alley. I thought about hiding behind a car, but then I thought that if the building did fall on top of me, a car wouldn't help. So I ducked into an alley, thinking that if it crashed on top of me, the buildings would break the fall."

Once in the alley, Suzanne made a phone call to her dad and left a message on his voice mail. "I told him I was OK and that I loved him." Her dad told her later that he saved the message for a long time—it had really scared him because she sounded "really whacked out."

She still couldn't breathe, so she started running down the street. "I found an office building that was open. I went inside the office building for a while. Wall Street traders were inside screaming and yelling. Everyone seemed to be freaking out. Then I knew I had to get back out there, so I tied my sweater around my mouth and went running outside. I basically concentrated that day on photographing people fleeing the scene."

Suzanne said most people didn't notice her or her camera. There was a notable exception. "I do clearly remember when I was photographing a bunch of people running toward me after the first building fell, and it was very quiet. I remember photographing two women holding each other as they were running away. I heard some guy yell, 'Take a picture of this, asshole.' It registered, but I just brushed it off. But I keep hearing that voice and thinking that's not what I'm doing. It is difficult when people don't understand what we're doing. Lots of people see photographers as pests. People patrolling the area of Ground Zero didn't understand what we're doing, and they didn't want us anywhere near, but then they'll see a photograph like Thomas Franklin's restaged Iwo Jima photograph [of firefighters raising an American flag]; they love it, and they'll buy a million copies. But in order for Thomas to get that photograph, he had to be there."

Suzanne said she used her camera as a kind of shield. "If you put the camera in front of your face, it's almost like you're superwoman and can do anything. But when you put the camera down, then you realize the magnitude of it. The camera was a protector in a way, because it gave me a reason to be down there. If I wasn't a photographer, I probably would have been running for my life."

While some moments of that day are crystal clear to Suzanne, other moments are out of focus. "I don't remember any sound. People keep asking me what it sounded like when the buildings fell down. I know that it must have made a big noise, but I don't remember any sound. Even the alley that I hid in—I can't find that alley. I've retraced my steps. Was I in an alley? I remember distinctly being in this alley, but it doesn't seem to exist. Maybe I just ran somewhere else, and I can't seem to retrace my steps." After the building fell, Suzanne said she does recall "a creepy, sort of haunted house sound, like a rumbling or metal bending."

Although she hasn't had any lasting physical effects, Suzanne was concerned about the dust she was breathing in. "It was really frightening because I didn't have a mask for quite a while. I was running around with just my sweater tied around my face. It was very frightening because I was definitely breathing in particles. My mouth felt like paste. It wasn't invisible dust; it was thick. My throat was covered and coated. I knew it was bad, whatever it was. The dust was strange. It probably was a lot of ground up glass. The first couple of days, I would sit down and it would feel like I was sitting on little slivers of glass. I showered and showered and I couldn't get it off, but that wore away.

"I was at a triage center waiting for victims to come in. There were hundreds of doctors waiting. Nobody was coming in because they weren't finding any survivors. I kept coughing, and one of the doctors gave me an asthma treatment. I felt fine after that."

Her next order of business that day was to transmit the photographs she had taken back to the AP bureau. "I had one photograph that I had to get out. I ducked into a vitamin/beeper shop—very New York—and asked for a phone. They said they had no phone lines, so I asked if I could just use their electricity. I sent three photographs to AP before the second building collapsed, just using my cell phone. Somehow I got a connection. I couldn't make a connection with anyone else during the day, except for the crazy message I left my dad and the AP office. But I somehow got the pictures out, and I wouldn't have been able to do that without my laptop. I was online about a half hour sending those pictures, and after that I couldn't contact anyone."

Suzanne said that no one in the AP newsroom knew where she was until she sent the pictures. They had paged her to go down there, and then they were wondering whether she was alive. "When I finally called in, everyone was like, 'Oh, my God!' They saw my pictures from the wire before they talked to me. So they knew I was around, doing something. But they didn't know where I was before the second building fell."

She continued to look for pictures everywhere she could. "I was thinking this is the most unbelievable thing I've ever seen, and I have to document it. I could take a picture of anything, and it was amazing looking. So many people were running by me. There were some people who were hurt, but I don't remember at the time thinking 'That looks gross' or anything. It was just 'This is what's happening.' I've seen a lot of stuff because I cover spot news—nothing ever the magnitude of this—but I was sort of prepared. Experience in covering things like this helped me go into my mode of being professional. It felt familiar because I've been doing it for eight years. The familiarity let me go find a photograph and send my pictures. I was able to follow my usual routine, and that is what got me through."

Suzanne didn't go back to the AP bureau that day, because she was able to send everything from her laptop. "I just stayed down there. Some editors had set up an overhead position. I went to an apartment and took some photographs from overhead so they could have an overall view of the scene. I walked around the city. I went to St. Vincent's Hospital and Chelsea Piers, where they had ambulances lined up. I wandered around and got home at 3 A.M. I went to sleep because I was just exhausted."

She didn't go into the office until Thursday. "I sent photographs from home or my laptop or wherever I was walking around. There is a cord on the back of my laptop that connects right into my cell phone. If I dial a certain number, I can get out to the AP server. I can send pictures directly into the system. Connections were spotty, but I was making them. I live downtown, and I didn't lose phone service from my home."

In spite of her professional approach, Suzanne said emotionally the experience was very difficult. "For weeks I had dreams, and everything was set in the rubble. I made it through emotionally and professionally until I went to Ground Zero. The second day I went out and photographed murals in my neighborhood. People were putting murals up right away in the East Village. That night I went down to Ground Zero. The very first day I was never right on the site. I had this extreme need to be down there for some reason. I felt like I was so close, but I hadn't gotten close enough. I have this strange guilt about not actually getting closer to it that day. I photographed Ground Zero Wednesday night into Thursday morning."

Suzanne retraced her route from the day before. "I actually was walking right on where the World Trade Center was and photographing it. It was absolutely indescribable at that point. It was therapeutic in a way just to be there, because I had been so close and actually wasn't there, and I wanted to go back. It was really late at night, and when I was trying to send pictures, I kept falling asleep. When I woke up the next morning, everything just hit me. I was really upset, and I cried. It was good because I got it out. I held out until that point, and then I went back to Ground Zero, and then all my emotions went out because it was so awful."

Compounding the strain was her inability to escape the aftermath. "My neighborhood and my street were used as a staging area for a lot of the dump trucks. There were lights and sirens. I couldn't get away from it. Even though I went home to sleep, I didn't really sleep. I was just exhausted."

The result, Suzanne said, was a kind of "shell shock." "Tons of times, I would be driving across the Manhattan Bridge, and I would suddenly imagine what would happen if the bridge collapsed, where I'd go in, and where I'd swim. I'd be halfway across the bridge and then go, 'What am I thinking? Stop it!'"

She found herself overreacting after a police officer told her in a normal voice to step to the side of the road. "I just bolted and ran to the sidewalk. My heart was racing." Seeing low-flying planes also made her tense.

In spite of being shell-shocked, Suzanne still found it difficult to seek support. Although she has a private therapist whom she had been seeing before September 11, she resisted going to see him after September 11. "It was the last place I wanted to go. I should have felt lucky to have someone who already knew my issues, but I just avoided going. I made it this insurmountable task to get there. I really pushed him away."

She did go to grief counseling sessions that the AP provided. "I went to those, and then realized I wanted to see my therapist. I didn't want to open up in front of coworkers I didn't know. It felt strange. It was thoughtful, but the whole thing was just odd. The third day, when I came into the office, they had a woman come and follow me around with her arm around me. She kept asking if I was OK. I really had a lot of work I needed to get done. But she kept asking me how I was feeling. I was like, 'Uh, OK.' At that point, I was pushing everyone away; I just wanted to be in a protective shell. I couldn't accept it all. It was too much."

Suzanne has turned to family for support. "My little sister came to visit me about a week after it happened to boost my morale for my first day off. Having my sister here really helped me get through it. I could put my camera down and go to Union Square and to a lot of memorials I hadn't been to. I experienced it as a New Yorker, rather than as a photographer. That was really therapeutic. Having a family member know where I've been was very helpful. We could just cry together."

She also is grateful to have shared the experience with her boyfriend. "We have since looked through each other's photographs. The way I covered it was completely different from the way he covered it, even though we were at the exact same point when the buildings came down. But what he shot was completely different. He might have been a little braver because he went right down to the site. He photographed firefighters and other people trying to get in, and I just stayed away.

"In retrospect, it makes sense that I was photographing people's reactions and how they felt. His approach was different. He wanted to get the scene and more of what happened there, while I was photographing the people on the outside, the victims. I don't know why we did it that way. It was just very different," Suzanne said.

She also credited the AP with looking out for her welfare. "For the first couple of weeks, they would only send me to 'happy' events, even though nothing was really happy at the time. For example, I covered two volunteers getting married. I know they did the same with some of the other photographers who were down there."

After covering "happy" events for two weeks, however, Suzanne had had enough. "I started wondering if the editors didn't think I was tough enough. I said, 'OK, I'm fine. I can go do the funerals. I didn't want to be treated differently because I was a woman. I had to go around to each editor and tell him or her that they could send me out because I'm fine. They started giving me regular assignments again."

She first went to an apartment AP rented that overlooks Ground Zero. "We give people shifts, and I've done a couple of those where we photograph the cleanup or bringing out bodies. The Cantor Fitzgerald [brokerage firm] funeral that I did was very, very difficult. It was in Central Park, and they didn't allow photographers inside for the memorial, so we stood outside and photographed people as they were leaving. There was a whole array of emotions from the people leaving. Some were saying we were vultures, and others were thanking us for being there to document them. I was wondering, 'Why am I here?' Then I realized I wanted to show the world how hard this is and what people are going through. There's a funeral for seven hundred people going on."

Suzanne had a friend who had previously worked at Cantor Fitzgerald. "I'd been up to the offices. So I remembered what those offices looked like. It was eerie. It really hit me when friends from my home state of Minnesota were calling me and bawling their eyes out. I suddenly felt like it was OK if I'm crying because people who aren't even near it are crying."

Suzanne does have a favorite among her many photographs. "It's a quieter moment with two women huddled together, looking very scared. They are very small in the frame. There's a lot of dust and a stoplight with a caution light on. It didn't get picked up a lot, but that's the one that reflects how I felt: just bewildered, walking through the dust. There was the intense moment of screaming and running, but there also was this bewildered fog that everyone was walking through for the next couple of weeks, not knowing what to do, and covered with dust."

Although she acknowledges that as a still photographer, she is biased, Suzanne believes a still image is easier to remember. "It sticks with you once you've seen it—it will come back to you right away. When you've seen videotape, you are not going to remember the whole sequence. But a still image is so permanent. You can recall it right away in your mind. It's like the Iwo Jima picture. Everyone thinks of it, and that is why the other one is so successful. I'm a still photographer so I feel biased, but I know the pictures I remember from September 11 are the still photographs. I remember seeing videotape of the towers falling, but capturing a moment is just completely different. It's a different way of thinking.

"If the towers hadn't collapsed, it would have been a smaller story. The towers were an icon, and now they're gone. The Pentagon can be repaired. If the Pentagon had disappeared, obviously it would have been a bigger story. But the towers were built at a time when the city was in a decline, and they brought up morale. So many people remember them being built and have this huge personal attachment to them."

Suzanne will most remember a huge bank of escalators at the World Trade Center. "I just loved them and wanted to photograph them. I keep thinking about them being gone. I have a sinking feeling when I see the skyline now. It looks like Boston, not New York. It's just a sick feeling, still. They are just gone. It's still hard to imagine."

10

Amy Sancetta, Associated Press, New York City

Amy Sancetta, the national enterprise photographer for the Associated Press, had been in New York City for two weeks covering the U.S. Open Tennis Tournament. The tournament ended on Sunday, September 9. Normally, she would have gone home the next day, but she decided to take a couple of extra days just to enjoy New York. She spent Monday in the AP bureau office, meeting with her boss and some of the writers with whom she works. On Tuesday, she planned to "hang out with friends, be a tourist, and enjoy the city." Amy said it was rare for her to take such time for herself. "I never do that. I usually go in to work and then go home."

Amy was staying in a hotel at Broadway and 52nd Street. She was in her room packing her gear away and getting ready to go out when the phone rang just before 9 A.M. "I got this frantic call from my supervisor at Rockefeller Center saying that a plane had crashed into one of the towers. They thought it was an accident, and I needed to get down there. Ten days later I finally went home. I never did the tourist thing."

Amy grabbed the gear she had been packing and hoped that her batteries were well charged. Since she's not from New York, her first challenge was to figure out where to go. "I'd never been down to the World Trade Center. I knew it was south. I really didn't know where they were compared to everything else." She got a cab on Broadway. She estimates that it took her about five minutes to get out the door and get the cab, but by then the second plane had hit. "But I went down there thinking it was an accident. The cab took me straight down Broadway. Broadway at 7th Street turns slightly to the east, and from there you can see the Trade Towers all the way down. Both had holes in them; both were smoking. Two holes in two towers didn't look like an accident, but I really didn't know what it was."

She got out of the cab twice, making the driver follow her along. "I shot people on the street just watching in horror what was in front of them. I stopped once to

Chapter 10

Amy Sancetta and her dog, Ellie

see if anyone was in the windows or if anyone was jumping out of the building, but I never did see anyone. It was just such a weird scene. There's almost no cars on the street, but the streets were just full of people, all standing there, dead silent, just staring."

After the cab driver took Amy as far as he could, she started making her way on foot south and east toward the towers. "I took the most convenient way I could, avoiding police blockades. I was shooting along the way until I got about one and a half blocks from the towers, just below City Hall Park. At that point, people were being driven back by police."

Amy said she stopped at that location mainly because the towers were getting too tall, and she was losing her perspective on them. She was using brand-new Nikon D1H digital camera equipment. Amy said she had an 80-to-200 medium-zoom lens on one camera and a fourteen-millimeter very-wide-angle lens on the other camera.

"I shot people fleeing the burning buildings and then turned my camera back to the south tower to look again for people in the windows high above. I shot frames as I watched it fall right through my lens. It was really weird to see the top of the building just come off," she said.

The sound is what Amy most remembers. "It was deafening, and it came from everywhere. I was in the middle of a lot of tall buildings, and the sound was bouncing around everywhere. Imagine 110 stories falling. Though it did not translate on television, it made one heck of a sound in person."

She compared it to a loud rock concert where the sound can be felt rumbling through the body, or the sound that the space shuttle makes when it goes up. "The sound is unbelievable. You feel it throughout your whole body. I don't know why I was so attuned to the sound, but that is what is in my mind all the time—that unbelievable rumbling and breaking metal and cement crushing against concrete. And then I became aware of all the people screaming and the pounding of feet on pavement."

Amy thinks she might have been so aware of the sound because she had her camera in front of her face, shooting as the building fell. "I shot the top of the south tower coming off, and as it began to fall behind another building in the foreground, I became aware of all that screaming and all those pounding feet, all running past me. I must have looked like an idiot standing there facing the building with everyone running away." She lifted her other camera with the fourteen-millimeter wide-angle lens. "I held it up vertically and shot forty frames. I know how many because my digital camera will allow me to shoot forty frames before it hits the buffer. The camera takes a break at that point to record the images on the disk."

"Technical stuff" was running through her head as she was shooting. "As I shot the tower, I knew I was right on it. It felt like shooting a sporting event when you're on a touchdown pass or you're on that play at the plate. You know you're there. So, when I actually shot the building, I was just a photographer. I was framing, and as I switched cameras to the wide lens to shoot the people running and the debris cloud coming toward me, what was really going through my head was, 'Are you straight up and down? Are you holding the camera perpendicular to the ground?' I thought, 'Boy, the sky is so blue and bright, and it's so dark down here in the street. I hope my exposure is good because I can't change it now.'"

She isn't sure what would have happened to her if she hadn't reached the camera's maximum number of exposures at that moment. "Frankly, if I hadn't hit the buffer on the camera, I probably would have stood there until the cloud came and hit me. I was so in the mind-set of the work. It wasn't scary when I was looking through the camera. It gives you enough of that separation. It wasn't until I stopped and I was away from it that I realized how frightening it had been. At one point, I thought, 'People are really screaming as they are running. I wonder if I was running, if I'd be screaming?'"

As people ran by her, Amy dropped the camera from her face and saw how big and close the debris cloud was. "I realized I needed to turn around and run with everybody else. I ran with the crowd. I looked behind me, and this debris cloud was big and fast and towering. I thought, 'I'm going to get hit.' I didn't want my cameras ruined. At that point, I wasn't thinking about getting hurt. I just didn't want my *brand-new* cameras trashed."

Amy turned right at the next street, but the cloud also turned right. "I thought I was going to be overtaken, so I took another right into this open parking garage. There were just some guys standing in it. I ran in there and turned to shoot as people

New Yorkers escape the area of the collapsed World Trade Center towers. Photo by Amy Sancetta

ran by. I turned around, and the whole street was white. You would see somebody emerge right in front of you and then disappear again. It was that thick."

Then the debris started coming into the garage, so she went to the back and down a stairway into the basement. "There was some debris there, but it gave me a chance to catch my breath and wipe off my cameras. I had worn a T-shirt with a button-down over it. When I was down in that parking garage, I took off my button-down. I put my cameras on over my T-shirt, and then I put my button-down back on over that so that my shirt would protect my gear. When I came back up into that cloudy world, I was able to put my shirt over my nose to breathe sometimes, because the air was awful. It really wasn't a very pleasant experience."

Amy was not alone in the basement of that garage. "There was a woman who was already there who was crying. I went over and hugged her and told her it was OK. She worked right near the buildings and had run. She was frantic because her pager kept going off. It was her son trying to call her, and she couldn't get a line out. I had a cell phone, so I stood there and tried to call her son for her. That's the first time I realized I was actually scared, because when I held my cell phone, my hand was shaking."

After ten minutes of trying unsuccessfully to reach the woman's son, Amy wrote down his number and promised to call him later and told her to get herself out of the garage and home. "The garage was filling up with soot. I thought, 'This is a really stupid place to get stuck.' Plus, I didn't know what else was going on. I don't live in the city; I live out in the woods. I kept thinking, if other things fall down, I don't want to get trapped in this garage. Nobody will know I'm here. I could be stuck here for a long time or worse."

She made the decision to leave the garage. "I came into that world of white silent soot with people just walking around in a daze. It was quiet, and it looked like it had snowed. Everything was white. The ground was white. The people were white. Everything. And there was no sound.

"The air was really acrid. It was not comfortable breathing. I actually tried to get water from a policeman who had a big crate of water. But he was just handing it out to other policemen," she said. "After ten days, I got home, but it was about five or six days after that until I finally had that smell and that taste out of my mouth."

Amy continued to shoot pictures in that white soot for a while. "At that point I ran into this photographer I knew from Boston who had been in town covering Fashion Week. He had not expected to be at something like this, either. We hung together for a little bit. Then we heard that huge rumbling sound again. I wasn't looking at the north tower, but two other photographers in the area who obviously knew each other were shouting, 'Run! Run! Run!' At that point, I was pumped up enough that I just turned around and ran. I just didn't know where it was coming down. The first one, I saw where it was, but this one I didn't see. I ran another couple of blocks with the crowd. Another cloud of yuck was coming. At that point I thought, 'This is really scary. I think I need to call the office and see what to do.'"

She dialed and dialed and dialed her cell phone. Miraculously, after about ten minutes, she finally got a line in to the AP bureau. "I got our executive news editor, and I told him what I had shot and that I didn't know where I was. I told him I was OK." He directed her back to the bureau, a four-and-a-half-mile walk to Rockefeller Center. "They edited my stuff, and I went out again. I ended up walking back to the scene, but I never got as close again as I had been."

Amy can't remember when she realized that terrorists had attacked the towers. "When I got back to the bureau, they were getting phone calls about other missing airplanes. After I went back out, I went down 2nd Avenue where all the hospitals are. I was walking with another staffer, and we were talking about how two planes had been hijacked, and at that point I didn't know they were passenger planes. We thought they were empty planes filled with bombs. I've been racking my brain trying to figure out when I understood that it was two commercial planes. I don't really know."

As she went back down toward Ground Zero, Amy said she was "pretty charged up." She walked along the street where the hospitals were located. "That was eerie because it was hospital after hospital of doctors or interns waiting out front with nobody coming. There were no ambulances, no scurrying about, just medical people waiting."

She walked back to Ground Zero, getting as close as she could, and then walked all the way back to the AP bureau. She returned to her hotel around 9 P.M. "My window looked right down Broadway, and I took a picture that night of Broadway with nobody there. Broadway at ten o'clock on a Tuesday night should have been packed with people getting out of the theater. It was a good picture because it showed how the city was completely deserted."

Sleep didn't come easily that night. "I was wide awake," Amy said. "I thought, 'I can't walk that again.' A good friend lived right down the block from where I was staying. So I called her and asked if I could borrow a bicycle. I went to her apartment and borrowed her husband's bike and borrowed some aroma therapy bathtub stuff because I had to calm down. I went back to the hotel and took a bath. At midnight I was lying in bed with my eyes wide open. I just wasn't sleepy. I wasn't tired, I wasn't freaked out, and I wasn't scared. It was just a restless night because I was charged up. I had to be up so I could go back to the scene for first-light pictures. So I was back on the bicycle at 5 A.M. pedaling down Broadway. I kept wondering which would frighten my mother more: that I'd been a block and a half from the tower when it collapsed or that I was riding a bicycle around Manhattan."

Amy encountered the police perimeter Wednesday morning. "Some people were getting in. God only knows how, because I sure tried but I didn't have any luck. But there was plenty to see just from the streets around it: debris everywhere, and down certain streets you could see the sides of the building that were stuck into the ground.

"There were quite a few of us there from the AP, a couple of our guys from Canadian Press and a couple of the New York staffers. We were all just walking the same perimeter, just trying to make pictures. I was really glad that I had that bicycle because at that point there was no way to get back and forth from the AP bureau.

We didn't have any messengers at that point. You couldn't get a cab back and forth because they had closed off Lower Manhattan. So I was able to gather everybody's disks at about 8 A.M. and ride the bike back to the bureau to deliver them for the early deadlines. Then I went back down. So I was photographer/bike messenger, which worked out well for us."

Thursday, it rained. "I had just been going and going and going. I was just done. I went down to the scene, and I couldn't get in. I was trying to make different pictures. I was soaking wet from the rain. I had just had enough. I called the office in tears and said I think I need to go back to the hotel and watch mindless TV and not think about this awfulness for a few hours. AP was great about trying to take care of those of us who had been right down there. They said, 'Don't go back. Let us know when you want to work again.' I just took a couple of hours off in the morning. Once the rain stopped, I was refreshed, and I went back out again."

Still, Amy faced many emotional moments during the next few days. "It was really hard because it was emotional, and you're working long days. You're very tired, and you've been through something really, really scary. Then, there were all those little flyers with people's pictures on them, like a Xeroxed photo of a guy with a little boy, and handwritten on it was, 'Have you seen my Daddy? He's this tall. He worked on this floor of the building.' Those started showing up everywhere. And that became part of the work in the days afterward, too. There were certain intersections you could go to where those flyers would be everywhere: on every mailbox and telephone pole, on cars—it was unbelievable. Memorials popped up everywhere in different parks, on subway stations, and firehouses. It was a very emotional time."

Amy intended to participate in AP counseling sessions, but she said they fell at times when she was out working, so she never did. "The work itself seemed to be good therapy. I wanted to do something. I wanted to do more. In fact, after I came home after those ten days, I wanted to go back. It was like working the story was helping somebody somewhere.

"I think there is some survivor guilt to it. You think, 'What more could I have done? Why didn't I do more? How else could I have helped?' But then you think, 'This is emotional for me, but lots of people died and others lost their jobs, so how bad are my feelings about it?' It's hard to put everything into perspective. I think, too, as a photographer or a journalist, you see a lot of things and carry things in your mind. For example, I used to joke that I'd been to more funerals of people I don't know over the years. You carry those things with you. You'll be thinking about something else, and something will jog your memory about a funeral you covered in Oklahoma City. And you'll see somebody's face. You see a picture in your mind. When I went into the city a couple of weeks ago, and as I drove among the buildings, I looked up at a tower and pictured the top coming off. You hold those images in your head because you saw them. Sometimes it's a lot to carry as actual personal experience."

Ironically, Amy doesn't do a lot of news stories. In fact, she refers to herself as "the happy photographer," because she prefers to do features that are uplifting and light, so this experience "was a little different" for her. Nevertheless, three of her images from the first day received a lot of play: the sequence of the top of the south tower falling, a vertical picture of people running with the big debris cloud coming through, and one horizontal picture of a white man in a beautiful business suit carrying a briefcase and holding the hand of a black woman who was running along with him. Amy captured that image when she first stepped into that parking garage. She was proud that the *New York Times* editors chose to run that one AP photograph along with their own staff-produced photos the next day.

Amy thinks that the still images she and other photographers captured during this national tragedy will be indelibly etched in people's minds. "I think your mind works in still images. As you remember things, even personal things—a party you had when you were six years old and you remember a still image of your dad carrying your cake. Or like President Kennedy's funeral—I have seen video of little John Jr. saluting his dad, but you remember the still picture. I think stills are what will come back to people's minds."

Amy has a theory as to why most photographers covering the attacks escaped harm that day. "It's strange. When the towers fell, most of the big debris went to the west. Most of the photographs seem to come in from the east side. Part of the reason is that the road that ran along the west side of the towers is where most of the rescue vehicles came in. Only one photographer was killed. You wonder why more weren't killed. There are so many professional and freelance photographers in New York City. I was at a point where I could have come in on the west side, also. But just the way the first police barricade was set up I went to the east, as did probably a lot of people. We were really a lucky lot."

In spite of the danger and horror she encountered on September 11, Amy is very proud of her profession. "I just like the work. If you're covering a football game, and one guy's running and the other guy is defending, there is a point when they crash together with this wonderful symmetry about them: their bodies, their helmets, the sky, and the ground. Maybe someone's toe is an inch off the ground. There is this perfect moment that you can catch that you might not even see when you are looking at it yourself. I like the composition of it, the way things fall together."

She understands the importance of her work as well. "I like doing something important like going to an inauguration knowing that I could take the picture that's on the front of everyone's newspaper tomorrow. I like that we provide information so that people can make decisions about their world. I like showing people things. Not everyone gets to go to the opening of the Olympics. But I get to go, and my colleagues get to go and show everyone what it is like. I didn't like being in New York on the 11th, but I hope that what I did helped show people what happened and gave them a chance to make a decision about how they are going to live their lives, how they are going to treat their neighbors, and how they deal with times that are difficult."

11

Gulnara Samoilova, Associated Press, New York City

Gulnara Samoilova was supposed to be in Russia on September 11 to photograph a family she is chronicling as part of a personal, ongoing project. Instead, she was nearly buried alive in the ash and debris from the World Trade Center as she documented the events of the day.

Because she doesn't report to work at the Associated Press New York bureau until noon, Gulnara was still asleep in her apartment when the first plane struck the tower five blocks away. The sound awoke her. As she lay in bed listening, she heard sirens. At first she thought the sirens signaled routine ambulance runs from a nearby hospital. But when they didn't stop, she thought something terrible must have happened.

She turned on her TV and froze. In her soft, Russian accent, she described what she saw on the screen. "I saw the first tower. It had just happened. The commentator on CNN didn't know what was going on. Somebody said it was a small plane. I am just watching it to learn what was going on. Then, the second plane hit the second tower. I saw it on TV, and I heard a powerful explosion. I realized it was a terrorist attack."

Gulnara jumped out of bed and quickly pulled on her clothes. "I was just running around the apartment, thinking, 'Do I need flash? How many rolls of film do I need to take?'" She had the black-and-white Tri-X film she prefers for her projects stored in her refrigerator.

Gulnara, an AP photo enhancer, should not have been in New York that day. "I was supposed to go to Russia on September 8 to continue a personal project, photographing a family in Russia I have been working on for six years, and I just canceled for no reason."

She grabbed her equipment and started outside toward the World Trade Center. "I didn't think I would be able to get close. I had AP ID but didn't have a police ID because I'm not a photojournalist. But nobody stopped me."

Chapter 11

Self-portrait of Gulnara Samoilova

People were running in the opposite direction from the Trade Center. "While I was walking, I was taking some pictures. Then I saw the towers. It was just amazing. I stopped at a church on Fulton across the street from the towers, but I could have gone inside the building or gotten closer because nobody was stopping me." Gulnara noted that she spotted three other photographers on the scene, all of them women. "We were all shocked. We didn't say hello to each other. We are running around photographing the scene."

Although she says she was in shock as she watched the towers burning, she got some shots. "Then I started concentrating on people around me—the victims and the injured. I couldn't even focus, it was so dramatic. I saw a woman whose skin was just coming off from burns. I was a little bit shy to photograph these people because they were in pain. I didn't want to just stick my camera in their faces. I'm not pushy. I shot the burned woman in color from the side. I couldn't do it from the front. I'm not a professional journalist. I'm not used to such a thing."

She said that it was important to concentrate not only on the event itself but on what was going on around it. "Reactions. People's faces. You must have a good eye to notice, not just the whole picture but little things," she said. "As a photographer, you have to notice everything."

For Gulnara, noticing everything included seeing people jumping from the tower. "I was so stunned I couldn't even lift my camera. I couldn't believe that people were jumping," she said. It never occurred to her that the towers would collapse. "I didn't realize how dangerous it was. They are so tall. I saw the fire, but I didn't realize there was a huge plane inside. I didn't know what kind of plane it was because I hadn't seen the news."

Gulnara said AP was in her thoughts. "This was breaking news. I hadn't seen any AP photographers, but at that point I was documenting it for my own purposes. Yet I definitely realized something big had happened."

A policeman tried to push her out of the area and asked her how she could try to photograph with so much going on. "I told him I had to document it. It's a big, historical event. I crossed the street and just kept photographing, constantly changing lenses."

Then she heard a tremendous noise. "I lifted my camera and took one shot before I realized the building was coming down. Someone said, 'Run!' and I started running. I was certain it was coming right on me. I kept thinking, 'It's not happening to me.' When it hit the ground, I fell. I thought, 'I'm going to die right now because people will run over me.' But nobody did. So I look back and I saw this unbelievable huge cloud of dust and debris coming right at me. I hid behind a car."

She compared being in the cloud of debris to being in a tunnel with strong wind pushing all around her. "I didn't have time to be scared. My heart wasn't pumping. I didn't have an adrenaline rush or anything. I just kept thinking, 'It's like I'm in a movie; I'm not here.'" Gulnara said being behind the camera helped her stay focused. She could view the scene as if it weren't real.

The wind settled down and then stopped. "Dust was going everywhere. I couldn't open my eyes. It was in my ears and my mouth. It was just very, very silent; and it was so dark. I couldn't see a thing. I don't remember how long it was. I started losing my breath. I was certain I was buried alive."

Then she realized someone else was hiding behind the same car, a man who asked her if she was OK. "I started seeing the lights from the car, and that is when I realized I was alive and would be OK. As soon as I could see something, I started photographing again. It was so silent. Paper was flying in the air. According to my film, I shot a couple of frames and my roll ended. All the dust went into the camera. I was in such shock that I changed lenses and film, but I don't remember doing it."

Her elbow was bleeding from her fall. "I started just walking home. I had trouble breathing and was in total shock. Somebody gave me a mask and water. Everything was amazingly organized. Immediately, people were giving out masks and water. People who worked at the Millennium Hotel got out chairs, towels, sheets, and water. They were ripping out doors to make into stretchers for people." She didn't

Survivors of the collapse of the World Trade Center towers make their way amid debris. Photo by Gulnara Samoilova

see a lot of panic. Priests were talking to people. Police and firefighters w~
professionally. "It was amazing to see that," she said.

"I got home and started mixing chemicals to develop my film. Because it was hot,
I put ice in the chemicals and waited for them to cool down. I was watching TV
when the second tower collapsed. I could hear it very well. It was just . . . well, when
steel goes inside of steel, only ten thousand times louder. It was very loud, like *crack!*
But don't ask me when the first building collapsed. I don't remember that sound."

She was aware of how powerful the collapse was. "My building just jumped, and
I thought it's going to collapse as well. Dust was everywhere. I quickly closed the
windows," she said.

"When I returned to my apartment, I went into the bathroom and shot two
frames, self-portraits, because I wanted to remember: Me, all gray from the debris.
My camera with dust all over it. My bleeding elbow. I just wanted to remember
how I looked because to me, it was really, really a big thing. I survived. I was alive."

Gulnara has a darkroom set up in her kitchen where she can develop film and
print pictures. As she started to develop her film, she realized she had shot one roll
of Ektachrome color slide film. "I never use that kind of film. It is still a mystery
how it got into my bag," she said.

Then AP was on the phone. "I talked to my girlfriend who works at AP. She
asked, 'Where have you been? I've been trying to reach you.' I told her, 'I was
there.'" After informing Gulnara that she was crazy for going to the scene, her friend
yelled to the AP bosses that Gulnara had film. They told her to come in as soon as
possible.

"So I developed the film, and it was still wet in the tank. I walked to work, clicking my tanks, because I didn't want to waste time drying it, and I could keep the
dust out of it. I thought by the time I would get to AP, it would be dry," she said.
"First, AP told me to get to a little office they had set up downtown. I walked there,
and my film is still wet. We were drying my film before the fan."

When her boss saw the film, he was shocked. "Black-and-white?" Gulnara
responded that she did have a roll of color film and that she was sure she got a
picture of the tower collapsing.

Her next task was to walk to the main AP office to deliver her film. The trip took
one and a half hours. "My hair still had debris in it. I was just able to change my
clothes. There was no time to take a shower.

"I scanned my images and gave them to my photo editor. The next day, my photographs were published everywhere around the world. They've been published in
magazines and Time-Life books. I definitely didn't think my photographs would be
published so well because they were black-and-white. I didn't get a lot of covers in
the U.S., because they are black-and-white. In Europe, yes, and in Asia, yes, but not
in the U.S." But she also noted that color film offered little advantage in this particular instance. "You couldn't tell in the pictures if the people were blacks or whites.
They were all just gray," she said.

While she was photographing the World Trade Center, Gulnara had considered running to a deli and buying some color film, but ultimately she didn't want to waste time doing that. So she stuck with the medium she has been using for twenty-two years. She thinks black-and-white is dramatic, bringing more power to the picture and evoking images from World War II. She's glad now that she got the only black-and-white shots for AP.

September 11 has had an impact on Gulnara's career. "It changed me, and hopefully it will change my perspective on the project I'm working on [in Russia]. Maybe I will see it differently. I'm going there in the summer. It changed my life, of course. I'm busy working; I'm trying to enter pictures in all kinds of contests. I got self-esteem, and I have self-respect. That is very important."

Although Gulnara was very proud that she went to the towers and that she did a good job, she still had a lot to go through. Other than to rescue her two cats, she was unable to get into her apartment for two weeks. She had no electricity, no water, and was without telephone service for two months. But, although there was dust everywhere, her apartment was not damaged. She bought an air cleaner to try to deal with the smell. She stayed with friends until she could go back home.

She also had to deal with the physical and emotional aftermath. "Saturday [after the attacks] I had to check myself into an emergency room because of the sharp pain in my belly where I fell on it. Then I went to the doctor for what they called the World Trade Center cough. I'm still taking medicine."

Gulnara said she also has been dealing with depression. "I have bad dreams and stuff. But it is getting better, much better." She participated in grief counseling with other AP employees, and she sought private therapy as well. She is aware that something deeper and more spiritual has developed within her. "I'm not religious at all. As a matter of fact, I was born Muslim. But I remember walking by a church, and I remember thinking there is something up there that guides me through all my life and protects me. And I really truly believed in that. I was so lucky—with someone's help. There is somebody up there who helped me in my life a lot. I didn't have survival skills. I was just so happy that I was alive."

Like many of the other women covering the World Trade Center attacks, Gulnara had to gradually resume ordinary activities. "At the beginning I was staying for a couple of days in Jersey City, and I was so afraid to go through the tunnel. It made me really nervous. A couple of months later I had to go to Florida. I was so afraid. My plane was the next day after the plane [Flight 587] crashed in Queens. Again, I was waking up to the sounds of sirens. There were a lot of sirens because of that crash. And I'm like, 'No! No! No!' I was afraid to turn the TV on. But I turned it on and saw that a plane had crashed in New York City. Again, the next day I had to fly, and I was so afraid . . . I was so afraid."

Gulnara said, though, that it was a relief to get out of the city. "About a week later after 9/11, someone invited me to the Hamptons. I stayed there for three days. And for all three days, I sat and stared at the ocean trying to clear my mind and to breathe to clear my lungs. I was just thinking. I couldn't cry before that. I thought something was wrong with me because I was so happy that I was alive. I saw a strange dog coming near me and then saw that it didn't have a leg. And I remembered the night before when I was glued to the television set, I'd seen a story about a policeman who lost his dog in the World Trade Center. They showed a picture of the dog. I just started crying."

Her first good cry triggered other dark thoughts. "That is when I remember people jumping. I was placing myself there; what if it happened to me? What would I do? Would I jump? I remember exactly a year ago I went to the top of the World Trade Center on the observation deck. I wanted to do skydiving, but then I thought, 'Oh, let me see what it would be like.' So I went to the top, and it was so high and so scary—all those little cars, and you couldn't see the people. I changed my mind, so I didn't do the skydiving. I have been living in New York City for nine years, and that was the first time I went to the top of the World Trade Center."

Gulnara bought herself a new camera. "I cleaned up the camera I was using at the Trade Center, but I had to do some shooting, and it was still in the repair shop. So I thought that was a great opportunity to buy myself a new camera because I had wanted to do that for the last couple of years—especially when I developed the film and scanned it. A lot of frames were not in focus. I just couldn't focus. But I was just in shock, clicking and clicking and clicking."

She misses the towers in the way most New Yorkers do. "It is very sad. Every day I go to the subway on Fulton Street, and I don't see the towers anymore. They were a big part of my life. I'm bad at directions. Every time I get off the subway, I'm thinking 'Where's north? Where's south?' But when I see the towers I know whether I'm looking uptown or downtown. For eight years I saw those towers from my bedroom, and I looked to them for direction. I always liked the World Trade Center, the beautiful gardens, and a park where I went [inline skating]. It was a big part of my life, and now it's gone. Every day it's a reminder of the tragedy. I have a lot of friends who had an office there or who lived around there who are still in shock and still struggling with that problem."

Gulnara, now a U.S. citizen, said she has always been treated well in New York and that connections between people have only improved since September 11. "New York is a very international city. We are used to accents. We understand each other. People are friendlier. I see it in the subway, on the street, in stores. It's like one big family."

She has not taken any pictures of the area of the World Trade Center since the day she rescued her cats. "I shot some pictures that day, but that's it. For a long time I couldn't even get close to it. One day I went there and saw what was left of the World Trade Center. It was so huge . . . a few stories up. And, again, I felt very lucky. I wish nothing like that will ever happen again."

12

arrogant if me! "

Beth A. Keiser, Associated Press, New York City

The most memorable aspect of September 11 for Associated Press photographer Beth A. Keiser is that she missed most of it. Beth was enjoying her dream vacation, a few days on Martha's Vineyard. She and her husband, a *New York Times* picture editor, along with her mother, had planned a leisurely day sleeping in and visiting with friends. But the telephone jarred her awake that morning. A friend was calling her to tell her to turn on her television set.

"I turned it on just in time to see the second plane hit live on the *Today* show. My first reaction: I just cried," Beth said. "The fact that two planes had hit the towers stunned me. And, to be honest, the fact that I wasn't there stunned me. I live on 19th Street near Park Avenue. That day would have been a regular working day with my shift starting at nine o'clock. I would have been getting ready to go to work and probably would have been down there before the second plane hit—if I had been there. But you can't dwell on the what-ifs."

As quickly as they could, Beth and her husband packed up the car, went to the ferry, and headed back to New York. "We were actually in the car on the way to the ferry when the towers collapsed. When I had seen them on fire, I said they would probably have to tear them down, and I was thinking this was a story that would go on forever. But when we got on the ferry, we had the car radio on, and we heard that they had collapsed. I didn't see the footage until about 6 P.M. that night, and I just couldn't believe it. I just kept thinking about all the people underneath it."

When Beth called the AP office, the first thing she asked was whether everyone was OK. "I was told that so far there had been no casualties. I found that astounding because I know how journalists work. We have the firefighter mentality to rush into buildings. We would have been in the lobby or at the base of the tower, shooting up at it. There is no question that the way that it fell saved another couple of thousand lives. The only thing that saved the journalists—and that I know from experi-

Beth A. Keiser

ence—is that their instincts told them not to be that close. Luckily, everybody made the right decision about where to go, and, luckily, the buildings didn't come down like trees. Those buildings fell in the right way."

Beth dropped her husband off in Times Square at 5 P.M. so he could go to work. She then went back to the apartment, dropped her mother off, and grabbed her gear. She headed toward Ground Zero at about 6:30 that night. Beth's first assignment was to photograph the skyline as the sun was setting from the top of an apartment building on 34th Street that provided both balcony and roof access. Her shot showed the Empire State Building, the Chrysler Building—and no Twin Towers.

"I went up with a lot of people living in the building who wanted to watch the sun set. You could see clearly to the south. There was smoke, but it was a beautiful sunset. Every color in the rainbow was in the sky that night because it was such a clear day. It was just a beautiful, beautiful sunset that unfortunately did not include the Twin Towers any more."

Beth transmitted the sunset photograph from the apartment building and then reported back to the office. She said her AP editors thought they had gotten solid images all day and had dispatched a night crew at the World Trade Center site. "I checked out blood-bank lines because we had heard so many people were giving blood. But by 9 P.M. they were closed. I was told to go home and get some sleep and be at Ground Zero by four o'clock in the morning. I got up at three, got my gear together, and because I live just above 14th Street, I put all my gear in a knapsack along with my laptop. I started walking at 3:30 in the morning down through the neighborhood."

Beth said that experience was a little unnerving. "There were lots of police officers along 14th Street and Canal Street, but I did walk through Washington Square Park and NYU [New York University], which was a little iffy. I picked bigger avenues. But there is this thing about New York: if you have this look of determination, usually people will leave you alone. There weren't many people out, but most who were out were somehow related to the disaster—the phone guys, construction guys, electric Con Edison guys, and police officers. So it actually wasn't too bad." Beth said she made that walk three days in a row at about four in the morning.

Another aspect of that first morning was unnerving. "I didn't know what I'd see when I got there. I had watched television all night long, and I knew that the No. 7 Tower had collapsed at around seven or eight that night. But just having gone down there just two weeks earlier to go shopping, I just didn't know what to envision when I got down there. So that was probably more nerve-racking. Also, I knew I was going to run into police blockades, and in this city that is a complicated process. I have all the proper credentials, but it doesn't do you any good in the city. So, it's just a matter of who you are going to run into and who is going to let you through and who's not. I knew that was going to be my biggest challenge that morning."

She was routed around by the police to the West Side Highway and was able to get to about Chambers Street, where the media trucks were parked, on the west side of the disaster. "I was just feeling out the boundaries, so I started walking more east. I had been told to find some overhead position to get an overall picture of the disaster. I didn't know at that time how easy or difficult that would be," Beth said.

Once she got to the west side, she moved up a few blocks to Church Street, which was as close as the police would let her get. "There was this really cool scene. You could see part of the collapsed rubble of the north tower that later on was called the Potato Chip. Some spikes of it were sticking up. Police were standing guard with masks on. The lights put on the debris so they could work overnight and the smoke coming up made it look like a Tim Burton movie set." She shot a couple of frames of police standing in the foreground and these eerie pieces of the Trade Center lit with the smoke behind them. She said she thought it was a really striking picture as she was walking up the block. Even though she thought the overnight crew had probably found the shot, she photographed it anyway. "It turned out to be one of the best pictures the next day. It got a lot of play and was in lots of papers the next day." It turned out that Beth was the first to get the shot.

As the daylight came up, Beth met a neighbor who had a building that looked down that block. She was able to go up on her roof and shoot down onto the debris that had been Building Seven. She then moved to the roof of a second building where she took additional pictures of collapsed Building Seven and the firefighters. "It gave me an idea of how much debris was there. You could tell it was about an eight-to-ten-story-high mountain of debris at that point. I hadn't been close enough to get the full scope of what it entailed because, until then, I still had a two-or-three-block buffer between me and the disaster."

Beth said the sun was rising when they got word that the police department was going to take some photographers into Ground Zero. "I ended up spending about two hours on a street corner waiting for the police department to organize this. They decided they were going to walk us all into the site so we could see it firsthand that morning. Much to my surprise, it did happen, around ten o'clock that morning. The sun was fully up. They marched about a hundred of us in, including television and radio reporters and a whole lot of still photographers. They marched us maybe a block to the northwest corner of the disaster, near Building No. 6, which was partially collapsed. You could see some of the debris of the south tower as well. The wildest part was they herded us like cattle down this sidewalk. We were wading through inches of white powder, which was obviously pulverized concrete of the building. There was paper just strewn everywhere. It was like walking through flour. It was coating everything, and because there were so many of us, it was rising up like a cloud around us—like cattle going through the dry dirt."

The other odd part, Beth said, was walking past one hundred or more firefighters, who had incredible looks on their faces. "They had all stopped what they were doing, and they parted just like a sea for us to come through on the sidewalk. They just stared at us in absolute disbelief. My first reaction was that they were angry at us for us being there. We still didn't realize how many firefighters had died, but they did. So it wasn't us. It was their anger and their grief at that time because they knew they had lost so many of their own. Their faces were really, really memorable. It was hard to take a picture of them because they were herding us in and out: 'Don't stop. Keep moving.' Also, the firefighters were staring at us, and we knew they were angry; we just didn't know why at that point. I did take a picture as I walked away from them, but not while I was in front of them, because it just didn't seem like the right thing to do."

Beth said she was not subjected to any abusive comments in those early days. "I've not had anybody except the cops give me a bad reaction. The police are the only ones that I've had become overly sensitive to the fact that I'm there. But victims' relatives, survivors, people in the neighborhood who survived who I met later didn't do any of that. Especially in the first thirty-six hours, I didn't encounter any of that from anybody."

On September 13, Beth was selected to become part of a fire department pool of reporters and photographers who were allowed to go back into Ground Zero. One of the AP reporters with whom she worked had connections within the fire department. He told the officials who were organizing the pool that he wanted to be in the one supervised by the fire department and that he wanted Beth to be included. The reporter's instincts proved invaluable.

"I stood on the pile of the World Trade Center," Beth said. "The firemen who were working there in the pile had dogs. And they would stop to listen for sounds of survivors. I was in the middle of everything, and not one of them had a problem with me being there. It was the police who kept saying, 'You're not supposed to be here.' My police escort would say that we were with the pool; it's OK. The firefighters who were on break were happy to talk. Even at the funerals later on, the families of the victims were OK with our presence. All of us worked at a reasonable distance, and nobody was obnoxious about it. We didn't get any backlash from anybody else."

When she was able to go into the site, Beth said it was visually overwhelming. "For a person like me who bases her life on visual things, to walk up to the base of this rubble and stand on the southeast corner of where the towers collapsed was initially overwhelming. I had to stop, absorb it, and look at it. There were hundreds of people combing through different sections of this pile. There were firefighters sprawled out on the edge of it. There was heavy machinery coming in. Where do you start when you look at a sixteen-block pile of devastation? And there were hundreds of people on every inch of the pile going through it. There were lines of men moving buckets, forming the bucket brigade. And there were other men at the end of the bucket brigade going through things. Then there were the dogs that were hunting. They would call out, 'Quiet.' Everyone would simultaneously stop what they were doing and just stand at the pile. That would allow the people with the listening devices and the dogs to listen for survivors. It was incredible to see the entire thing come to a halt and become completely silent.

"One of the things that really struck me about Manhattan during the first twenty-four to thirty-six hours was how quiet the city was. There weren't cars moving; there weren't people moving; there weren't horns honking. It was just incredibly quiet. But to stand at the base of all that disaster and have everyone completely to stop what they are doing and be silent was breathtaking."

In spite of the unbelievable scene before her, Beth knew it was time to start taking pictures. "I saw the flag on top on the rubble, about in the center. I concentrated on that because there were bucket brigades weaving up this hill with the flag on top of it. Then there was a group of men working in some rubble much closer to me that I was able to use the wide-angle lens with. I just slowly found areas that I could see would make nice pictures. I tried varying my lensing so I could shoot wide-angle to show the scope of what I was standing at and also use my longer lenses to show the faces of the men working on the pile. Those faces were astonishing and determined and covered in dirt."

At one point that day, Beth and some of her fellow photographers had a close call. "We were underneath the Millennium Hotel when they sounded three horns. They did that when they thought a building was unstable. They certainly thought the Millennium Hotel was unstable at that time. The escorts there with us shouted, 'Run!' We just went running north up Broadway. Us, the firefighters, everyone was running because we weren't sure if One Liberty Plaza or Millennium was going to come down. They were obviously worried about our security and our safety because they had brought us in." Beth said that experience unnerved her at first because one of these other towers could come down on top of them while she and the workers

A postcard of the World Trade Center towers is taped up in a damaged fire station across the street from Ground Zero. Photo by Beth A. Keiser

were there. "Both buildings ended up being sound, but they were shifting, which obviously made people nervous."

Beth also knew that she had a time limit, because fire department officials had escorted her in. "Even though I was there for almost two hours, that was the only time that any of us from the media were allowed to go in and spend so much time there. It was a real luxury because when the police took us in, we had fifteen minutes to get in and get out. The fire department walked us about 75 percent around the whole site. I never got to do it again." Beth said she and her colleagues were able to move fifteen to twenty pictures, providing a lot of different views from Ground Zero.

This was not the first act of terrorism Beth had photographed. She also covered the Oklahoma City bombing. She said she walked to the base of the Oklahoma City site and remembered how overwhelming that felt. But New York City was an even more intense experience for her. "It caused me to really concentrate and to work quickly because I knew I only had so much time. I tried to be as diverse in my images as I could be and not to spend too much time in any one area. I'd use a long lens and then change lenses and move to a different part of the pile. I'd photograph that and then put a wide-angle on to show the dimension of what I was over-whelmed by seeing through the lens. Ironically, after we stood on the southeast cor-ner, we moved around, and there was a fire station right across the street—Engine 10 and Ladder 10. The building was still there, but all the windows were blown out, the trucks were gone, and some of the men were gone. It was the building where all the men in that area were working in and out of. They had set up a little triage center there so that doctors could remove irritants from their eyes and treat minor cuts and scrapes as well. We went there to talk to some of the men."

Beth said there she saw an image she vividly recalls. "The front windows were blown out and someone had pulled from the rubble a postcard of the Twin Towers at sunset. They had taken duct tape and taped it in the blown-out frame of the window. Here I am standing at the base of this rubble of the World Trade Center and here is the postcard with this beautiful image that no longer exists taped up in place of the window of the fire station. There were firemen all around it, decom-pressing before they went back into the pile. I took pictures there that really stayed with me.

"I was in Miami during Hurricane Andrew," Beth continued, "and I can see what a hurricane can do to half of a city. In a way what helped me process what I was seeing at the World Trade Center disaster was the fact that I lived in Dade County and worked in Miami when the hurricane hit. And to see blocks and blocks of noth-ing but rubble in a way compares to what I saw at the World Trade Center. It was just a level of destruction that you can't fathom. In a way, it helped me process what I saw at the World Trade Center disaster because Hurricane Andrew was spread over so many miles."

In addition to the Oklahoma City bombing and Hurricane Andrew, Beth has covered four plane crashes (including the Queens plane crash in November 2001), tornadoes, and floods. "I've seen a lot of disaster leading up to the World Trade Center disaster. I'm always the photographer who flies in and deals with the aftermath of it. To have this disaster in your own backyard is a much different thing. I regret not being here that day because I wasn't able to be a part of the first wave of people in there. I can't imagine what it would have been like to be there on September 11 and have all these visual things happen—towers on fire, people jumping from the towers, and then the towers coming down. Those images—I have no doubt I would have captured them."

Beth knows that there is a chance that she might not have survived it had she been there, but that doesn't dilute her regret. "I was back in the same pattern of the way I've been covering disasters. I came in after the initial wave of it. In a way for me that is how I dealt with it. I missed the initial day, but I was now on cleanup in terms of covering the disaster. That is what I've always done, but now I'm in a prolonged version of it. It is still in my backyard, and it will be the one thing I cover for the next year. I knew this is how it will work based on all the other disasters I've covered. Until you hit that one-year anniversary, it's the biggest story that you have in your town or in that part of the country.

"Oklahoma City was like that, too. I went back for the one-year anniversary. I felt bad for the photographers who were based there because I knew that is all they had done for a year—cover anything and everything that had to do with the Oklahoma City bombing. And that's how it is with the Trade Center. That's the pattern I'm in now—the three-month anniversary, Christmas, and New Year's at Ground Zero—that's all I'll do until September 11, 2002.

"But no question, I think without experience it would have been harder to collect myself and get on with what I needed to do. You have to get into that mode, and it's a hard mode to get into, but you have to. That is the only way you make the images. I had a lot of responsibility at that time, too, because I was working for everybody else as a pool photographer. There was extra pressure because all the other agencies and all the newspapers are relying on you to make those images because they couldn't get in. So I had to be even more thoughtful about what I made that day and on my tour because I knew that a lot of people would be looking at what I made—not just from my company but all the other agencies. So it made me focus a little bit harder."

By the third day, Beth said workers at Ground Zero were still optimistic they would find people, but they were beginning to realize that it was a search-and-recovery operation. Soon after that point the media pools began to dry up, and security at the site was tightened. "Even at four in the morning it was very secured. The National Guard came in on the morning of the 12th, and once they got there it really got secure. It was a very difficult environment because if you played by the rules and obeyed the police, you didn't get closer than two blocks. The only other way to do it was to sneak around and find a friendly cop or go all the way to the very tip of Manhattan and come up around the south side going through parks and all sorts of things."

Beth said there were stories about photographers who impersonated firefighters, who went with welders and other workers, or who joined the Red Cross or other volunteer groups in order to get access to the site. "By the 12th, people realized that to photograph the actual site of the World Trade Center required doing some fairly unethical things, which I did not partake in. I was in the mind-set that I am an Associated Press photographer, I'm a legitimate news source, and I had a legitimate right to cover this event. I didn't want to partake in that kind of dishonesty. In some ways it cost me because I didn't produce the same pictures that those who sneaked in did. They are more dramatic, more telling, and will probably last longer than some of my images. But, ethically, I thought it was wrong, and AP agreed with that. So we relied on pools a lot to get in there and do what we could do. I'm very grateful that on the 13th I was able to get in there."

Beth encountered difficulties with transmitting her pictures back to the AP office because of the lack of cellular communication in the days following the disaster. She said either the photographers had to hike out and get a subway back, or they had to use bicycle messengers to transport images back.

Beth was using AP's digital Canon DCS 520 equipment, and she was pleased with the way her equipment held up. "Someone pointed out to me that if we had been using regular cameras with film, the film plane would have been scratched up. But, although dust got into the digital cameras, it was easily cleaned up."

She said the digital age means there is a different process for archiving important photographs now. "Great pictures last no matter how they were taken. There are great pictures from the early days of photography that are glass negatives. Prints of those pictures still exist today. Even some of the great pictures taken with film— some of those negatives don't exist anymore. Some were lost by fire; some were stolen, damaged, or just moved from the archives. So I think lasting images have absolutely nothing to do with the format in which they were made. It's the image itself that's lasting. There is always going to be a print, a copy negative, and a way to preserve that image. I think that's true even in the digital age." Beth said that most photographers who use digital cameras take personal responsibility for preserving their best images. A computer glitch can mean a lost image, so many photographers back up their own work rather than counting on a company to preserve it.

For Beth, dealing with both mental and physical exhaustion was an everyday thing. "For me, my day was wondering, 'How do I get in? How many times will I be harassed? How do I get through roadblocks?' But I also walked miles and miles for days on end because that was the only way to get around, which was physically exhausting as well.

"There is no question that we breathed in some really nasty stuff. The first day I took a bandanna with me that I used to breathe through and to keep my equipment clean. By the 13th, I was using a mask full-time because it really burned my lungs. I'm a contact wearer, and the dirt in and out of the contacts was difficult. But none of it seems to have been long-term. I resorted to using a mask because the air was very caustic. The smell lingered until late October."

Beth opted not to participate in the counseling sessions that AP supplied, but she thinks she has been dealing with her emotions, at least most of the time. "I think there are times when I deal with it better than other times. I'm in full working mode these days, but on my days off I don't like to go down there. I don't go to the restaurants in that neighborhood any more. I find it difficult because I did spend so much time down there the first couple of weeks. I saw such a level of destruction."

Through the end of 2001, Beth was going into Ground Zero with a pool every two weeks, usually with a visiting dignitary. "AP has an apartment that we rent that overlooks the site. I try to go down every couple of weeks and spend a day photographing it. I've really watched the amazing transformation of the site from what I first saw to what it is now. It absolutely blows my mind that in four months it has gone from eight stories of twisted steel to four levels into the dirt.

"I think I've dealt with it pretty well. My husband is a picture editor, and lots of my friends are photographers. We've all talked about it. The hardest part for me has been that I wasn't here on September 11. In a way, even though I've been a big part of covering this great disaster, to have missed being a part—at least the initial day—of the biggest news event in U.S. history—at least in my lifetime—has been harder to deal with than what I've seen at Ground Zero. In some respects, I feel selfish about that, but it's honest. One of the surprising things is that I'm not alone. I've met a few other photographers who are based here in New York who, like me, were on vacation and out of the city. They also felt they missed being a part of history, which is why we do what we do. Wire service people in particular do this because it allows us to be a part of history. I feel like I missed a huge opportunity to be a part of history. I can't make that up in any way. And for me that has been the hardest thing to deal with."

Two weeks before the attacks, Beth had taken her husband shopping in the mall below the World Trade Center. He had suggested that they go up to Windows on the World, but Beth told him they should wait for another day. "So we didn't go to the top of the World Trade Center," she said. "Who knew there wouldn't be another day?"

13

Madge Stager, Associated Press, New York City

When the first plane hit the World Trade Center, Associated Press enterprise photo editor Madge Stager's first call was to Amy Sancetta, AP's national enterprise photographer. "Amy was in town, and she had to be there. She reports to me, so I knew exactly where she was and that her plan was to spend her day off going to museums. So I thought she'd still be in at nine o'clock in the morning. I called her up after the first plane hit. I told her that a plane had hit the World Trade Center. We didn't know at that point that it was an attack. The conversation was very short. I just said, 'A plane hit the World Trade Center. You have to get down there.' She said, 'OK, I'm on my way.' And that was the end of that."

Initially, Madge didn't realize the implications of the assignment. In fact, she wouldn't know for several hours whether she might have sent Amy to her death. It was even more unfathomable at that point that she herself would be considered missing in action for part of the day.

In reality, Madge represents many of the editors working in New York City on September 11. They knew they had the biggest story since the bombing of Pearl Harbor, and no one was expecting the quick collapse of the Twin Towers. They didn't know where their reporters and photographers were when the towers collapsed, because usual communication modes—cell phones, pay phones, and computer transmissions—were suddenly unavailable. While watching the story unfold on television in their offices or homes, these editors spent a long day waiting for word or, in Madge's case, photos to arrive to confirm that their reporters and photographers were safe.

The day started out routinely for Madge. She arrived at the AP office at about 7:45 A.M. She learned about the first plane crash when another AP photo editor, Bernadette Tuazon, received a phone call from her husband telling her that a plane

Madge Stager

had hit the World Trade Center. Bernadette broadcast the news to the rest of the people in the office.

"Bernadette stood up and said, 'My husband just called and said the World Trade Center is on fire.' Nobody else really reacted at first. I was across the room from her, and I stood up and said, 'What?' So we all jumped and turned on the TV set to NY1, a local channel, because they tend to cover things in the city really quickly. We left CNN and MSNBC on, but we jumped on NY1 right away. We then saw the building on fire and thought that maybe a small plane hit it."

Madge said that everyone immediately started working on the story. Bernadette lived in an apartment barely two blocks from the Trade Center. "Usually, we'd be running around looking for a hotel room. But since Bernadette had an apartment there that was the natural thing to do. The response was, 'OK, go.' She ran out of here even before the second plane hit. We knew the important thing was to set up a base. The trick would be to get as close as we could to the World Trade Center."

All the editors were deciding what to do next. "We thought it was a small plane at first. But we knew this would be big. When the second plane hit, we knew it was a terrorist attack. There was no doubt about it. We knew we had to get more people down there. So it was decided that myself, Mike Feldmen, and Bill Pilc would go to Bernadette's. I took long enough to tell my husband there were terrorist attacks, and I had to go.

"Bernadette planned to set up a temporary office in her apartment," she said. "Then, when the second plane hit, the three of us left to go to Bernadette's place because we knew that it was going to be *huge*. We were going to help Bernadette set up and transmit from there."

They first tried to get a cab to take them as close as they could get, but the driver told them they were crazy. They ended up taking the subway. "Basically, I spent the collapse of the buildings on the subway, probably under city hall. We actually felt them come down, although we didn't know at the time that's what was happening. The decision had been made to stop the trains. A man on the train with us said his wife was in the tower. He jumped out and ran across three tracks. His wife may have lived and he may have died. I'll never know what happened to him."

Madge had seen the towers burning from 50th Street. "When we came out of the subway on 7th Avenue and we looked down, there was just smoke. Bill looked at me and asked, 'Why is that smoke so low?' I said, 'Bill, something has happened, but I can't get my mind around it. We have to go east to my apartment.' My mind could just not register that the towers were gone. We picked that information up as we were running across town. That's a lot of what got people heading north, because it was just so unreal."

"It was amazingly calm," Madge said. "When they show the video of the buildings collapsing, you hear people screaming, but away from that—and I was not that far away from there when I came out of the subway—the city was amazingly quiet. The police did not run their sirens all the time. Thousands and thousands and thousands of people were just quietly streaming north up 5th and 6th Avenues. If they bumped into someone, they said, 'Excuse me.' It was the most amazing quiet and calm I have ever experienced. And I've been in the city during blackouts and all kinds of things. I have never experienced people being so calm. It was probably shock. Everybody just headed north."

The three of them found themselves heading the other direction. "We were having to cut through people. Wherever there was a television set, anywhere from a handful to one hundred people were gathered around watching television. There were groups of people praying on the street, but it was eerily quiet. So there was not the horror and blood and guts and the gore. My sister works down there and was in her building when both of the buildings came down. And when she came out, it was just so quiet."

Although Madge and her coworkers weren't concerned at that point, their colleagues in the AP office and Madge's husband feared for their safety. "Mike, Bill, and I were missing for a couple of hours. We couldn't communicate with anybody because the cell phones were not working. That's why, when we came out of the subway, we decided to go to my house just north of 14th Street (about one and a half miles from the Trade Center), which is where they set up the demarcation line to let people through. We tried to set up things there because it was closer to Ground Zero than the AP office was, but it was outside the barricades.

"For the two hours we were out of touch, I didn't know if Amy was OK. So, my

first thoughts when we came out of the subway and learned the buildings had collapsed were that Amy and Bernadette had been crushed. When I got to my apartment, the first thing I did was call the office. I didn't even call my husband. That's
just what you do."

Madge said they made contact with the AP desk right after they arrived at her
apartment. "I was on the phone with them while Bill took my digital camera and
ran out to 1st Avenue, because I live right near Beth Israel Hospital. There is a whole
hospital row on 1st Avenue. As we ran across town we saw that Beth Israel had one
hundred stretchers outside, ambulances, and all their personnel that were waiting
for casualties. Bill shot some pictures of that while I talked with the office and Mike
set up the computer. Bill took my digital camera, ran up to the roof of my building,
and started shooting pictures of where the World Trade Center used to be. Mike
was trying to set the computer up and get the connection going, so that when we
did have pictures, we'd be able to transmit them. The pictures weren't very exciting
because as everyone knows now there were never any casualties. Then Bill came back
and started working with Mike on setting things up."

When Madge called the office, she was amazed to learn that she and her two
coworkers were listed among the missing. "We had no idea that we were missing.
There was a shout across the office from the person who answered the phone that
we were OK. I gave them my phone numbers and directions to my house and told
them what else we were going to need to be able to transmit. We couldn't confirm
that Bernadette and Amy were OK immediately. I was worried about them. We
were trying to figure out where everyone was."

Then they learned that Gulnara Samoilova, an AP photo enhancer who was freelancing that day, was somewhere in the vicinity of Madge's apartment and that she
had film. "So I knew we were going to need a scanner. The office found a messenger
service that was still operating, and they messengered down a scanner shortly after
Gulnara came in, shocked and covered with dust."

While she was in contact with the desk, Madge learned that Amy and Bernadette
were safe. "We dried Gulnara's film on the fan in my living room because you can't
really look at it and work with it until it's dry. Otherwise you can really ruin it. We
got the light box out so we could look at it."

While Gulnara's black-and-white film was drying, Madge also was calling around
to see which lab might be able to develop her one roll of color film, which was of a
type that was hard to process. "We called around, but most of the labs were closing
down. We called a few of the labs we knew, but most of them were, 'Nope, I'm
sorry. We're closing down.' The city was very quickly coming to a standstill."

Gulnara kept saying that she was fine, but Madge wasn't so sure. "She was wan-
dering around a little saying, 'No, no, I'm OK.' Finally, she said, 'Maybe I'm not
really so fine. Could I have a cup of tea?' I actually gave her a cup of Sleepy Time
Tea, but I had a feeling it wasn't going to put her to sleep," she said with a laugh.

"We were drying her film. The office was shipping us a scanner; we were shooting
pictures off my roof and trying to establish a phone line to transmit them," Madge

said. The scanner arrived, but it didn't work. "It worked out just as well that the scanner wasn't working because it got Gulnara and Mike back up into the area where they could get the color processed at the Time-Life lab. I stayed in my apartment basically waiting for anybody who needed to come there because they couldn't get up to the office. But not much of that happened," she said.

Meanwhile, Bernadette made it to her apartment just moments before the towers fell. Madge said that if Bernadette had been five minutes later getting there, she might have ended up crushed under the rubble. "When she went in, the street was full of people, but when she came out they were gone," Madge said. "Where were they? It wasn't for a day or so that everybody began to get the idea that the dust we had all over us was part remains. Fortunately, Bernadette's building remained standing. She was able to shoot a couple of pictures and transmit them from her laundry room before police made her evacuate the building.

"I'd gone into work at a quarter to eight, and then I stayed at my apartment waiting for people to come, and they never did. So I just paced around for hours," Madge said. "Amy came around four or five in the afternoon with some stuff she had shot on the street—signs for blood donors, a lot of medical people standing around NYU waiting for casualties. Rather than going back to the office, she came to my house, and we transmitted from there. Then once we were done with that, I went back into the office and was negotiating with freelancers for pictures. I worked through the night until about 8:30 the next morning. I just stayed on the overnight shift basically for the rest of the week. The whole thing is very much a blur. It would have been disorienting even if we had been able to sleep. And we had a lot of people on the main desk and four people on the Enterprise desk, and one of them was on vacation, and the other three just immediately jumped in to help with the spot stuff. Two went over to help with the editing and captioning of pictures as they came in, and one of them ran up to the Metro desk and ended up spending a week up there helping out."

Madge said that AP's routine process was in place regarding photography selection. "It's kind of hard to describe the photo selection process because it eventually becomes instinct. I think even for people who are new at it, it's instinct. A good picture is a good picture. There is always going to be a photograph like the one of someone jumping out of a building or a body being dragged through the streets of Mogadishu in Somalia. These are things you have to take a moment and figure out the best way to handle them. It's really not that different."

Madge said she didn't deal with any photograph from September 11 that was very graphic. "We didn't have that many. The people jumping out the windows is the one situation that would have needed a flag on it, meaning that we would put a flag in the front of the caption just to let editors knows that it's graphic and that they need to look at it. I did not actually edit any photo that was graphic. There was no blood and gore, just pulverized people. That is the horror of it."

Madge manages the AP's Enterprise photo desk. "On any given day I am working with editors and photographers, reporters on illustrating Enterprise stories. They can be the top news of the day, but on the side of it—the more in-depth stuff and picture packages. We're not the on-the-spot desk, but we're next to it. I primarily concern myself with making sure that we have stories illustrated nicely and fully. I work with photographers who have ideas and try to inspire photographers to have ideas and to work on projects that are picture-rich. I try to hook them up with writers and vice versa. That is what my department does, and I oversee that internationally and domestically."

On any given day Madge would be looking through the reports of the day. "I now concern myself more with what happens to people after the plane falls out of the sky—that kind of thing. It's not the heat of the moment, usually. I can get pulled back to the main desk when there is a big story, such as Kosovo. We are primarily the people who are stopping and taking a breath and making sure we have striking images and layouts and thorough, in-depth work. The spot desk is concerned with what comes up in front of them and what is happening at the moment. It is our responsibility to see at the Enterprise desk that we are taking that further."

Unlike the projects she routinely handles, this one was personal for Madge. "That was what was so different about this story from almost anything I've ever been around. In most places where there is breaking news, especially in a war situation, you have an idea that you're in a war zone. But to go from being a beautiful, quiet, kind of boring Tuesday in New York City to a war zone adds a whole element to this that I've not experienced before. Then I was suddenly thinking, 'Oh, my God, I'm the one who sent Amy down there, and I didn't know whether she was alive or dead.' I realized that my husband thought there was a possibility that I might be dead, but the first phone call I made when I got to my apartment was to my office. . . . It was kind of amazing to see the way the instincts work and how we managed to really kind of take the stuff that was so personal, so intense, and so frightening and just keep moving.

"AP staffers have talked among themselves about the fact that everyone came out alive. I didn't know that I was missing. So that was the first time in my life to hear the cheer go up in the office and to have my husband and sister calling the office to find out how I was. When Amy came into my apartment later that day, I gave her a hug. I'm very grateful that I would not have to feel guilty that I sent Amy. I'm very glad that I don't have to deal with that. I've talked to photographers within a day of their being killed, but this felt different. When I came in to the office that night, one of my bosses said, 'I can't tell you how worried I was.' And she came out and gave me a hug. It's really amazing that we all came out of it OK. We have kind of talked about it, but not as a group. A lot of us have a different appreciation for each other. Amy and I have now been to a place that we hadn't been to before. Gulnara was in our apartment, and there is a bond there that wasn't there before. I was really happy to see her, and she was really happy to be alive to get that cup of tea. We weren't really thinking about it, but it sunk in later that we could very easily have been killed. If our train had been allowed to go to one more station, or if I had been able to get out when I wanted to, there is a very good chance that I would have been under the building. So, whatever the powers that be are, I guess it was more important for us to tell the story than to *be* the story that day."

Madge said she had a lot of nightmares at first. "I didn't sleep for a couple of weeks, basically. I don't know if that is even over yet in terms of being jumpy. I didn't have to fly until December, but I know most of the time on the plane I tried to envision what it would be like for the plane to be heading into a building. We didn't have planes flying over New York except for fighter jets for a while. When they let commercial planes start flying again, it was a little nerve-racking. People will look up. I still look up at the buildings. It was the lack of sirens that was the crazy thing. For the first thirty-six hours, for the most part, they didn't run their sirens. I was grateful for that. But I grew up in New York, so if I don't hear sirens I worry. But I have to say at night if I hear them longer or hear two or three go by, I wonder if something has happened. Then we had that plane crash in Queens, and that didn't help."

Madge also had some physical symptoms. "I smelled, as many people did for several weeks afterward. We had what we affectionately called 'the smell.' When the wind shifted, it would come from the southern part of the island up, and it was awful. I had an upper respiratory infection. Most of the people I know had some kind of respiratory problem or sinus infection. You didn't have to be that close to get the physical effects. That dust was in the air for a long time, and fires burned for a couple of months. They officially announced that the fires were out in December, a week or two before Christmas."

Madge explained how the digital age has "hugely" changed photography. "It's not just the digital camera but also transmitting by cell phone and transmitting digitally. In the United States it used to take eight minutes to transmit one picture in black and white. And that would be after you went through the time of processing film, making a print in the darkroom, typing a caption, pasting that on the print, putting it on a drum, and establishing a phone connection. Then it would take eight minutes. Domestically and internationally we moved seventy-five to one hundred photos a day. Now we can run a thousand. We easily have a picture thirty minutes after the event. In the old days, you had to have a whole team of people. And depending on where you were working, such as South America, it could take you hours to get a picture out. So it's a completely different ball game now."

To transmit photographs, photographers plug a computer or laptop into a telephone landline or cell phone. They can dial up an AP phone number and transmit digitally by FTP. Madge said the photographs just land on her desk.

The debate about whether negative or digital images are better continues, but Madge expects the argument to subside. "Some people think the quality of negatives is better than the quality of digital images, which eventually just won't be an issue because digital quality is changing so rapidly. On this stuff you can't really tell which one is film and which one is digital."

Whether black-and-white photography is now passé is another question. "The argument I use with photographers is that if you shoot in black and white, you are basically locking in where the picture can be used and how it can be used. You have taken an option away. It's something I deal with when photographers on the Enterprise desk want to do a package in black and white because they say it's stronger, but I would say it actually can be a gimmick. If the image is not strong in real life, then it is not strong. If you have to make it black-and-white in order to make it strong, then there's something wrong with the image. That's my personal opinion."

Madge points out that from her point of view, the AP is not a single publication. "We're trying to be basically everything. That's why it's so important that we don't ever alter pictures and that the world knows that is our cardinal rule and we can be trusted with that. It's as simple as that. You can take pictures that are shot on film and put them in the computer and alter them. Shooting digitally is not at all different than shooting with film. It's the advent of the computer itself and PhotoShop that's the issue. We don't have a problem with that. You can crop them, and you can tone them just as you would in a darkroom, but that's *it*. We don't alter them. We don't do anything but what's there."

Madge thinks that television video can have a great impact at the moment it is being shown. "When you are seeing video pictures live from Jerusalem after a shooting, and sirens are blaring and everybody is running around, I think that has a lot of impact at that moment. The actual impact on history, I think, will be the pictures of the person bursting into tears as an ambulance driver goes up to them—and that in a still frame. I think still frames have a huge impact in terms of the history of something. You can sit there and look at the picture and study it. You can look at people's faces and background. Then you can go back to it and look at it again. You can't do that with video. You just have to keep running it."

Sometimes AP uses "frame grabs" from videos. "That's always an interesting thing for us to do," Madge said. "Sometimes there's an event going on, and we don't have somebody right there, or we haven't heard from the photographer. You see the video, and it seems so dramatic. Then you try to do the frame grab—trying to pull out the one frame that tells the story for the rest of time. Very often it's just not there." Madge points out that it's not cassettes or DVD that are coming out to capture September 11 but rather coffee table books. "They are coming out by the dozens because of the images and the ability to study them."

Madge had to review all the images from September 11 for AP's year-end wrapup. "I'm the one who gathered all our stuff together. Then a bunch of us sat down to pick out our year-end package. But I had to go through everything picking out the possibles. I spent two or three days in late November and early December just going through all of September 11 again. The nightmares came right back."

Madge said she dislikes the comparisons between the flag-raising Iwo Jima photo and the one taken of the firefighters raising the flag over the World Trade Center rubble. "I think it is absolutely bizarre for it to be cast like that. The Iwo Jima photo was taken during a war, and it was a victory. It annoys me that people compare those two pictures. It's a good picture, but it's not September 11 for me personally."

There are images that for Madge are representative: a picture of a man in a white shirt falling upside down next to a building, and one black-and-white photo of Gulnara's of people covered in dust. "Actually, there is one of Amy's photos of a man with a briefcase walking in the dust that just haunts me. And Suzanne Plunkett's photo of people running with the cloud behind them."

Madge may have more images in her head than do most people. "Because I see so many, I don't often have the same picture in my mind that someone from my family would have. I'm looking at them for nine hours a day, and from all over the world and with every story. Some will just jump out, and those are the ones that stick with me. I have physical reactions to some pictures and not others. If I don't have that physical reaction, it doesn't mean it's a bad picture. It just means that it didn't do it for me."

Madge spent the Christmas holidays in Europe with her husband's family. She said people didn't know how to talk to her about it, so most didn't. She said she found that to be more upsetting than talking about it. She was happy to return home. "It was nice to get back to New York where everyone is traumatized. No one is telling you to get over it, like the Europeans did. They'd say, 'Well, it's been a while now.' But not for us. It is still real new."

14

Mika Brzezinski, CBS News, New York City

Mika Brzezinski usually comes into work at CBS News in New York at eight o'clock in the morning. She reads the paper, has a cup of coffee, and brainstorms story ideas for the *CBS Evening News*. That's how her morning began September 11. She was feeling happy, because the night before she had had her first package on the evening newscast. She'd been back at work at CBS for just four days.

But then she looked up at the television monitors in the newsroom and saw CNN video of the World Trade Center tower on fire. It was right after the first plane hit. "I was thinking 'Oh, my God! What in the world! What an idiot!'" She thought a small plane had hit the tower—that someone had made a mistake. "But within ten seconds this felt worse, and it started to look bad to me. I thought, 'I need to be there.' I went downstairs to touch base with the national editor who told me to go. I found my producer, Mike Noble, and we ran outside.

"On my way out the door, I saw Andrew Heyward [the president of CBS News], kissed him, and thanked him for having me back at CBS. Then I jumped into a cab. I thought this was a normal plane crash story, terrible, but 'normal.' We were sitting in the cab, and I realized we were going nowhere. Traffic was gridlocked. CBS News is located on West 57th Street at the West Side Highway. It's about three or four miles north of the World Trade Center. And we were totally going nowhere. I'm thinking, 'I'm a reporter, and I can't get to the story.' So I took my shoes off and told my producer, 'We are going to run down there.'"

Mika is a runner, logging about five miles a day. When she started running south on West Street, she could see the World Trade Center burning. She had a cell phone, but no camera. She was running and holding her shoes and trying to call in, but the phone was not working. She wanted to report what she was seeing. "What I felt was not a good feeling. I had a looming feeling in my stomach."

While she was running, the second plane hit. "I saw crowds of people in clumps

Mika Brzezinski

listening to the radio. Some were walking away fast but turning and looking back. Radios in cars were turned up high. That's when I heard about the second plane hitting. It hit behind the tower that I could see. I looked up and could see Metropolis burning above us.

"I was speechless. I was trying to get down there. I took all my money out of my pocket. I wanted to pay a sanitation worker to take us down there on a golf cart. One finally agreed. The cart made that beep-beep-beep sound. A female police officer jumped on board with us. The officer's brother was down there. She held up her badge, and that got us through the crowds. We got close—I think it was the corner of Murray and West Street, about a block and a half from the World Trade Center. It felt way too close. I had to put my chin way up to see the building burning. We were at the yellow police tape, and I was thinking, 'This feels way too close. If this building falls, it will fall on us. If it falls sideways, it will hit us.' I don't know why I was thinking about the building falling. No one had thought it would fall."

The police barricade didn't seem to Mika to be far enough away from the World Trade Center towers. She remembers, "It was just chaos down there. Nobody with emergency management knew what they were doing. This was so big. So much was going on. Where to place the barricade was the last thing they were thinking about."

"I had a bad feeling in the pit of my stomach. My husband is a reporter for Channel 7 in New York City. I have two young daughters. I knew my husband was down there reporting somewhere because he goes into work early. Somehow I found [CBS reporter] Byron Pitts in the crowd. He also had no camera and no phone service." By this time Mika was being beeped by CBS.

"I heard a low, loud rumble, like a huge vacuum sound, like the wind. I looked up. Byron was counting people jumping from the World Trade Center. The top of the building just crumbled—it fell away from where I was standing and onto a crowd of people near us. I heard screams. I saw it go down. I was not getting it. It was not reality. It was not happening. I didn't scream. I just stood there and watched with my mouth open. I just stood there. I had to look at it. Byron did the same thing.

"I don't know how to describe this or where to begin. The building is coming down. A waft of soot and debris starts rolling toward us. Byron says to me, 'Now we have to go. We have to go.' Reporters in front and behind us were hysterical and screaming. I was silent, standing there. People were pouring around us to get out. Byron took my hand and led me out. The crowd was moving at stampede level, and we had to keep up. We ducked into PS 89 [a public elementary school]. The debris cloud rolled by. I heard the click-click-click of stuff in the cloud hitting the building. It was like being chased by a cloud. It went black inside the school. I remember when the school went dark, I started thinking, 'I could die.' This was the first time I had felt unsafe.

"The school was full of kids. They were being lined up, ready to evacuate. We stayed behind in the school, hoping we would not be noticed. We hid in there. We were looking for a working phone line. We found a room that had one."

They used the phone in PS 89 to call CBS News and say, "Put us on the air." Mika began relaying live reports to Dan Rather, who was anchoring the network's coverage. Dan tossed to Mika and she talked about what she had just seen—the top of one of the towers falling off onto a crowd of people.

Then Byron went on the air with Dan, and Mika went outside. Firefighters were coming into the school, coughing and sweating. They had run from the debris cloud but had been hit by it. Mika remembered, "They were covered with a layer of thick, sticky debris. It was like cement, heavy and thick. It was on their mouths and noses." Mika found some boxes of fruit juice and water that were there for the students and gave them to the firefighters. "One firefighter was crying. He had just been on the phone with his wife Cherrie when they were cut off. I brought the firefighter over to Byron. Byron put him on the air. The firefighter said, 'I'm OK. If you hear me on the air, call my wife and tell her I'm OK.'"

Mika started to realize, "So many people down here aren't going to make it." She was grasping the magnitude of the number of people who had probably died when the building collapsed. She brought a mother and her son into the school for safety; she pulled them in from the street. She gave them water and fruit juice and offered them the phone to make a call. "We put them on the air, but they didn't say much.

"Byron came in with the head of security for the World Financial Center. This head of security had heard that a Channel 7 News truck had been crushed in the collapse. It was my worst thought. This scared me. The second we heard a van was crushed I thought I would die. I thought my husband was dead. I called a producer at CBS and said to call WABC and see if my husband is alive. Then I was on the air with Dan again. I didn't hear back for a while."

Mika was trying to report on the people who were coming into the lobby of the school. She doesn't remember now what she said in her reports. Her producer in the control booth at CBS finally told her that her husband was OK. Then she started crying. She realized others wouldn't come home that night.

She continued to report live from the school. "Firefighters came in all day. We felt that the building was not safe, and we considered leaving. Then we heard another huge vacuum sound. It was overwhelming. I didn't know what it was. I felt a huge pressure of something happening. But we stayed in the school for several hours that day."

At noon, Byron left to join a CBS live-truck crew on the West Side Highway.

Mika interviewed a father who came to the school. "The father was hysterical. He lived near the World Trade Center. He had left his three-year-old daughter with a nanny in his apartment that morning. The windows of his apartment building had been blasted out when the tower collapsed. He found his daughter's shoe and Barney doll in the doorway. He ran to school where his son was supposed to be. He was running around hysterical. We both were crying. He couldn't find his family. In this day of beepers and cell phones and instant communications, he couldn't find anyone. We got him some help to find his son [who had been evacuated with the other kids]."

Mika dug around in the clothing donation bin at the school and found a pair of Army boots that fit her. She put those on with her designer suit and walked up to Canal Street and then to West Street to join the live-truck crew and Byron. It's a twenty-minute walk. That's when she realized her suit was covered with soot. She was walking in "deep gray stuff" on the streets. She still has the boots and the suit, which she can still wear now that it's been dry-cleaned.

When she joined the live-truck crew, she continued to report live all day. She remembers "a big, gaping hole down the street where the World Trade Center towers used to be." They reported live for a week. Mika lives in Westchester County (north of New York City) but didn't go back home for several days. She stayed in apartments with friends who live in Manhattan. She had five or six hours off each night. She was reporting for the *CBS Evening News* and the West Coast edition, which airs three hours later than the New York edition. Then each morning, she was up early to report for the *Early Show*. She said CBS didn't want its reporters to leave their posts because they didn't know whether they could get back in. She didn't want to leave, anyway. "Something takes over you as a reporter on a story like this."

Mika said nothing could have prepared her emotionally for this story. "I remember thinking to myself during the 2000 election when I was the person for MSNBC handling all the changing vote numbers in Florida, 'This is the biggest story I'll ever cover!' I was so wrong. I have yet to fully remember everything I saw, heard, and said, but I believe that is my brain protecting me from myself at this point. In terms of *how* I reported on this story, it's what I have done for a decade. The reporting part was easy. It's what I do. The emotional part is something I am still working through."

Mika does not personally know anyone who did not make it out of the buildings. She drew strength from her two children, three and six years old. She considers them her greatest achievement. "The images of their beautiful, innocent, pudgy faces . . . knowing they are too young to understand or experience this—that gave me peace, that there was hope that we can get through this as a society by cherishing our children. When I returned home for the first time after six days at Ground Zero, my three-year-old was telling her friends, 'A plane accidentally hit a building, and Mommy was helping tell people where to go.' And I thought, 'How I wish that's what it was.' I am just so lucky to have them to guide me. I did a lot of praying for them while I was there. When I cried, it was after speaking to them on the phone because I missed them."

Mika has had both nightmares and insomnia since September 11. "I was on sleep medication. I was experiencing extreme negative thought about the future. All this has subsided somewhat, but once in a while I will have a bad night."

She has some words of advice to reporters, especially to women getting into the field. "*Don't* put off family and love for this business. It all comes together if you really want it. But an opportunity to have a family only comes once or twice, and covering a story like this, *you really need your family*. Many young people in this business make greedy decisions that leave them morally empty-handed later in life. Don't be one of them if you don't want to be."

Mika hasn't heard much feedback about CBS coverage of September 11. She's been too busy. "I feel a little guilty taking compliments for doing my job. And, quite frankly, I feel guilty doing this interview because, relatively, my story and pain are *nothing* compared to the victims, their families, and the tireless rescue workers. There was a lot of human greatness in that one spot where the World Trade Center once stood."

15

Susan Harrigan, *Newsday*, New York City

Susan Harrigan is a *Newsday* business reporter who lives at 7th Avenue and 14th Street in the Chelsea neighborhood of New York City. The World Trade Center is about a mile south of her home. Her beat is Wall Street. It was about ten minutes till nine on September 11, and she was outside, walking her dog on the east side of 7th Avenue. The Twin Towers are visible from the west side of the avenue, but not from the east side.

She remembers, "I saw some fire trucks race down the street. The speed of the trucks is what got my attention. One of the trucks was a 'high-rise unit.' I'd never seen one before. A high-rise fire is a real serious thing in New York. I went back to my apartment, and the doorman said a plane had hit the World Trade Center. He said someone in the building had seen it. About that time I heard a plane overhead. I now believe it was the second plane going down Park Avenue, heading for the second tower."

Susan raced upstairs to her apartment. Her husband had already gone to work. She tried to call her editors at *Newsday* to tell them she'd go down to the World Trade Center site. She says, "I figured I was the closest reporter they had. I had a duty to go. I thought it was a small plane. In the 1940s, an Army Air Corps bomber had hit the Empire State Building. That was a big story, and obviously this was a big story." But Susan couldn't get anybody at her office to answer the phone, so she left messages telling her editors she was going down to the World Trade Center site. Then she "just went."

Susan had been working in New York in 1993 when the World Trade Center was bombed. She remembered that the West Side subway (which ran to the World Trade Center from her neighborhood) was shut down when that happened. So she took a crosstown subway, then a southbound East Side subway. It was about 9:05 when she got on the subway. She had not heard about the second plane. She remembers,

"No one on the subway knew about the first plane. They'd been on the subway for some time already that morning. It was an odd thing, an odd feeling. I'd never covered a major disaster. I was praying, 'Please let me do the right thing.'"

"When we reached Lower Manhattan, someone got on the subway and said a second plane had hit the World Trade Center. I started interviewing him. He told me that two planes had hit the towers, that people were stampeding out of the buildings, that the sky was full of debris."

Susan had a reporter's notebook and two ballpoint pens with her. For the rest of the day, she followed the basic reporting routine of getting names and ages and addresses of interview subjects, as well as home phone numbers so they could be contacted later. Very few people said no to her requests for an interview, and all those interviewed gave her their home phone numbers, even in the middle of frightening situations and choking smoke.

She got off the subway at Wall Street, and "I walked into hell. But it was nothing compared to what people in, or closer to, the Twin Towers went through. I walked west on Rector Street to an area in back of the American Stock Exchange. I was interviewing people about what happened. People were telling me the planes were big, what color they were, about bodies falling out of the sky. Formations of teenagers with backpacks from the area's schools trotted past us, doing double time.

"I was looking for people who got out of the buildings. I walked closer to the Trade Center and then a little bit west to a group of people that contained some escapees from one of the towers. At the time, I wasn't paying much attention to where I was, and the smoke made seeing signs difficult. From going back a few weeks later, I know that I ended up on Washington Street, which runs north-south. I was about two and a half blocks south of the World Trade Center between where Carlisle and Rector Streets, which run east-west, intersect with Washington.

"There was a horrible view of the two burning buildings. In the process of doing interviews with the group of people, I turned around to face them so my back was to the buildings. They were looking at the towers while they talked to me and said that people were jumping. Then one of them said, 'Gee, look at the tower bow out. They're going to come down.' I was thinking, 'Nah.'"

Susan did not turn around and look at the jumpers because to her it would have been voyeuristic and "would have robbed them of dignity." She said it was an instinctive personal decision. "I don't know if it was a good journalistic decision, but I don't regret it." She said it was bad enough to see the buildings burning. She had spent time at Cantor Fitzgerald, a brokerage firm with offices on the upper floors of One World Trade Center. "I knew people there. I knew dying was going on there.

"Two minutes later, police were running down the street, putting up yellow tape, telling us to move back. Then someone shouted, 'The buildings are falling.' I turned and ran. I looked back. There was nothing there. The building wasn't there. I had expected to see something fall. What I saw was nothing. Then a multistory cloud of debris roared around the corner as I was looking back. I felt like I was being chased by an animal. I don't remember any sound. Everything was just loud. The roar of the fire was huge. It was a very noisy environment.

"This cloud, who knew what was in it? Cement? Fire? Steel? I knew I couldn't outrun it. I turned right, toward a building with a revolving door in it. I thought things would start falling out of the air. It was getting dark, completely black, like midnight.

"The revolving door was locked. I pressed myself into it because it at least made an indentation into the building, providing some shelter. That was probably a bad idea, because I would've been surrounded by glass when the debris cloud hit. Then I heard people going through another small door perhaps five feet away. I dove through that door and hit the marble floor just as the cloud arrived.

"I lay on the floor and tried to prepare my mind for death. I'd been in places that were under artillery attack in Vietnam, but this was ten times more terrifying. I was out of the debris cloud, but I thought that the falling tower would land on the roof of the building I was in. I didn't see how anything could withstand such force. At best, we'd be buried alive."

The tower had fallen at 9:59. "From looking at photographs and news accounts later, I saw that although it mostly imploded straight down to the ground, the top forty stories did fall outward the way I had expected. But they fell east and north, not south, where I was.

"For a long time later it felt wrong to have been there. I don't know why. Wrong to go there? Wrong to live? Wrong to be shaken by the experience? I hadn't even seen dead people like so many others did. I wasn't close enough to the towers to see the bodies at the bottom.

"There were about ten people in the building with me, including a couple of dazed security guards. (I went back later and saw that it was an unused facility for the Bank of New York.) The immediate problem was to get out of the building. The door we had come in through was jammed. The building was filling up with smoke, fumes. It was hard to breathe and see.

"We walked up and down staircases and around the hallways trying to find a way out, and I had to make a really tough decision. Nobody else had noticed that the only door to the basement was on automatic lock, meaning that we couldn't get back in there once we left. I thought that if we couldn't get out of the building, the basement might end up being the safest place to stay. The only thing I had to jam the door open with was my reporter's notebook. So I did it, figuring that if I didn't live to file a story, the notes wouldn't be worth much.

"In a few minutes, someone found a way out. I heard them calling—we'd all been calling to each other as we explored the building. Before I followed the people who were leaving, I went back and retrieved my notebook.

"It took us about half an hour to get out of the building. Everything looked fur covered because it was underneath several inches of whitish-gray ash. Washington Street was lined with shoes that people had literally run out of. I don't know what happened to people who'd stayed out there, but a man walking with me had a broken shoulder. We went to the end of Washington Street, where there is a fence and then a highway. Firefighters were there with flashlights, helping us get over the fence and telling us to head for the water. It was very dark.

"Right after we went over the fence, I started doing interviews again. At the end of the day, I had twenty-one interviews in my notebook. People were wrapping shirts around their faces to try to keep out the ash, and it was hard to see where we were going. I didn't wrap anything around my face because that would've made it harder to talk to people.

"We got to Broadway, and we were told to keep going toward the East River and then north to the Brooklyn Bridge. I turned right on Liberty Street—I know it was Liberty because I saw the New York Federal Reserve Bank up the street. Just about then, the smoke became even thicker, and more ash and paper rained from the sky. Someone walking with me said the other tower had fallen. That would have been Tower One, the north tower.

"We got to Water Street, right next to the East River, and started walking north to the Brooklyn Bridge. Some people stopped at the ferry landings, hoping to get boats to New Jersey. I'd been trying to call the office ever since the first tower fell, but my cell phone was not working—there was no signal. Everyone else was having the same problem. When we went through the Fulton Fish Market, people held out paper towels and cups of water to us and offered to hose down the shirts people had wound around their faces. I was asking people, 'What did you see?' and 'What happened to you?' and getting their names.

"I saw a courtyard with trucks in it and stopped. It turned out to be the City Department of Environmental Protection. I asked to use their phone. I wanted to call in and say, 'I'm OK,' and give them my notes. I was one of the first people to come in. Then more people came in to make phone calls. We were all covered with ash.

"I got through to *Newsday*. They put a fellow reporter, Jim Bernstein, on the phone, and I looked at my notes. I noticed I couldn't see very well and suddenly realized that my glasses were gone. I figured they must have bounced off my face when I hit the floor in that building. I'd hit it pretty hard—the next day I was black and blue. A woman who worked in the offices lent me her glasses so I could read my notes over the phone. I dictated my notes to Jim as fast as I could. I'm not sure what time it was, but I'd called in time to make the special edition *Newsday* had decided to do, and I think the deadline for that was at noon.

"I gave Jim everything: the quotes from people I'd interviewed, names, ages, addresses, phone numbers. Then my boss, Rich Galant, asked me to dictate a first-person story about what had happened to me. I had to be really quick. Other people wanted to use the phone, and I was finally told to get off it. For quite a while after September 11, I regretted doing the first-person story because I didn't go down there to write about myself."

Susan cleaned up a little and returned the glasses to the woman who had loaned them to her. "I could have gotten away with taking them, and I'm embarrassed that

I even thought about that. But for the rest of the day, I couldn't find a place open to buy another pair, and I had to dictate from outside telephones in order to see my notes at all." She was wearing a linen pant suit because it was warm that day. And she had on good shoes with a good tread, no high heels. She later had to throw the outfit away because it was covered with gray ash.

"A church had opened up in the next block. I believe it was St. James. They were giving out sandwiches and water. They were offering bathrooms and counseling. I ate a sandwich and did more interviews with people who were covered with ash, a sign they would have a story to tell.

"I called in, and my boss at *Newsday* said, 'We don't know what's going to happen. Go to the New York Stock Exchange.' I did. I got through the barricades. They were not very organized yet. I did more interviews with people who were walking out or, in a couple of cases, sitting on a park bench trying to get themselves together. I'm still amazed that so few people declined to be interviewed at such a terrible time for them. Maybe talking helped them deal with the situation. Maybe they saw it as doing a good turn for someone, making something useful out of their experience. I came out of September 11 with an even greater respect for humanity.

"I got as far as a block east of the New York Stock Exchange before police stopped me. I was on Wall Street where it intersects with William—they wouldn't let me go any closer. I stood there in the ash all the rest of the afternoon. Tribune Company, which owns *Newsday,* requested that I call some of its TV stations, and they interviewed me live from a pay phone at the street corner. I think the stations I called were in Denver and Los Angeles. I told them what people coming out of the buildings had told me and what it looked like and sounded like. They asked how I felt, and I couldn't come up with any answer. I just described the scene. They put you on hold before you go on the air, and you hear what's being broadcast. I was touched by hearing people in Denver and on the West Coast describe their feelings about what happened in New York.

"I have a very strong mental picture of that afternoon, of building maintenance staff standing outside and looking at the layer of ash and paper and shoes and wondering what to do. Some had brooms in their hands, but brooms were obviously so inadequate that they didn't move them. Someone started to hose a sidewalk, and someone else yelled at him to stop because they needed water pressure. People were stunned. The air was full of smoke and ash and hurt my eyes and throat.

"In the late afternoon, it was decided that for the morning paper, I'd rewrite my first-person account and flesh it out. I went north from the Wall Street area to New York Downtown Hospital—the one just southeast of city hall—to do that. It was chaotic, filled with people waiting for medical help, but there was no smoke inside. I tried to stay out of the way while I sketched out a better version of the story in my notebook.

"But I couldn't dictate the story from a pay phone inside the hospital because there wasn't enough light in the phone booths for me to see the notes well. So I went back out and found a street phone to dictate. While I was on the way out,

Building Seven of the World Trade Center came down. By then, seeing a crowd of people screaming and running down the street, and more stuff in the air, didn't startle me. I guess I was pretty numb. I dictated as well as I could—it was a little dark again—and started home, after checking with my boss to see if there was anything else they needed me to do. It was between six and 6:30 P.M.

"Weeks later, I read a first-person account by a reporter who had a much closer call than I did when one of the towers fell, got out, and then hitched a ride with an ambulance to get through barricades and back to the Trade Center site in the late afternoon. She spent the night there. I don't know why it didn't occur to me to try to do that. I hope it wasn't cowardice. I don't think so, although not being able to see well may subconsciously have made me less confident. My mind was telling me the story was over. It obviously wasn't over, in terms of rescue efforts and things that needed to be witnessed. If I could do anything over again from that day, I'd go back.

"I walked back to Chelsea. In Chinatown, huge, silent crowds were watching the fires. In Little Italy, the streets were hung with glittering tinsel for the upcoming Feast of San Gennaro. There was a kiddie ride, completely empty, with smiling panda-bear faces on the gondolas. It looked so incongruous compared to what happened maybe a half-mile away. In the Village [Greenwich Village], churches were open, and people were sitting on the curbs on 6th Avenue, where you get a clear view of the World Trade Center. They were hugging but not talking. At St. Vincent's Medical Center, two blocks south of my home, the emergency entrance was floodlit, and people on gurneys were out on the sidewalk. I can't believe this now, but it didn't register on me why they were out there. I actually asked a policeman if there'd been a bomb scare. Of course they were people from the World Trade Center.

Susan's husband works about a dozen blocks north of the World Trade Center, just north of city hall. He had heard both planes hit and had seen the second tower fall. When she called *Newsday* from the City Department of Environmental Protection, Susan had asked *Newsday* to let him know where she was, and that she was all right.

When she got home, she called her nineteen-year-old daughter, Anne, a student at Berkeley who was in Argentina for the semester and was worried about her. Susan apologized to her for accidentally having a close call. Especially because Anne has worked at the student newspaper, Susan didn't want her to think that being a journalist meant deliberately getting into dangerous situations.

Susan had an extra pair of glasses at home. She went to work the next day and worked all the rest of the week and Saturday as well. The financial markets were trying to open up again after the attack; she covered that story and had to write every day.

She says the aftereffects of September 11 only came to her slowly. What does it mean that about three thousand people died? She says it's hard for her to get her mind around that. On Wednesday, she was still numb and came into work a little late. On the way to work Thursday, she walked by her local firehouse where the high-rise unit had come from. She realized the firefighters she had seen on the truck that day never came back to the firehouse. She went in and talked to some firefighters and started to cry.

She thought she was OK for one and a half to two weeks. But when the adrenaline rush of writing continuous stories about the Wall Street reopening died down, she realized she was having trouble concentrating. "I made two mistakes in the newspaper that we had to correct. I was having trouble finding things on my desk, and I was not paying attention. There was noise in my mind and in my head. I was disorganized and forgetful and grief-stricken. At home, I saw visions of the buildings burning, and I felt like crying a lot. I went to see a psychologist. It was like there was a hole in my soul.

"I felt bad for writing a first-person story. I felt bad because so many had died. I had only been frightened, not hurt, and it didn't seem right to write about myself. I had real trouble with the fact I'd been near a killing ground, and it had stopped before it got to me. I felt wrong to have been there and wrong to be living. I'm OK now. But I still get gusts of grief for all the lost lives, especially for people I knew. These were people I knew from phone conversations, mostly—I hadn't met them in person. They were good people, trusted sources in the banking and securities industry and on Wall Street."

Three weeks after the attacks, Susan retraced her steps of September 11 and went back to see where she had been that day. She went back to the unused Bank of New York Building where she had sought refuge from the debris cloud and looked at the marble floor when she had thrown herself. She spoke to the doorman and told him what had happened to her that day. That was the place where she had lost her glasses. "He had my glasses in a drawer. He had picked them up and saved them. That was a wonderful thing for him to do, and I'm glad I went back."

She remembers the day as "so chaotic." The paper made counseling available for staff on Long Island almost immediately. But it didn't offer counseling to people in Manhattan, where Susan is based, for several weeks. She got her counseling on her own by going to a psychologist she already knew. She went to see him four times.

As far as doing her job on September 11, "What would have prepared me to do better might have been more disaster coverage. I had done accidents and drownings, but never anything on a large scale. But I've been a reporter a long time, and interviewing people about who, what, where, and why is automatic and my purpose for being in any situation. It's automatic. And that's what I did that day. I asked people about what was going on. I thought about doing my job. There was no room for fear. I had to get details, names. I involved myself in my job. I didn't feel terrified except for that moment alone on the floor."

Susan has no idea how covering this story will impact her career. "I don't think of it in those terms. I'm happy doing what I'm doing. Since I was there, it's good to be able to understand what other people in the financial district went through. Maybe I'll be a little more sensitive to the changes this will produce in their lives."

"I Knew We Couldn't Outrun It"
By Susan Harrigan
STAFF WRITER
September 12, 2001

I was interviewing a group of people who had seen the planes hit the World Trade Center. We were about three blocks south of the two towers that had been hit.

Smoke was pouring from what looked like enormous bites that had been taken out of the buildings, and the edges of the gaping structural wounds were bleeding flames.

People were jumping—I didn't want to look.

Witnesses who had come from closer to the towers were telling me that the ground there, and the tops of nearby buildings, were strewn with body parts.

All of a sudden, police officers came down both sides of the street. I heard one of them saying "Pentagon," and they told us to move back.

As we began moving, someone yelled "The building is falling," and we started running.

I looked over my shoulder and saw what looked like a several-story-high cloud of debris roaring up the street. From its speed, I knew we couldn't outrun it and looked for shelter.

It suddenly struck me as a little ridiculous to think that I might be about to die at a scene that looked like something created by a special effects unit on the set of a disaster movie.

At what seemed like almost the last moment before the cloud hit, I saw a revolving door and what I hoped was a solid building. The door was jammed, so I decided to press myself into the wall and hope for the best.

Then I saw a middle door that was open. People were scrambling in. I think I was the last one. I threw myself flat on the floor inside and waited for not only the cloud, but for what I thought might be an entire World Trade Center tower to fall on top of me.

I've wondered before what I might think of if I was about to die, and I concentrated on that while I squeezed through the door. You don't get much time to think. I thought of my daughter, my husband, and two words of a prayer, in that order.

While I was on the floor, the air outside turned black and the building went dark. But there was no crash—just thick, acrid smoke filling the building. I don't know what happened to the people who were running with me and didn't make it inside.

There were about ten of us in the building, but no one panicked. We looked for the exits, fearing that the air would soon be unbreathable. It took about half an hour to find a way out.

Back out on the street, everything was covered with ash, and the air was black with smoke. There were shoes, many of them women's sandals, lying there.

Above, there was the buzz of another low-flying airplane and a helicopter. Everyone looked for new cover.

A firefighter helped us climb a fence and get into a park area. One man who was with me had a broken shoulder. The firefighter told us to head for the water, then others suggested the Brooklyn Bridge.

That called for some navigational guesswork as the smoke was so thick it was hard to

Susan Harrigan

tell north from south. People put handkerchiefs or whatever else they could use over their noses or mouths and stumbled on. When I got as far as the Federal Reserve building on Liberty Street, I noticed a huge new cloud falling from the sky. A few minutes later, I heard that the second tower had fallen.

We went as far east as we could and turned north alongside the East River. We passed workers in front of a Chase Bank branch who were holding big bottles of water of a type that services water coolers. They offered people a chance to drink or soak their handkerchiefs or sweaters.

At the Fulton Fish Market, workers held out paper towels and Kleenex. One held a hose out, offering to wet down anyone who needed it. We were all covered from head to foot with ash.

There was never any panic, and even at the worst moments, such as when we were trying to get in the door of the building ahead of the debris cloud, I never saw anyone push other people out of the way. People were touchingly willing to share their stories of what they had seen and felt—even a man who couldn't find his wife and son, and feared that they had been on the 74th floor of Tower One.

After reaching the Brooklyn Bridge area, I turned around and went back. I got as far as the corner of Wall and William streets and as close to the New York Stock Exchange as I could, according to the police.

The streets for blocks and blocks were covered with several inches of light gray ash that was constantly being churned up by emergency vehicles. Few people wandered through, some of them brokers and other financial district workers who had stayed where they were, figuring the bridges might not be safe and knowing that public transportation was not working.

Almost everyone wore surgical paper masks or had created makeshift ones.

Trinity Church still stood at the end of 12th Street, its graceful spire almost invisible in a thick cloud of smoke and dust.

The streets were carpeted with paper that had obviously blown from the falling towers. Some of them were meticulous sheets of bid-and-ask prices on stocks. One memo recommended a trainee to the person's manager. Another discussed a contract.

An outdoor restaurant not far away from the stock exchange was deserted, its tables, gay umbrellas and hanging plants covered in ash. A woman's shoe lay on one table. There were shoes in the street even there, including a couple of mismatched Nikes, along with a flattened pair of reading glasses. (Copyright © 2002, Newsday, Inc.)

16

Charlotte Hall, *Newsday*, Long Island, New York

Charlotte Hall was listening to the radio at her home on Long Island the morning of September 11. It was shortly after the first plane hit, so she knew then they were going to have a big story to cover that day. But then the second plane hit, and Charlotte began trying to contact her staff from her home. Then she headed to her office on Long Island, a fifteen-minute commute. She is managing editor of *Newsday*, the fifth-largest metropolitan newspaper in the country. Residents in Nassau, Suffolk, and Queens Counties in New York State consider it their "local" newspaper.

As managing editor, Charlotte's job is to oversee the paper's coverage overall, setting directions for the reporting and mobilizing the staff. Her first thought was to get staff from the *Newsday* bureau in Queens across the East River and into Manhattan. But that proved difficult because of the enormous transit problems caused by the attack. "They really couldn't get there," Charlotte explained.

On September 11, every reporter who could "just went" to the story. Charlotte said reporters instantly and naturally move toward a story. Whether they are women or men makes no difference, so there was no debate for her about whether to send women. On September 11, whoever was in Lower Manhattan for *Newsday* went there, and several of them were women.

Susan Harrigan, a *Newsday* business reporter who lives in Greenwich Village, was near home and walking her dog when the first plane hit. She immediately headed downtown. The first-person account she wrote for the paper that day is included in the previous chapter. She was two or three blocks away when the first tower collapsed, and she ran for her life. She squeezed into a building before the wave of debris could hit her. She thought she would die. The first-person account she wrote for the paper that day is included in the previous chapter.

A second *Newsday* reporter, Jessica Kowal, was also in Manhattan. She was sched-

Charlotte Hall

uled to cover the New York City mayoral primary that was to be held that day. Jessica was at home on the Upper West Side when the first plane hit, and she, too, immediately headed downtown. She took one of the last subways to City Hall. When she came up from the subway, the first tower collapsed and she also had to run for her life. She was a leading reporter on this story for the first three days, although her beat is education.

Charlotte reached her office about 9:30 that morning, before the first tower collapsed, and gathered her staff together. They were watching TV and talking about how to mobilize the staff for the day when they saw the first tower collapse. "There was silence in the room when we realized the tower was gone," Charlotte recalled.

The editors and reporters had many decisions to make quickly. One was whether to put out an extra. They decided they had to. The copy was delivered to *Newsday*'s Long Island presses by three o'clock on September 11, and the extra edition was available on Long Island by 3:30. A limited press run of fifty thousand copies was produced that day and delivered by truck to 7-Elevens, which are the paper's main point-of-purchase site. Charlotte calls the twenty-four-page extra "pretty impressive." It contains all staff-written reports, AP photos, Susan Harrigan's first-person account of the morning of September 11, graphics of the planes' flight paths, and a history of the Twin Towers.

Newsday ran stories with 132 bylines on September 12. "Everyone at the paper was working on this story," Charlotte remembered. "One of the good things to come out of this experience is that the story broke down walls between departments. Reporters worked on this story whether they 'belonged' in sports or arts or business.

The production of the paper changed. People were 'out of place' in the normal sense. They were doing the job that had to be done." Another big decision was to tell the human stories, of individual lives, and the staff started right away working on profiles of the victims. This project is called "The Lost" and was still running in the paper months later.

Charlotte also got the foreign staff into action immediately. She moved four reporters and a photographer into Pakistan within a few days. She wanted full, rounded coverage on this, *Newsday*'s biggest story ever—in a national, world, and local sense.

The *Newsday* staff ran into unprecedented communications difficulties that first day. The paper's main New York City operation is in Queens. Its reporters already in the city went to the site and stayed there. But the big problem was communicating with them by cell phone and regular phone. The phones just didn't work during the early hours. Then the city shut down. The subways shut down. The buildings shut down. Long Island was cut off from Manhattan by that afternoon. There had never been a day like that. Charlotte went home late that night to rest but was back at work first thing next morning and worked for days after that.

She said what prepared her staff for this level of coverage was experience gained from other big stories the newspaper had covered. For example, when the crash of TWA Flight 800 occurred off Long Island's south shore in July 1996, it was a national tragedy right in the staff's own backyard.

Charlotte found the 9/11 story to be unusual in many ways. First, she and her staff felt it personally. "There was a lot of sadness and stress in the newsroom. Reporters and editors are trained to maintain composure and be professional, but sometimes they cried. Doing work is where journalists find comfort, even though the work for this story was exhausting emotionally and physically," she said.

Charlotte said her bosses gave people breaks from the story to get some rest or go to counseling. She knew the needs of the reporters and editors in her newsroom. She made some people take time off after the first few days, but some felt there was nothing for them to do at home. "They wanted to work, and the discipline of work kept them focused. Work was a way to deal with it. They were doing something worthwhile. They were putting out a paper, performing a public service, and there was affirmation and comfort in that."

Charlotte does not know anyone directly who was killed in the attacks. But she knows people who know people. "This is very typical," she said. "There are no more than one or two degrees of separation between those who covered the story and those who were killed. Everyone on Long Island knows somebody or somebody who knows somebody, and the same is true in the newsroom. One sports columnist lost a brother in the Pentagon attack. Everybody has been personally touched."

The first Saturday after the attacks, Charlotte went into Manhattan and walked past the firehouses and makeshift shrines with photographs of those missing. She said the firehouses were heartbreaking and that she could see smoke at the site of the Twin Towers and the surrealistic lights burning at night for the rescue workers.

She has gone to Ground Zero frequently since the attack, trying to understand the impact of what happened.

Charlotte doesn't know what long-term effect this story will have on her career. But on the paper she said it will have a positive impact. "The newspaper will change forever because of this story. There is more a sense of Long Island being connected to New York City now, and New York news has become more important to Long Islanders. We changed some of the beats in our Washington bureau and created a new homeland security beat there. At the same time we're closely covering the civil liberties issues that have grown out of the attacks. Overall, our staff worked better together on this story than ever before, and strong teamwork is to everyone's advantage."

She said there has been great support and very little criticism of the paper's coverage. The paper did run one photograph of a man jumping from the World Trade Center. "We needed to run it," she said. "It was an important, although horrific, part of the story. We couldn't hide this."

In Charlotte's opinion, women are already doing everything and anything in her newsroom. "They are experienced reporters, and we sent two of them to central Asia. Tina Susman went to Pakistan but broke her leg in an accident near Kashmir, and we had to get her out for medical treatment. Letta Tayler went to Tora Bora and did some very gutsy reporting during the bombardment of al Qaeda caves in the hills there."

Charlotte had no qualms about women covering the war and wanted to make sure women were among those sent. "One, because it's right. But, more importantly, because they are terrific reporters. And they're both very brave." Both women she sent had foreign reporting experience and knew how to handle dangerous situations. Charlotte said an added advantage for a female reporter in Pakistan and Afghanistan is easier access to women as news sources, since for some women there is a cultural taboo against talking to men who are not members of their family. "But I would never say that women should cover only stories about women or that men shouldn't cover those stories. In fact, a male reporter did our most extensive story on the reemergence of Afghan women."

Both abroad and at home, the women on her staff have performed extraordinarily well, Charlotte said. "I want a good mix of people working on every story. I value the perspectives and diversity of our reporting staff. The richness of our coverage comes from the mix of talents and backgrounds. And I believe it's important to treat people well, enable them, and take care of them while they're covering a story."

17

Cynthia McFadden, ABC News, New York City

It was nine o'clock in the morning on September 11 when Cynthia McFadden walked into ABC's offices for a morning meeting. The offices are on the Upper West Side of Manhattan on Columbus Avenue between 66th and 67th Streets. Her assistant Devon Binch had the TV on and said to her, "Cynthia, something terrible has happened." Cynthia looked up at the TV, saw the World Trade Center towers on fire, and called the ABC news desk. She was the first ABC correspondent to call the news desk. She also called the executive producer of ABC's *PrimeTime Live,* who told her to report to his office for a briefing.

She was asked where she wanted to be posted. Cynthia recalled, "In a crisis, as often happens, there's a vacuum in the middle of it. There's a lot of leeway in what to do. I could have gone pretty much wherever I wanted." She knew that ABC had other people already heading toward the World Trade Center site, and she felt ABC needed people at many different venues, so she suggested going to the command post for city emergency services being set up at Bellevue Hospital on the East Side of Manhattan. The city's emergency services command center had been inside the World Trade Center. It is where the mayor and the ambulance, fire, and police services would have coordinated their efforts.

By the time Cynthia headed south with her crew, one of the World Trade Center towers had already collapsed. "I knew it was catastrophic," she said. "As we were driving south down Fifth Avenue, we realized all the people were going north. We were the only people going south."

She and her crew got as far as the United Nations on 49th Street and 1st Avenue. They had to walk the last mile, lugging their heavy camera equipment, because they could not get through on the streets. They interviewed people they met along the way, people who were covered with white dust, people who appeared to be in shock. Cynthia stayed in touch with ABC News by satellite phone and essentially kept an

129

Cynthia McFadden

open line to the ABC control room. "We walked with our heads down, looking at people's shoes. We interviewed people whose shoes and clothes were covered with the most dust. We suspected they had been closest to the towers."

Cynthia said there was no discussion whatsoever at ABC News about whether to send women to cover this story. She volunteered for the assignment and then went about doing her job: reporting the news. She took her assistant with her. "Devon had never covered a breaking news story before, and I wanted her to see it. I also knew we'd need her help." Besides Devon, Cynthia's crew consisted of a satellite truck crew, two news producers, and videographers.

Cynthia and her crew reached Bellevue Hospital "somewhere around eleven o'clock." Two hundred to three hundred people were already there, ready to give blood. She and her crew were the first television crew inside the command center. Security checkpoints were set up everywhere inside the hospital. Hospital officials took her inside, and "It was disquieting because it was absolutely silent inside. This is where they were coordinating the emergency response of New York City. This is when we realized the damage must have been massive. All the normal emergency systems had been knocked out."

Cynthia lives across the street from ABC's offices, three or four miles north of the World Trade Center. The relay station for the phones in her building had been on top of one of the towers, so after the attacks there was no phone service at her apartment, where she had left her three-year-old son, Spencer, with his nanny that morning. She remembers it was very difficult to communicate using a cell phone. She did have a satellite phone and recalled, "We were covering New York City as if it were a foreign country, using our satellite phone."

She and her crew left Bellevue Hospital in the early afternoon because they felt they needed to be at the Chelsea Piers, where emergency medical cases were being handled. They were told fifty temporary operating suites had been set up there. She and her crew walked across Manhattan to the Chelsea Piers. "It was a long walk. It was amazing. It was early afternoon, a beautiful fall day, and New York City was deserted, all cordoned off." She stayed at the piers, waiting for rescued victims to be brought in. But no one came.

She was on the air Tuesday afternoon doing live reports "almost constantly for Peter Jennings." Her first report was on the phone from Bellevue Hospital shortly after noon. She reported from the Chelsea Piers all afternoon and was on the air "once an hour or so" until three o'clock Wednesday morning, reporting what rescue workers were telling her and giving eyewitness accounts of what was happening around her, such as the number of rescue vehicles and ambulances she could see going by and the smoke rising from the World Trade Center site about a mile to the south of the piers.

Cynthia went home from the Chelsea Piers about 3 A.M. and was expecting to return to them at 4:30 A.M. to report for *Good Morning America*. "When the driver picked me up Wednesday morning at 4:30, he said we were going to St. Luke's Hospital. I thought he was wrong, and I insisted he take me to the Chelsea Piers. When we arrived there, I saw there was no one at the Chelsea Piers. I was overwhelmed. It was clear no one was being rescued. There were no survivors to be treated."

On Wednesday she reported from St. Vincent's Hospital and kept a vigil there the rest of the week. St. Vincent's is the trauma hospital closest to the World Trade Center site; it is where rescue workers were brought. She reported live all day long, every day. She had the first reports from medical personnel returning from the scene. But much of her reporting was with families desperately looking for loved ones. "It was heartbreaking. People came up to us and begged us to put pictures of their missing relatives on the air. The hard part was being there for these people, especially because as the hours clicked by it became increasingly clear most of their loved ones would not be found."

ABC News was on the air virtually round-the-clock that first week. Reporters from *World News Tonight, Good Morning, America, PrimeTime Live, Nightline,* and *20/20* all covered the story. Cynthia normally reports for *PrimeTime Live,* which is a news magazine, but she was covering this story for all the other ABC news shows as well.

Cynthia and her crew worked on the streets of Manhattan for five straight days—Tuesday through Saturday. They literally sat on the sidewalks because there was no place else to sit. She was able to go home for about four hours a night, to clean up and rest.

"What prepared me to do this? I don't know. I've been doing this for a while now. I have been, regrettably, at some of the worst places on earth—at brothels in Bombay where eleven-year-olds are sold into sexual slavery, at a mental hospital in Mexico where conditions are so bad we wouldn't hold animals there. I have learned how to try to absorb the experience and communicate it. I suppose stamina helps. I tell myself, 'This is a job I need to do.' It's a job I could do. I felt that if I was able to absorb the pain of these people and communicate it, I was doing something important. This was a professional role I could play. Like most Americans, I was thinking, 'What can I do to help? What do I know how to do? I'm not a nurse or a doctor or a firefighter.' Reporting is what I know how to do. I wanted to be calm, clear, accurate, and compassionate. I hope I was.

"A very informing experience about this for me was being a mother. Most of those who died in the attacks were young fathers. I spent day after day with women with little kids who were looking for their husbands. I spent a lot of time holding back tears. I *felt* this story for these women. It was *very* difficult. This was an attack on *my* city, and I was very worried about my own little boy. We live near Lincoln Center. After the attack, our phones went out. Our nanny had a cell phone, but I wanted to be home with my little boy. One of the toughest moments for me personally came on Wednesday when I was told while on the air that they thought there was a car bomb across the street from my home. I called the nanny and got her and my son out of our building, but it was tough being part of a story you are covering.

"But to me, being a journalist is not just a job. I felt I had to do it the best way I knew how. Nonetheless, it was very difficult to be away from Spencer. By coincidence, I had bought him some new books on September 10. So as I'd leave in the wee hours of the morning for work, I would write him a note and leave him a new book. Later in the day I'd call him on the phone. I wanted him to know that Mommy was coming home."

Cynthia knows several people killed in the attacks, but none were close friends. She doesn't know whether she was in any personal danger covering the story but doesn't think so. She remembered, "There were some air quality problems, and we wore masks at St. Vincent's Hospital, which the hospital people brought to us." She became very sick afterward with a massive staph infection from being on the streets for a week. "I was sick for three months." On Friday of that first week, she had moved to the Armory, where the family assistance center had been set up. "It was pouring rain. I had been up since four o'clock that morning, there were no tents, and I was standing in the rain all day. I came back to the ABC building later in the week, and my little boy came for a visit. We later found out there was anthrax in that same area of the newsroom, so both of us had to be tested. So I suppose there was a psychic toll."

At the Armory on Friday, Cynthia had half an hour between live shots to get some coffee. On one of those breaks she went into the Armory. "I walked in, and I lost it. I cried. I was completely exhausted. Crying was cathartic. I was looking for one of my closest friends who worked in Tower One. I ran into a woman from the Red Cross. My friend was not on the list of survivors. But I went back outside, and I did a live report! It turned out my friend was in London the day of the attacks, but we didn't know that at the time. It was all mentally hard. I had to take a lot of information, and I had to figure out how to report it."

Cynthia felt supported by her colleagues at ABC News. As long as ABC wanted her to stay put at her post, she wanted to stay. She says she knows relief was only a phone call away. But it was up to her to call if she wanted to be replaced. Actually, she felt sorry for others at other networks who were on a regular rotation clock to be replaced. "I felt ABC's coverage was strong in part because all of us stayed put for long stretches. Staying at my post meant I felt the ebb and flow of the day. I got to know the rescue workers who were there. It's ABC's philosophy to leave people in position, and I think it's a good one. As one of our producers says, 'Sleep is for sissies.'"

She did not feel a lot of competition covering the story. She loaned her IFB (earpiece) to a CNN reporter who lost hers. They shared guests. She remembers a lot of cooperation with other correspondents and networks.

Families came to her and asked to be on TV; only occasionally did she seek them out. "Our producers found people in the crowds who had amazing stories. They would come up to me and say, 'We know you from *PrimeTime*. Please tell our story.'" She said this happened a lot between live shots. "At first we recorded these interviews and sent them to the network. It was heartbreaking. I couldn't say to these people, 'We're not doing any more.' We rolled on everybody. I let anyone talk. I told them, 'I don't know if this will be used, but I'm sending it back uptown.'"

"I'm really proud of how ABC covered this story," Cynthia said. "I am enormously proud of my colleagues. We did a great job under very difficult circumstances. We exercised appropriate restraint and used our reporting skills. I think Peter Jennings handled his role perfectly under horrendous circumstances. Peter stayed on the air for hours—his job was so complex—I figured I ought to be able to handle reporting from the scene for as long as he could sit at the anchor desk. Peter's true citizenship of the world was on display. I was moved by so many of my colleagues, by their sensitivity and their passion to do the job. The news division feels closer now. I suppose people in foxholes learn the strengths and weaknesses of their colleagues."

What sticks with her still is what a beautiful fall morning September 11 was. "It's heartbreaking. Every time it's a beautiful day, I remember, 'So was September 11.' It's hard for me to get on an airplane now, and I travel a lot. But it's not hard to be in New York City. I have a house in the country, but I never thought about moving out of the city and going there during this time." She was asked to go to Afghanistan and Pakistan but declined because she does not want to leave her son.

Cynthia does not know what impact covering this story will have on her career. "I just don't know. I know I learned a lot doing it. Tragedy often is what makes

journalism careers. In this instance I played a small part in covering a very big tragedy with a group of people I have great respect for. It's a role I wanted to play. It
may sound odd, but I am honored to have been able to do this job."

Cynthia remembered what CBS News producer Fred Friendly once told her: "A
professional is someone who knows what to do when the roof falls in." She added,
"Experience showed in the coverage of this story. People with the most experience
did the best work, by and large." She would tell young journalists not to forget the
human aspects of whatever story they're covering. "There's a human side to a
story—it's not just tonnage and debris and geopolitics. It's important to explain the
human price of all of this—that's the story that needed to be told. It's easy to move
away from the human tragedy. Covering ideas is covering people, too. Always
remember to cover the people."

18

Ann Compton, ABC News, White House Press Corps, Sarasota, Florida

ABC News White House correspondent Ann Compton was in Sarasota, Florida, with President George W. Bush on Tuesday, September 11. She was scheduled to travel onboard Air Force One that day while the president promoted his education bill. Covering his trip was part of her regular beat for ABC. Tuesday was the second of two days on the road with the entire White House Press Corps, which included print reporters, camera crews, and White House staff.

Shortly after 9 A.M. on Tuesday, the president was speaking to a class of second-graders at Emma E. Booker Elementary School. Shortly before walking into the classroom, Bush had been informed in a telephone conversation with National Security Adviser Condoleezza Rice, who was in Washington, that a plane had hit one of the World Trade Center towers. Chief of Staff Andrew Card was in a holding room outside the classroom where Bush was speaking. A few moments later, at 9:07 A.M. by Ann's watch, Card entered the classroom and whispered into the president's ear that a second plane had hit the other World Trade Center tower. Bush's face became visibly tense and serious. Ann was standing at the rear of the classroom and remembered, "The look in the president's eyes betrayed the dread. Months later Bush told us Card whispered, 'America is under attack.'"

President Bush spoke briefly at the school at 9:31 A.M. and called the two plane hits "an apparent terrorist attack." Then he and his entourage of Secret Service agents and a small travel pool of thirteen journalists abruptly left. They went by motorcade to the Sarasota airport, where Air Force One was parked. "In a matter of minutes, President Bush was rushed to the steps of Air Force One, engines revving for the flight back to the capital." Ann was able to call in to ABC's live broadcasts on her cell phone from the speeding motorcade. "I called from a van en route to the plane as we first scrambled out of Sarasota. The driver quickly cut off her radio when she discovered she was hearing me from the dashboard and from the back seat."

Ann Compton

While the motorcade was en route to the airport, a plane hit the west side of the Pentagon, which is located in Arlington, Virginia, immediately across the Potomac River from Washington, D.C.

"At the airport, there was a dog and hand search of all press bags. At 9:54 A.M., Air Force One was 'wheels up' from Sarasota. President Bush was being evacuated—a term the White House would only use 'off the record.'

"Once airborne, the news of the crash at the Pentagon made it clear President Bush could not return to Washington, so Air Force One turned west to Barksdale, but we were not told where we were going." Air Force One was taking the president and his entourage to Barksdale Air Force Base, a secure military base outside Shreveport, Louisiana. Ann was one of thirteen members of the press corps on board. At 10:10 A.M., a commercial jetliner crashed in Somerset County, Pennsylvania. At 10:29 A.M., a weak television signal from the ground brought Ann and the others onboard a live picture of the second World Trade Center tower collapsing.

"I marked each moment in my reporter's notebook because, as broadcasters, our lives are ruled by clocks," Ann recalled. "At 10:55 A.M., there was a noticeable increase in the plane's altitude. Air Force One climbed past forty thousand feet. We were headed west, away from Washington."

Around 11:30 A.M., Ann noticed air force fighter jets flying off Air Force One's right and left wings. The jets continued to hover near both wings of Air Force One during its descent at Barksdale. Once on the ground, the plane was surrounded by Air Force personnel wearing full combat gear and carrying M-16s.

Reporting this story was going to be difficult because, as Ann remembered, "We were not told we were going to Barksdale. Upon landing we were told not to turn on our cell phones since the president's location was secret. However, local press guessed as much and were camped outside the base gates and saw Air Force One land. When we informed Ari [Ari Fleischer, White House press secretary] about the local media, he gave us permission to tell our colleagues where we were. The national press held the information, as requested, until Ari gave the OK. We were told not to turn on our cell phones and two-way pagers because the president's location could be traced."

The president made a brief statement at Barksdale and then reboarded Air Force One.

Ann was the only broadcast reporter allowed back on board with him. "Ari allowed one print reporter, Sonya Ross of the Associated Press, a still photographer from the AP, and the two-man CBS television camera crew to continue traveling. These five journalists would have to represent all of their colleagues as President Bush traveled in secret.

"Onboard Air Force One, there was no discussion in our presence about who would stay, who would go. The two most senior women on the White House staff were *not* present—counselor Karen Hughes and National Security Adviser Condoleezza Rice. Among the reporters onboard, two of us were allowed to remain, both women: Sonya Ross of the Associated Press and me. We were both veteran White House correspondents."

For the remainder of that day, Ann filed reports for all broadcast operations. "I was required by the rules of White House pool coverage to 'pool' my information about President Bush with all the rest of the White House Press Corps still stranded in Florida and in Louisiana before I could report for ABC News or try to reach my own family. That pool information was relayed by telephone landline through ABC News in Washington. Then I filed by phone to ABC television and radio. Only then was there time to try for my family, to no avail. I did leave my husband's office phone number with a gentleman at the air force base in Louisiana, asking that he try to call my husband and assure him I was OK, onboard Air Force One—then I wondered whether that was much of a reassuring message. By then, of course, he had already heard from others who had heard my reports on the air."

Three digital clocks are mounted on the forward wall in each of the passenger compartments onboard Air Force One. The clocks show the time in Washington, the time at the current location, and the time at the plane's destination. Ann recalled, "After a hasty refueling at the air base in Louisiana, and after leaving most of its passengers and some of its crew standing in confusion on the tarmac, Air Force One took off with the president of the United States and a handful of others, bound for the safety of a secret location. The three clocks read 1:36 P.M. eastern daylight time, until the destination clock snapped to central time, 12:36 P.M., our only confirmation that Air Force One was again headed west, away from Washington.

"It was the first time in twenty-five years of flying on the president's plane that I felt a chill of foreboding. F-16s shadowed us just off the wing. No place seemed safe. I was the only broadcast reporter on the plane, assigned to represent all my colleagues. For the coming hours I would have very limited means to tell the American people and the world of the condition of the president of the United States."

Air Force One was flying the president from Barksdale Air Force Base in Louisiana to Offutt Air Force Base in Omaha. Offutt is the command post of America's nuclear forces and one of the most secure military installations in the United States. At Offutt, the president would lead, by video phone to Washington, a meeting of the National Security Council with Vice President Dick Cheney and National Security Adviser Rice.

"As we were en route to Offutt, Ari came to the rear of the plane and told us he could not say where we were going or when we would ever be back in Washington. He offered reassurance that we would be cared for wherever the president waited out the crisis. Nearly five hours had elapsed since the hijacked airliners had destroyed the twin towers of the World Trade Center and a section of the Pentagon."

Ann wrote in her notebook, "At 2:47 P.M., Air Force One descended over flat, agricultural territory to a medium-sized city. We were not told that we were landing at the headquarters of the Strategic Air Command in Nebraska, but local news crews figured it out. We had the eerie sensation of watching ourselves landing live on the local TV channel broadcast in our cabin."

Reporting this news was also difficult. "In Nebraska, Offutt Air Base was in a 'lockdown,' but a sympathetic custodian agreed to let us into a well-equipped conference center with ample phone jacks and power outlets for the Comrex Hotline unit I carry to feed radio reports.

"My first responsibility was calling in details in a pool report to all the other broadcasters and reporters who were left behind. Through ABC News Radio in Washington and through the TV desk pool telephone system among the five television networks, I dictated long narratives, trying to sound as if I were on the air live so the information could be used even by our competition. Several times I was able to call in to ABC's live broadcasts, usually on a cell phone. Twice, I was live on the air when I had to cut off the broadcast in near panic. I interrupted Vic Ratner, the radio anchor in Washington, because we were suddenly hauled back out to the airplane. At another moment in a live voice report on television, Peter Jennings [ABC news anchor] asked where we were going in such a hurry. I could only be honest: 'Peter, I have no idea.' In retrospect, not a reassuring message to millions of our listeners."

Ann had a variety of equipment problems that day. "I was unable to use my computer because I was never in any one location long enough. It was like the old days—relying on my office to brief me on other developments and relying on my eyes and ears. Cell phone service was frustratingly unavailable nationwide. In Louisiana, where Air Force One stopped first for refueling, my cell phone never connected with anything. I was on the air with ABC's live coverage on a landline only. By the time we reached Nebraska and the Strategic Air Command Headquarters, the cell came alive, and there was a voice mail message waiting. 'Mommy,' the voice complained, 'Why did you have time to tell Peter Jennings you were OK and not have time to call me?' Of course, I had tried to call my daughter in her Texas dorm room—in vain."

Air Force One left Offutt Air Force Base in the midafternoon. It was 6:47 P.M. eastern time when it touched down at Andrews Air Force Base, its home base in suburban Maryland, a few miles outside Washington, D.C. For Ann, "Still, there was no sense of safety. I had only minutes for one last live broadcast as we literally ran to the waiting helicopters. Peter Jennings asked if the president would take Marine One [the presidential helicopter]. I had to answer that we were instructed not to tell our offices or the public. President Bush was indeed about to fly back to the White House lawn. He would be flying past the thick smoke still rising from the damaged Pentagon. It had been an intensive ten hours on the move. It was 7:22 P.M. when I returned to the ABC News booth at the rear of the White House press room, my pool responsibilities over. Only then did I begin to hear the names of those lost and missing in the day's attacks—journalist Barbara Olson and a fraternity brother of my college sons. That's when I sat down and cried."

Ann is an accomplished and seasoned network correspondent. The fact that she was one of only two reporters in the White House Press Corps allowed to stay on Air Force One that day is a testament to her skill and professionalism. Her years of experience in journalism and in life helped prepare her to report this story. "Reporting prepares you to take unspeakable events and translate them into coherent stories. Life trains you to weep when you are done.

"Back at the White House, I prepared to cover President Bush's address to the nation at 8:30 P.M., and then I appeared live with Peter Jennings for a full report on the president's day. Then I wrote and recorded a long diary spot for *Good Morning America,* which I was back in before dawn the next morning to open and close live on the program. We all continued to work through the week as President Bush and his national security advisers all met at Camp David [Maryland].

"On Friday, when air travel was still restricted, President Bush took only a normal pool of thirteen journalists with him to Ground Zero—one each from television, radio, newspapers, magazines, a TV crew, wire writers, and still photographers. I chose not to be among them, remaining at the White House to broadcast from there. I was honored to see Ground Zero for the first time at Thanksgiving—not with politicians or news crews. We drove up with our four children so we could, as a family, see for ourselves. It was a very dramatic moment, to show your children something that will shape their future lives."

19

Lesli Foster, WUSA-TV, Washington, D.C.

Lesli Foster usually reports during the early morning shift, which begins at 3 A.M. During the week of September 10, her schedule was changed so that she was to work the day shift from 10 A.M. until 6 P.M. On September 11, Lesli was supposed to anchor the noon newscast and report in the afternoon. It was before nine o'clock and she was at home, getting ready for work, when she saw the news on TV about the World Trade Center attack. It takes Lesli only twelve minutes to get to work by car, and she quickly went on to work.

The WUSA offices are in upper northwest D.C., near the National Cathedral and about fifteen minutes from the National Mall grounds. "We were all in the newsroom," Lesli remembered. "I was putting on makeup when I looked up at the TV monitors and saw the CBS News coverage. Bryant Gumbel and Jane Clayson were on the air. I heard them say that the Pentagon had been hit and was on fire. This was shortly after nine o'clock, and the entire newsroom went into emergency mode. Newsroom managers were planning to send anchor Gordon Peterson to New York . . . but soon after decided to regroup and keep all news personnel in Washington. I asked, 'Where do you want me to go?' "

News crews from the station were quickly dispersed to various locations in and around Washington. Lesli was sent with a photographer in a news car toward Capitol Hill. They had police scanners and two-way radios in their car, but their cell phones were not working. "The assignment desk basically said to us, 'Get out there. We'll tell you more later.' " On their way to Capitol Hill, they were listening to the scanners and to radio news and hearing reports about alleged car bombs, bombs at the State Department, and reports that the Capitol and the White House were targets. Then they began hearing that Union Station, which is just north of Capitol Hill, might have received a suspicious package.

"All federal employees were dismissed from work after the attacks, so there was a

Lesli Foster

major traffic jam in Washington," recalled Lesli. "Cars and people flooded the streets. No one knew what was happening. We didn't know if the White House or the Capitol might be the next target."

Lesli was sent from one site to another as the story changed throughout the morning. "I did not do any live reporting on air that first day. After the Twin Towers were attacked, the station needed me in the field rather than on the anchor desk. Because of the traffic gridlock, we were unable to make it to a live position in time to get on the air. As a result, my colleague Wayne Myers and I ended up working as field producers throughout the day. We were able to get sound and video from various locations across the city. At the U.S. Capitol, Chamber of Commerce representatives from North Carolina were meeting with congressional members. They were evacuated and were trying to figure out how to get home. We got sound bites [brief interviews] from them. They were shaken up. I'm not sure the words *terrorist attacks* truly had sunk in.

"The assignment desk redirected us [from Capitol Hill] to the city government's emergency post in the Reeves Municipal Center. There was a news conference to talk about the city's response to the attack with Washington, D.C., Mayor Anthony Williams and his deputy mayors. The mayor of Los Angeles, who was in town for a meeting, also attended, but he didn't know many details about what had happened.

"A big issue turned out to be the city's emergency response immediately following the attacks. Many people believe Washington was truly vulnerable because the city did not have an adequate emergency preparedness plan ready for an attack of this sort. The city's emergency broadcast system was never activated. Cell phones were dead. City leaders couldn't communicate with each other. Top leaders were supposed to have satellite phones . . . but none of them had them. They were apparently stored in an office. D.C. police responded in the best way they knew how: they activated a joint operation center . . . but even they did not appear to have a formal response plan. Other local police agencies were faced with the same problem."

After the news conference at the city government's emergency post, Lesli was sent to a church gathering at the Metropolitan United Methodist Church, near her station, where people had come to pray for people who had perished in the attacks. "It was an impromptu gathering. Prayer services were springing up all over the city. People were putting out flags. Later that evening there were candlelight vigils on street corners."

Lesli said there was no discussion in her newsroom about whether to send women to cover this story. "If there was, I wasn't privy to it. I didn't think about that. They sent all of us out to get news as it was happening. My colleague Dave Statter got to the Pentagon during those first dark minutes. He is a former firefighter himself, and we were the first local station to show the Pentagon damage and go live locally from the scene."

On September 11, Lesli didn't file any stories with her name on them. She called in information to writers who wrote up brief stories, and all of her video was used. Lesli left work about six o'clock Tuesday evening. "They told me they needed me back the next morning at 3 A.M. I watched TV till midnight that Tuesday. I tried to call my sister in New York and my family.

"It was a pretty scary day. We didn't know what we would encounter. There were moments of concern and fear, but we had a job to do and we approached it that way. I've never covered a war. This was uncharted ground for me. There were so many rumors that day about buildings being targeted. I just put fear out of my mind."

Lesli said she was "not really" in any personal danger on September 11. "There was the element of danger. There might be a bomb. We didn't have specialized gear to wear—no gas masks, no terrorist protection kits. We just went out there and tried to report what we saw. We didn't know what was in store for us."

Lesli was sent to the Pentagon on the second day, Wednesday, September 12. "We were confined to a media staging area about a quarter of a mile away from the Pentagon. We had to set up [our equipment] in the parking lot of a military gas station. There was a large cadre of media in this particular area. We were sequestered there for a good two weeks. I came in [on September 12] at 3 A.M. and worked until 3 P.M. The thing I noticed the most when I arrived that morning was the pungent smell of smoke. I was amazed by the extent of the damage to this icon building, and my heart felt heavy for the people who perished and their families.

"Over the next two weeks, I really came to appreciate the Salvation Army. What a job they did! The Salvation Army set up a canteen area for the hundreds of emergency and rescue workers with snacks and meals available throughout the day. Another canteen area was set up in the media area. I think I gained a few pounds during those two weeks at the Pentagon. Citizens from the area would bring food to the Salvation Army to say thank you.

"The dissemination of information about the search-and-recovery efforts was very organized," Lesli said. "There were two press conferences each day. The city manager for Arlington, the police chief for Arlington, the fire chief or the deputy fire chief for Arlington, members of search-and-rescue teams from Maryland, Virginia, and other states, along with members of the armed services, all participated in the briefings. Many people may think the Pentagon is in Washington, D.C., but it's actually in Arlington, Virginia.

"We were allowed to interview search-and-rescue team members about what they saw and what their job was like, but local news crews had no access to the immediate physical Pentagon site during those first few days. On the first day, before it was cordoned off, several photographers got some shots of injured people coming out of the Pentagon after the attack.

"Each day, officials would update the search-and-rescue efforts. They would tell us the number of bodies recovered, how the shoring-up effort was going, the number of injured, the mental state of the workers. It [the staging area] was a little city in front of the Pentagon. The Salvation Army, Red Cross, FBI, military police, and heavy equipment operators were in constant motion. They all seemed so focused, so dedicated to the enormous task in front of them.

"Several days after the attacks, more than a dozen journalists were taken over to view the physical site up close. Our access was controlled and monitored by several police agencies. We had maybe ten or fifteen minutes to shoot all of the video and make all the observations we could before being escorted back to the media area. We were told, 'No interviews, no questions, just video.' The Department of Justice did release their own video, and so did some of the search-and-rescue teams. But most of the first images of the Pentagon site were disseminated by the military.

"What we could see at the Pentagon was the enormity of the task at hand. Hundreds of people were there. Rescue teams worked tirelessly. They had American flags on their hats. We saw the heavy equipment being used, but we couldn't see the actual wreckage, the debris, or the ongoing search itself."

Lesli did not personally know anyone who was killed in the Pentagon attack. On the first day she was near the Pentagon, even though she was a quarter of a mile away from it, the smoke from the fires was so thick that she had trouble with her eyes. Smoke got under her contact lenses; she developed a severe eye irritation and had to wear her glasses on the air for the next two weeks.

"There is nothing at all that could have prepared me to cover this," she said. "At twenty-seven, I'm one of the youngest reporters in the market. During the days that followed, . . . I'm not exactly sure where I drew strength. My faith in a higher power played a huge part. Also, I kept thinking about all the lives lost and how many families would never see their loved ones walk through their doors again. It reminded me of why I am in this business."

She said no one in her newsroom checked to see how she was doing emotionally. "Everyone was in task mode. With the attacks taking place in our backyard, there wasn't much time to stop and think about our own emotional state. But, certainly, we were concerned about everyone else. And, while on duty, many of us tried to reach our own families to assure them that we were OK. My significant other was worried about me. We couldn't reach each other [on the phone] for hours on September 11. My parents were concerned. I was unable to contact my sister in New York. She was panicking, because she couldn't reach me. I eventually reached my partner, and he contacted my family for me."

During the two weeks of reporting from the Pentagon site, she remembered, "There were a number of scares from time to time about aircraft in the controlled airspace near the Pentagon and whether they belonged there, people phoning in bomb threats with rescue workers having to get out of the building quickly. One time there was a scare, and police told us at the media site to move back immediately, so we ran."

Lesli feels that September 11 and the days immediately following had a definite impact on the Washington press corps. "There was a noticeable spirit of cooperation among all of the correspondents, photographers, and producers. We were all good journalistic citizens trying to serve a mission. Considering we were confined to one space near the Pentagon, we really didn't have any other option. All of us knew how important it was to get the story—and get it right. And, in the process, if someone needed a light or help with a power source for a live shot . . . the crews managed to work it out."

The Washington reporters didn't encounter people going on TV and searching for relatives in quite the same way New York City reporters did. Pictures weren't plastered on city streets. Pentagon officials directed families to a local hotel for information. Families brought pictures and mementos to that location. A number of families did check area hospitals, and, soon after, the Pentagon set up designated places for them to go. "New York City reporters and photographers had unprecedented access to the World Trade Center," Lesli said. "But we were kept at least a quarter of a mile away from the Pentagon site. Busloads of family members would be taken into the Pentagon site, but we weren't allowed to talk with them."

Lesli had trouble sleeping for the first couple of days following September 11. "I felt an incredible sense of sadness. I knew, like most Americans, that I would never be the same. And, in those first few days, weeks, and months after the attacks . . . it was quite remarkable to see the landscape of Washington changing. It became a more warm and feeling place.

"People were more courteous. I almost wondered if this was truly the same city. I think September 11 was a defining moment for me as a journalist. In just weeks I felt like I attained greater depth and understanding of what this business is all about. My most important objective during that time, and at all times, was to use my moral compass to guide me in the right direction. I knew that more than ever we all had to be responsible about the words and images coming across our airwaves."

Like many television news organizations, WUSA decided to edit the images shown after the first day, according to Lesli. "We stopped showing shots of the planes going into the Twin Towers and decided not to show shots of people jumping to their deaths. We were very sensitive about that. I think our managers made the right call regarding that footage. They didn't want our community, and especially those who lost loved ones, to keep reliving that awful moment again and again.

"An article in the *Washington Post* criticized us for treating the story like it was a snow day. But, when you consider that school districts were releasing students early, and thousands of federal workers and others were dismissed at the same time, . . . people were searching for the best escape routes out of the city, . . . and we had an obligation to tell people what the best routes out of the city were. We had an obligation to tell them what streets were cordoned off . . . how they could get to their children, their families. The area has close to a million federal workers and family members in and around the city. So in addition to this huge breach of national and local security, these were things local people needed to know."

Lesli feels that covering this story had a definite impact on her, believing it underscored how important news information is to the well-being and survival of individuals and that it strengthened her commitment to using the basics in covering the news. "I was observant, I asked lots of questions, and I tried my best to be objective," she said. "I used everything I had—how to approach a story, how to tell a story, how to talk to people in a difficult situation. I told myself, 'The fundamentals should get you through.' I trusted my judgment. I worked as a member of a team. I knew we had to be sensitive to what people were going through. I knew that we had to constantly think about the basic human principles of compassion and courtesy."

20

Elizabeth Cohen, CNN, Atlanta, Georgia

Elizabeth Cohen was on the phone in her office at CNN headquarters in Atlanta on the morning of September 11. She was talking with Ken Shiffman, a producer with whom she was doing a one-hour special on obesity. She had already done two live shots, at 7 A.M. and 8:15 A.M., one on stem cell research and the other on obesity. She was scheduled to do another live shot at nine o'clock. Elizabeth had her back to the CNN monitor in her office when Ken told her to turn around and look at the monitor. It was about 8:48 in the morning, shortly after the first plane hit the World Trade Center. CNN was carrying live pictures. The scene shocked her.

She said there was no discussion whatsoever about whether women would be sent to cover this story. She and her producer Miriam Falco (a senior producer with CNN's medical team) just decided, "Let's go." They asked permission from their supervisor, CNN's director of medical coverage, Carol Kinstle, rented a van because the airports were now closed, and piled in along with a photographer and a sound technician. They were on the road to New York early Tuesday afternoon. They took with them their regular gear—video cameras, cell phones, computers, and Palm Pilots.

Elizabeth had attended college in New York and did not want to stay in Atlanta as this story unfolded. She called her husband, who "urged me to go, telling me it was very important that I go to New York to help cover this story."

Elizabeth and her crew reached New York City about five o'clock in the morning Wednesday. As they approached the city from New Jersey to the south, she could see the damage immediately. "I could see the hole in the skyline and smoke rising from the site. It was very shocking." It would take them another four hours to get into Manhattan. "We had a hard time getting in. We tried the George Washington Bridge and then made a clockwise effort and were finally able to get in through the

Elizabeth Cohen

Midtown Tunnel." Having lived in New York and learned how to navigate the city was a benefit for her and her crew on this story.

"We immediately went to New York University Medical Center on 1st Avenue. We thought there would be hundreds of injured people to interview—like there had been in Oklahoma City. But we quickly found out that this was not like Oklahoma City. The city's finest trauma surgeons had been called in, and one hundred surgical beds had been set aside. But there was nothing for the surgeons to do, no one to put in those beds, no one for me to interview. The story wasn't at the hospital—it was on the street."

The New York City Morgue is on the east side of the city, near Bellevue Hospital. "On Wednesday, September 12, families were gathered at Bellevue Hospital waiting to see if their loved ones had been admitted there for treatment. The families were literally going hospital to hospital in search. We followed one of these families around as they searched, and we produced one story about their search. We wanted to put a human face on the missing."

On Thursday, September 13, Elizabeth was stationed at the Family Center that had been set up at the Armory at Lexington and 26th. She and her crew spent three days at the Armory (Thursday, Friday, and Saturday); Elizabeth said the families' stories were "wrenching." She worked from eight to fifteen hours a day, doing several live shots every hour. She and her crew were staying at a hotel in Manhattan and took time to eat and sleep. "But at work I was surrounded by these families of the missing, and it was hard to leave them sometimes. I feel I gave desperate family members and friends an outlet to tell the world about their loved ones who were missing. I'd never seen anything like this. Families were handing out fliers to the media, hoping for some news on their relatives.

"I felt their sadness, their desperation. It was heartbreaking and emotional. There was a wounded numbness about it, total shock. The families were walking around with photos, begging the media to show their relative's pictures. It was difficult, but the families were strong. The families sought out the media, not the other way around. International people did, too, since everyone knows CNN."

Every day, the Salvation Army and others, such as people living in the neighborhood, offered food and water to Elizabeth and the other journalists who had no time to leave their posts. "There was simply no free time at all," she explained.

"I got to know some of the families during this time. I felt I was helping the families and that the families wanted my help to find their missing loved ones. The families seemed to feel that if they could show their loved one's photograph to viewers, someone might recognize the person and call and say where their family member was being treated."

Elizabeth said covering the families' stories at the Armory was something she could do and something that helped the families in a way. People came to her to be interviewed. "The families told me there are always a couple of people who are saved in the rubble of buildings, even in small disasters. They believed that even more people would survive in this disaster since it was so much bigger. They believed if only someone saw the pictures. . . .

"It was not difficult to work with the families. I was doing multiple live shots every hour—for CNN Headline News, CNN/U.S., and CNN International. There was lots of air time for everyone who wanted to be on, there was room for everyone, and I didn't have to turn people away or choose from among them."

Elizabeth and the families received many phone calls from people they knew, and this was important to them—this evidence that people were connecting in the face of this overwhelming tragedy.

"I was prepared to cover this story because I had helped other people in my personal life deal with the loss of someone close to them. Helping them through their loss made it easier for me to do this work with the families at the Armory. There had been occasions in my own life where I'd helped others. I'd done it before. This life experience helped me ground myself for this story. I had also done day after day of live shots before, so it was somewhat routine in that way; I'd had lots of practice over the years. On one day during this time, I was on the air for fifteen hours, doing live shots several times an hour.

"My husband was very supportive, and we talked a lot on the phone. We have two young daughters at home. My husband could tell I was safe and could tell I was taking care of myself because he could see me on the air. Also, because I arrived in New York City fifteen hours after the attack, there was a feeling that the terrorist deed was already done and over with. I also credit my ability to continue with having a good producer. My producer is very supportive, and we've been an amazing team for two years. My supervisor, CNN's director of medical coverage, also stayed in touch with me over the phone and was very supportive."

Elizabeth said she and her crew were able to focus by "just doing their jobs," adding that it was very clear-cut what had to be done.

On the fifteen-hour drive up from Atlanta, she had called college friends in New York City. All of them were fine, except for one whose friend had died in the attack.

Elizabeth said she was never in any personal danger when she was covering this story. "On Wednesday, when I was walking around, I noticed many people with masks on; but I did not have one, and I found it hard to breathe sometimes. Some debris blew into my eye, and I called my doctor in Atlanta, who could see the problem when I was on the air doing live shots. An eye infection resulted, and my Atlanta doctor called in a prescription for me over the phone."

She has not experienced emotional problems as a result of covering this story. She says she's had lots of opportunities to talk—with her producer, her husband, her parents, her friend in New York City who lost a friend in the attacks. "During the month of December we vacationed outside the United States and found that people didn't talk so much about it there. I missed talking about it. Talking about it seems to help."

Elizabeth has no idea what impact covering this story will have on her career. She has heard no criticism of her work. She said many women were already "out there" in the workforce when this story happened. "There are many women working in TV journalism on the air. People expect to see women and men on the air. It wouldn't look right to the audience for there to be one group and not the other. Both are needed, and the audience wants both."

Looking back on the events of September 11, Elizabeth said, "Reporters are trained to be dispassionate, but there was a lot of emotion in this story. I felt very sad. But people needed me to continue to tell their stories. Human contact is important for grieving people. As a television reporter, I was a conduit on this tragedy, a way for people to tell other people about their missing relative."

Elizabeth had already experienced days when she'd done hour after hour after hour of live shots, so she knew going into this story that she could handle very long live-reporting shifts. Not surprisingly, then, her advice to up-and-coming reporters is, "Get all the live-shot experience you can; just do it, do it, do it, do it."

21

Miriam Falco, CNN, Atlanta, Georgia

Miriam Falco was sitting at her desk at CNN Center in Atlanta on the morning of September 11. She had come in early that day to produce several live shots on stem cell research. She had already produced two live shots that morning and was making phone calls to arrange other stories for the next day. Miriam had her back to the television monitor in her office when she rolled back in her chair and saw CNN's picture of the first World Trade Center tower on fire.

She shouted to everyone nearby to "turn up the TV—the World Trade Center's on fire!" She sat there "mesmerized" listening to the anchor and trying to figure out what was going on. The anchor said a plane, an airliner, had gone into the tower. Miriam was thinking, "How could that be? We must be wrong about that." Elizabeth Cohen, a medical correspondent with CNN, was with her. They were watching the monitor and saw the second plane go into Two World Trade Center. It was a "far-off" picture of the plane, shot from CNN's New York bureau's rooftop camera at Five Penn Plaza. The permanent camera is normally used for live shots and shows the skyline of New York City. CNN focused that camera on the World Trade Center and had a continuous "clear shot" of the site that day.

After seeing the second plane go in, Miriam and Elizabeth both knew in their hearts that "this was no accident." Miriam checked with Carol Kinstle, director of health coverage, CNN medical unit, and the CNN assignment desk in Atlanta. She was thinking they should start calling hospitals in New York City since the New York CNN Bureau staff would be overwhelmed by this story. Miriam said she and Elizabeth were "glued to the TV," heard about the Pentagon hit and also about the fourth plane that may have been headed for Washington, and decided, "We have to go to New York."

Miriam said there were no discussion about sending women specifically. Her supervisor did ask her, "Are you sure you want to go? This might be dangerous."

Miriam Falco

But Miriam said, "There was no way not to go. This was the biggest story ever. We initially thought there'd be medical stories to do. But when the towers collapsed, we felt few would survive and starting thinking about peripheral stories to do."

Miriam volunteered for this assignment. With CNN for thirteen years, she had worked in the newsroom for eleven years and had produced newscasts and stories during the Persian Gulf War, the Oklahoma City bombing, and the crash of TWA Flight 800. She knew from experience how many people it took to cover such stories—and this was going to be a much bigger story. This was also going to overshadow an entire file of stories she had been working on. Months later, many of those stories were still not done. They were timely before September 11, overshadowed later. The debate about stem cells and cloning, for example, has died down.

Miriam went home to pack. Her fiancé had already started gathering together a few things for her. She knew she and a crew could not fly to New York, since the airports were now shut down. They checked about rail travel, but the train would take too long, so they decided to drive. They called about renting a car, but all the rental car companies' cars were sold out, since all the planes were grounded in Atlanta. They thought about taking one of their own cars. She needed enough room to take a camera crew and their equipment, so they would need a larger vehicle than a passenger car.

The CNN assignment desk in Atlanta paired Miriam and Elizabeth with a photographer and sound technician who were en route back to Atlanta from covering President Bush's trip to Sarasota, Florida. The crew came in on one of the last planes to land at Atlanta that morning. They finally found and rented a fifteen-seat van from a local company. Then CNN rented the local company's entire fleet of vehicles. A second correspondent had been assigned to go with them to New York, but she was reluctant to go and declined. Miriam had her crew together, and they were on the road by early afternoon, 2:30 P.M. They knew they were going to be gone for "a while" but didn't know how long.

They drove straight through the night. Miriam was driving the van as they approached New York City. She was giving their photographer a break from driving since he would be carrying a thirty-pound camera on his shoulder for several days to come. It was five o'clock in the morning when they drove past Newark Airport. As they were approaching Manhattan, it was dark because of the power outage in the city. She could see a giant cloud of smoke rising from the World Trade Center site. But it was what she could *not* see that made her sad and gave her goose bumps. She could not see the signature Twin Towers of the World Trade Center.

Miriam said this made her "very, very sad." As they were driving up to New York, Miriam's colleague Elizabeth had talked with a college friend whose close friend had lost her husband in the tower collapse. So they were experiencing some of the emotion of what had happened in New York City while they were on the road.

At five o'clock in the morning Wednesday, as they were approaching Manhattan, they called the CNN New York bureau for directions on how to get into the city. The bureau told them to go to the George Washington Bridge, since the tunnels were closed. On the George Washington Bridge, they were stopped by police officers who asked each of them to produce two picture IDs. One of the crew had IDs that didn't match. The sound technician had his full name on his driver's license but his nickname (instead of his first name) on his CNN ID. As a result, police officers would not allow them to cross the bridge. They were told to head for the Tappan Zee Bridge in Westchester County, far to the north and away from Manhattan.

"We were driving around New York City in rush hour traffic finding bridges and tunnels closed to us," Miriam remembered. "The sun was coming up. Traffic was bumper to bumper. Trash trucks were driving past us, carrying debris from the World Trade Center site. We couldn't get into the city. We drove around until nine o'clock in the morning. We stopped and bought some gas near the Queens/Midtown Tunnel [where] we talked with some police officers who finally let us through."

They drove to New York University Medical Center, where Elizabeth had contacts. They interviewed doctors and nurses there. "The doctors had been standing around for hours but saw no patients. There were no medical stories to speak of there.

"We were standing outside NYU Medical Center so Elizabeth could do a phone interview with CNN about what she had seen so far. We were waiting, standing with our crew at 1st Avenue, across from NYU Medical Center. While Elizabeth was on the phone, a young woman with an older woman approached me. The young woman was holding two pieces of paper—a photo and a copy of a photo. She said, 'Can you show these pictures of my brother-in-law on TV?'" This became the first of many interviews Miriam and Elizabeth would produce with family members who were looking for missing relatives. It was Wednesday in the middle of the morning when this began.

The young woman had come up to Miriam voluntarily. Obviously Miriam was part of a TV crew. They were there with a video camera, cell phones, tripod, microphones, videotapes, batteries, and cables. They had no satellite truck of their own; they planned to go back to the CNN bureau to edit tape. They shot video as they followed this young woman, who was looking for her brother-in-law, from hospital to hospital. As they shadowed this young woman, they found other families doing the same thing she was doing.

"At NYU Medical Center, there was a long line of people waiting to see the list of survivors, of people being treated," Miriam said. "Families were literally going from hospital to hospital to check these lists. We saw more and more people with flyers and photos as the day wore on. The families thought this would help. They believed their loved one was 'the one who got away.' They believed their relative was in a hospital, in a coma, with no identification. They believed that showing their picture on TV would stir someone's memory. They were giving out their home phone numbers, asking people to call them. The woman who had come up to me was named Naomi; she was twenty-four years old and was doing this on behalf of her sister who was at home. Naomi's missing brother-in-law had worked in the Twin Towers, and he also was a volunteer firefighter. She and her family were completely convinced that he was alive."

Miriam and Elizabeth reported Naomi's story on Wednesday. They went back to the CNN bureau, wrote and edited their story, and left the bureau at midnight for their hotel. "Forty hours after arriving at work in Atlanta, we finally were asleep by 2 A.M. in New York City. In my case, I had to switch rooms because there was wet paint in the first one, thus the late hour."

They got up early Thursday morning and were assigned to go to St. Vincent's Hospital to cover more of the searching families. After arriving, they were reassigned to the Armory to relieve the correspondent there. "By now, the city of New York had established the Armory as the central place for families to get information and ultimately leave information about their missing relatives," Miriam explained.

"We began doing live reports starting about two o'clock in the afternoon. We did a live shot at least once an hour from the Armory. We were on the air from 2 P.M. till 10 P.M. or so on Thursday. I remember this as a day of multiple live shots for all CNN networks (CNN/U.S., CNN International, CNN Headline News). I believe we did at least fifteen live shots on Thursday and maybe as many as twenty. It's all a blur now," she said.

"Thursday was a bizarre day. More and more people were showing up on the streets with poster boards and flyers of their missing relatives. I remember we did one live shot that was twenty minutes long. Crowd control became an issue for me because I had to cover the photographer's back to keep people away from him at the same time I was lining up people for Elizabeth to interview. I remember feeling crushed by people wanting to be on TV. The families were feeling desperate. I found this work with the families incredibly hard to do. The crowds around us were getting bigger. I felt we needed to take a break, because we could lose control of the crowd. The perimeter around the crew was getting smaller."

On Friday, they started working at 7 A.M. and worked all day. They did multiple live shots for twelve hours straight. Miriam believes they did maybe thirty live shots on Friday. People kept coming to them, crowding around them, wanting to tell their story and show pictures of their loved ones on TV.

"The work was nonstop. We were producing live shots each hour for multiple CNN networks. My job as a producer was to organize the live shots and coordinate them over the phone. I had to coordinate with CNN's Atlanta news desk, with CNN's New York news desk, with control rooms in Atlanta and in New York, and with the satellite truck crew, who were using walkie-talkies. While the reporter concentrates on what she'll say in her live report, a producer has to make sure the reporter will be seen and heard, which requires a lot of coordination between the live location and the studio." Live-shot technology requires coordination in much the same way an orchestra requires a conductor to keep everyone together.

Miriam remembered Friday as "a very long day." They had left their hotel at 5:30 A.M. They were at their live shot location diagonally across from the Armory by six and did their first live shot at 7 A.M. President Bush was scheduled to come to New York City that day, Friday, and he did, but details about his movements were sketchy until the moment he arrived. Miriam and her crew worked till ten at night on Friday.

Miriam would go back to her hotel each night to rest, but she would wake up every hour or so all night long, every night she was there, thinking about what had happened and what needed to be done the next day.

She had worked for CNN for thirteen years. But she had done her work from "inside" CNN Center, putting shows together. As a result, she didn't usually see the news firsthand in the field. She didn't really know what to expect on this story, but she did know the expectations of those in the control rooms and in the newsrooms. On the streets of New York, this story "came to them" in the form of the family members. Her job was to take this information, this grief, this sorrow, and assemble it into a coherent form. She says she relied on "instinct" to help her.

"Elizabeth and I helped each other. We found it incredibly sad to hear these stories. The number of families we put on the air was a fraction of those who were around us. I felt an immense amount of sadness about this story. I didn't know anyone personally who was lost. I realized these folks who were missing would not be found. I felt a hopelessness about it.

"Bits and pieces of kindness and humanity I observed in New York kept me going. I remember an outpouring of kindness and gentleness and generosity around us. People were giving out food and water to anyone who needed it. I remember two twenty-year-olds walking around with gallon-size water bottles filled with flowers—roses and carnations. They were handing out the flowers on Lexington and

26th to people with the flyers [about their missing loved ones]. I would see them two or three times a day. Another woman was walking around on Sunday handing out Hershey's Kisses. I remember volunteers at the Armory handing out sandwiches that a first-grade class had prepared. The first-graders had written little personal notes and enclosed them with the sandwiches.

"On Friday I had taken a cab from our hotel to the Armory at Lexington and 26th. The cab driver asked me what I did. I said I worked for CNN and was covering the families who were looking for missing loved ones. The driver dropped me off right at the entrance to the Armory. It was six o'clock in the morning. He said there would be 'no charge. Just do your job. You're doing a great job.' I explained that I was on an expense account, but he would accept no payment and no tip, either. I remember ten cabs with Hindu drivers outside the Armory. These drivers had volunteered to take the families anywhere they wanted to go at no charge. I remember a restaurant across from the Armory letting people use their tables and phones lines to set up a computer so people could register their missing on the Internet. I remember a pizza shop where they sometimes didn't charge, or just charged minimal amounts, for food and soft drinks. I remember this generosity and that no one was mooching."

Miriam said she never felt in any personal danger in New York, not where she was posted. She felt safe in New York and believed that the terrorists "were done." "There was no 'normal' crime, either—just nothing."

On Friday, as they were waiting for President Bush to visit Ground Zero, she noticed an increase in the number of police officers on duty. She said there was also a plane overhead. People waited for three hours and the sidewalks were filling in. While they were waiting, Miriam's cell phone went dead, and she passed the phone through the crowd to a member of her crew near the back wall. She later passed her purse back through the crowd to another member of her crew. She says she was not afraid. She felt safe in the crowd.

"But I remember when we were leaving Atlanta on Tuesday that CNN was evacuating nonessential personnel from the building. I had never experienced an evacuation at CNN headquarters before. I remember thinking, 'No one would bomb CNN. The terrorists needed CNN to get the news out.'"

Miriam said her sister in Philadelphia was a little worried about her being in New York. Her fiancé in Atlanta, however, was not worried about her being there. On that Thursday when Miriam was in New York, her fiancé was one of thirty-five people laid off from their CNN/*Sports Illustrated* jobs. She says, "The poor timing made me angry, and I sent an e-mail to CNN's top executive telling him how outrageous it was to do this while CNN news crews were working their hardest to cover this story in New York and cover it well for the company."

She felt some competition in New York but did not feel a lot of competition for news where they were located. "Multiple TV cameras were set up on that corner of Lexington and 26th near the Armory. People went from camera to camera telling their story. Because I was working for CNN, which is a twenty-four-hour news operation, I felt I may have been working longer hours than some other producers, but that's because CNN's programming is different, because it's nonstop. There's no downtime for the crews. I felt confident we could tell this story from where we were located."

The reality of what had happened in New York would hit her late at night when she was in her hotel room. "Then the tears would well up," she said. "I tried not to cry in public. I cried when I was alone. It just erupted sometimes. The families touched me. The visual images touched me. I took pictures of where the American flag was cropping up in New York—in window boxes, on top of satellite trucks, in store windows, and on so many cars. I lost that camera before I left New York, but I'll never lose those images. I remember seeing an old man taking care of a dog for a financial services executive who was lost in the World Trade Center collapse. The dog is a giant basset hound. The old man had taped a picture of the dog's owner to the dog's leash, and I remember seeing them together on the streets of New York. I remember seeing a college student putting up pictures on Sunday. Someone from California wanted him to put the pictures up. It's images like those that stay with me."

Now she wonders how the families are doing. The families left an impression on her. The "money distribution thing" is the saddest thing for her. She feels the families haven't been able to grieve because they have been overwhelmed by paperwork.

Miriam doesn't know whether the impact on her career of covering this story will be "for better or worse," but "the big boss at CNN knows who I am now." That's because she wrote him that angry e-mail when she found out her fiancé had been laid off on September 13. She does believe that she grew as a journalist because of this coverage. She had only a small amount of in-the-field experience going into this story, less than many others. She feels as a result of this story that she's "a lot better field producer now." She also thinks she has a new sense of perspective.

Miriam is not aware of any criticism of CNN's work. "Afterward, people told me they turned off the TV because they couldn't take the sadness anymore. They were saying, 'Enough already. This is too much.' I also heard that during the Persian Gulf War. I tell people, 'We [at CNN] are on over and over again. Don't watch TV all the time. Turn it off after a while.'"

Miriam feels women reached a higher profile with this story. Women were there in the field, covering various facets of the story, which may help them in the news workforce. She thinks women proved they could do it, demonstrating a positive contribution.

Her advice to others is that "talking about tragedy helps. Sharing what you experience is beneficial. Talk about what it was like. Don't bottle it up." Miriam says she has taken this approach herself. She observed people suffering, but she was not in danger herself. She "saw one side of an extremely sad, multifaceted story."

Miriam left New York unable to comprehend the number of people who had died in the World Trade Center collapse. On Saturday, she finally went inside the Armory. It had been closed to reporters because the police were very protective of the families inside. She had met a chaplain from San Diego, and he took her into the Armory. He showed her where the families had gone to look at the list of survivors. "On every wall were hundreds and hundreds and hundreds of pictures of missing people. It was eerie and overwhelming to be in there." People knew after seeing the lists that their loved ones were not there. Miriam still can't comprehend losing that many people at one time.

She didn't go to Ground Zero, but she could see the pile of debris. "It was so large it looked like a building. It's all impossible to comprehend."

She says every day in New York had a different nuance, each day was different. Friday, it was raining as they interviewed the families. Saturday, three girls showed up and sang gospel songs to the crowd. Miriam put them on TV. One lived nearby, near the Armory. They came to share what they could share—their voices. Sunday, more people came to the Armory to look at flyers than were going to register missing family members. They brought their children. In the afternoon, people were reading the flyers, lighting candles, bringing flowers. People were looking at literally "walls of flyers." Artists were drawing murals.

While Miriam was in New York, she began receiving e-mail on her pager from people she knew in Germany where she had grown up. German people were telling her they were appalled by what had happened and that they felt solidarity with the Americans. Miriam told the families of the missing that people all over the world were thinking about them, which served as therapy for people who were hurting.

She feels she was compassionate in doing her work with the families in New York. "I felt I was providing a public service and that helps me cope. I let people tell their stories in their own words on TV. I helped them let the world know that their loved ones mattered."

Miriam had been on vacation in Philadelphia when TWA Flight 800 went down off Long Island in 1996. She volunteered and went to Long Island to cover that story for CNN. She was sent out to interview family members of those killed in the crash. She remembered thinking at the time that that was a difficult assignment, but it may have prepared her for this story in New York City.

"Years of doing what you do prepares you for something like this," she said. "I didn't force people to talk to us. People came up to us and asked, 'Can I be on TV?' Or, 'Can you just show this picture?' Some just wanted to talk. I would ask them, 'Do you want to be on camera?'"

22

Gabrielle DeRose, KDKA-TV, Pittsburgh, Pennsylvania

Gabrielle DeRose was at home in Oakmong (a Pittsburgh suburb) when the phone rang. Actually, both of her phone lines were ringing. Her friends were calling her and telling her to turn on the TV. She did. Gabrielle anchors the weekend evening newscasts at KDKA-TV, the CBS affiliate in Pittsburgh, and normally reports day shift on Mondays, Tuesdays, and Wednesdays.

This particular Tuesday she was scheduled to fill in for a colleague in the evening, so she was still at home when the phone rang. She said she was in total disbelief as she watched the first World Trade Center tower on fire in New York City. It was just before nine o'clock, just after the first plane hit. She was thinking it must have been a terrible accident. Then she watched the second plane hit the second tower and was starting to grasp that this was no accident. She called into work and told them she'd be right in. She still had to shower and drive forty-five minutes to the station, but she was there by 10:30 A.M.

Shortly after ten o'clock, while Gabrielle was en route to her station, United Airlines Flight 93 crashed in southern Pennsylvania. Gabrielle described the scene in her newsroom when she reached it as "amazing." "Department heads from all over the station had come into the newsroom to help in any way they could. The general manager was there, the sales manager, the marketing manager, and the news director, all of them helping to coordinate coverage of this breaking story. Everyone was working together to get the job done."

Gabrielle had come to KDKA in January 2001 from the CBS affiliate in Altoona, near the crash site. The feeling in the newsroom was that she had worked down there for eleven years, knew many people there, would have good access since it was her old territory, and could help the station get "first video" for the story. The station had already called sister station WTAJ in Altoona. KDKA had already sent two crews; reporter Mary Berecky of the Greensburg bureau was part of one of them.

Gabrielle DeRose

Gabrielle was part of the third crew now being sent to the site. Jennifer Antkowiak from the five o'clock anchor desk was part of a fourth crew being dispatched at the same time. It was 11:30 when they left the station. The site was two hours and eighty miles to the southeast in Somerset County.

"There was an optional evacuation that morning of all tall buildings in downtown Pittsburgh," Gabrielle remembered, "and I ran into an immense traffic jam driving out of the city. It was hard to get anywhere because the Pennsylvania Turnpike was jammed with outbound traffic."

Gabrielle arrived at the crash site at 1:30 in the afternoon. WTAJ's live truck was already there, and KDKA's was on the way. Gabrielle began filing live reports that consisted of a general overview of the situation—what local, state, and federal agencies were doing at the site. She said it was still chaos when she first arrived. Rescue personnel at the site included the Red Cross, ATF (Bureau of Alcohol, Tobacco, and Firearms), FBI, state police, FEMA (Federal Emergency Management Agency), and PEMA (Pennsylvania Emergency Management Agency). A lot of coordination was taking place among representatives of those agencies.

When Gabrielle arrived at the site, FBI and state police were setting up a command center to handle the media and relaying information as best they could to the many media who were there. "There was a huge pool of reporters there, dozens of different media outlets. It was wall-to-wall media by early afternoon," Gabrielle said.

The actual crash site was out in a field near an abandoned strip mine. Gabrielle and her crew took a rural route to get there faster. "The site was already cordoned off when I got there. It was about a mile down the road from the command center. Reporters were only allowed to stand on a hill overlooking the site in this vast valley. All we could see was this small crater, about eight feet wide and ten feet deep. No smoke or debris. It was very disturbing to think all the remains just disintegrated."

One crew member from each television station was being escorted to the crash site by police officers. A woman who was in charge of the command center recognized Gabrielle as the former main anchor in Altoona. This woman allowed Gabrielle to go to the site later in the afternoon, even though another crew member (Jennifer) from her station had already gone down there.

"There were no large pieces of airplane, no human remains, no baggage. It looked as though the nose of the plane had hit the ground. There are woods a few hundred yards past the crater. I thought perhaps the plane had nose-dived and flipped into the woods, and perhaps the wreckage was back there."

Gabrielle's reports that afternoon consisted of setting the scene. She covered briefings and filed initial reports on what state, federal, and local officials were doing at the scene. "Officials were setting up the perimeter of the site as a crime scene. And they were initially only treating the crash as a 'possible' terrorist attack."

She said her station provided continual coverage throughout the day September 11. Whenever Gabrielle had an update from the Pennsylvania crash site, she and her colleagues went live for her station in Pittsburgh. She filed several live shots during the first hours she was there at the site on Tuesday afternoon.

"At 7:30 that night, the governor of Pennsylvania came to the crash site. The command center had been set up. And news briefings were now being held only when there was new information. KDKA management decided to have only one crew remain at the site that night. Jennifer Antkowiak did live shots at ten and eleven. I went back to the station. I was glued to the radio as we drove back to the station. I was just shocked and numb from the day's events."

Gabrielle did one more report that night. "I interviewed a helicopter pilot who had been at the crash site. The pilot had worked air rescue that day and gave me the card of a US Airways pilot who was sent by federal officials to do an assessment of the site and what might have gone wrong with the plane. I called the US Airways pilot, but the airline didn't want him doing any interviews. So I interviewed the helicopter pilot who had taken the US Airways pilot over the site and had shown him around. I went live from the newsroom with what the helicopter pilot said. I stayed at the station until 11:30 that night."

On Wednesday evening, Gabrielle covered the many candlelight vigils that were held throughout Pittsburgh. "The sight of them was incredibly emotional. I had covered the aftermath of the bombing of the Murrah Federal Building in Oklahoma City in April 1995. These candlelight vigils had much the same feeling. People crowded into churches like it was a Sunday service. All the services were packed. All ages attended, young and old, all praying together. At one church I attended, the pastor said, 'You pray the way you need to pray.' It wasn't a traditional mass. Soft music was playing. There were several different groups of people kneeling on the floor and praying. Parents with their kids, brothers with their sisters, and neighbors holding hands. I was overwhelmed by how united everyone was. At one point I was just struck by the realization it was *my* country this time dealing with such inconceivable grief and sadness. In the prayer services, people were just sobbing, holding tightly to their children, and saying prayers."

Thursday would normally have been Gabrielle's day off, but she came into work anyway and covered the new security restrictions at the airport in Pittsburgh.

Gabrielle did take her day off on Friday to rest up, knowing she'd need to be sharp for anchoring on Saturday and Sunday. "As it turned out, there were no scripts for the Saturday and Sunday newscasts; we ad-libbed the entire broadcast as the news was still unfolding."

Station managers didn't approach Gabrielle about counseling. She says she couldn't see anything at the site anyway; it was more baffling than gruesome, and she didn't feel she needed help.

What she remembers most from covering the crash was that she had a job to do. "I immediately focused on my job, on getting information. I didn't focus on myself and how it affected me until I got home. I cried *after* I got home, when I finally sat down and watched all the coverage in the middle of the night. It just seemed so surreal and horrifying that this had actually happened.

"It was an overwhelming emotion when I first heard what happened that Tuesday morning. I wanted so much to do something to help. I remember feeling so thankful to be a journalist, because I could at least do *something* to help people make sense of what was happening. I at least could inform them of what was going on in the Pittsburgh area so they might feel some sense of security at such an unsettling time."

When Gabrielle watched the coverage of the World Trade Center ruins, she says she experienced that same sense of shock and disbelief and numbness that she had felt in Oklahoma City back in 1995. "It was extremely emotional talking with family members as they looked at the Murrah Federal Building, praying that their loved ones would come out alive, saying, 'This just doesn't happen here.' It was unbelievably sad to hear rescue workers tell me how emotionally scarred they were after digging for hours trying to reach the person crying out [to] them in the ruins, only to find them dead when they finally got to them."

On Monday, October 1, 2001, Gabrielle went to New York City herself to see Ground Zero. She's a native of New York City and was born in St. Vincent's Hospital there. Friends of her family died in the World Trade Center collapse. "The site was just surreal," she said. "I toured it with my mother. People there just look, but no one speaks. They just watch. Teams of police officers and firefighters go into the site and come out, but no one speaks. Everyone is affected the same."

Gabrielle is not sure how this experience may impact her career. "What I do know is that it reaffirms for me the honor and responsibility I feel in being a journalist. When such horrifying things happen in the world, we have an opportunity to bring some sense of understanding to the public by educating them of what's happening around them, and in doing so, we can feel a sense of pride in being able to do something beneficial."

23

Emily Longnecker, WTAJ-TV, Altoona, Pennsylvania

Emily Longnecker had switched schedules with a colleague that Tuesday. Normally she covers the afternoon/night shift, but on September 11 she came into the WTAJ-TV (CBS) newsroom in Altoona at about 9:15 A.M. to work the day shift. The reporters were standing around the assignments desk watching the events in New York City unfold on the television monitors in the newsroom when they heard a "plane in distress" call come over the scanners. It was about 10 A.M., and they all looked at each other and said, "What's going on?" "No way!" "This can't be related!" "It must be a random plane in trouble." They knew from the scanner that it was a big plane, a 757. It was flying low near Cambria, in Somerset County in southern Pennsylvania.

The plane in distress was United Airlines Flight 93. At 10:10 A.M., it nose-dived at full speed into a field in rural Somerset County about sixty miles from Altoona, an hour-and-a-half drive south from the station.

Emily immediately asked to be sent to the crash site to cover the story, but another crew from the station was already in Cambria County, covering a preliminary hearing. They were the closest to the crash. Later in the day, the evening anchor was also sent to the site. They were all men. Emily pushed for the story assignment and was frustrated when it didn't come her way the first day.

The WTAJ crew that was sent to the crash site was the first local crew to reach the crater, and they fed video to CNN. (WTAJ has a video-sharing arrangement with CNN.) The plane was so broken up that the reporter and photographer said there was "just a big hole in the ground." They couldn't even tell what kind of a plane it was. According to authorities at the site, the largest piece of wreckage was reported to be no larger than the size of a phone book.

Emily fielded calls at the station all day Tuesday. "The phone was ringing like

Emily Longnecker

crazy. I don't remember from whom—just news calls. I was totally focused on that first day to hear from an Altoona man we later found out was in Tower Two.

"They sent the closest crew first. I don't think it had anything to do with my experience. Because the story was so big, they made the decision to send a main anchor to the scene, too. Later, I heard comments from staff that they should have sent the female main anchor just to even out the coverage. The first day, I did stories on a local family, the Schmittles, whose son escaped from Tower Two at the World Trade Center. By the time I interviewed Mrs. Schmittle, she had heard from her son John at noon that he was indeed safe. I had spent most of the day Tuesday trying to reach John Schmittle by cell phone (regular phone lines were down in New York, and even cell service was awful in New York) to conduct a phone interview with him for a story at 11 P.M. I finally reached him and did a piece from the set. It was a real coup to have someone from Altoona who could describe the horror firsthand."

Wednesday morning Emily pushed again to go to the crash site, and this time she was sent to cover the sidebar stories, the reaction stories, and the stories with the victims' families. There was no discussion of the gruesome nature of the story and no effort to discourage her from going. She and a photographer were sent to the site with standard TV equipment: camera, tripod, microphone, and cell phone. The station's satellite truck was already at the scene. A media staging area had been set up. The Red Cross and the Salvation Army were providing food. A row of portable toilets had been set up. The WTAJ reporter originally sent on Tuesday continued to cover the investigation side of the story. By the time Emily arrived at the site on Wednesday, it was roped off and under the control of the FBI and United Airlines. Authorities kept her and others too far away from the crash site for them to see anything of it.

Emily filed three stories on Wednesday: town reaction for the five o'clock show, security measures at the Cambria County airport for the six o'clock show, and the medical examiner angle (the effort to identify remains using dental records and DNA from hair samples) on the eleven o'clock show. On this day, Wednesday, September 12, U.S. airspace was still closed, so the victims' families could not easily get to the site. The WTAJ crew stayed Wednesday night at a Cambria hotel. They also stayed Thursday night but began driving back and forth every day after that.

On Thursday morning, Emily began seeing signs and flags go up in people's yards and thought she'd do a town reaction piece in nearby Somerset, a town of about eight thousand people. "There were signs in the town that read 'Praying for Families.' There was also a lot of anger and emotion there. One sign read 'Paybacks Are Hell.'"

The victims' families stayed at the Seven Springs Mountain Resort in Somerset. The news crews went every morning, beginning Thursday, September 13, to the resort and asked whether anyone wanted to talk to them. Emily recalled that the crews tried to be very respectful of the families, who had gone through such a great loss. On Thursday, only one man talked to the media. He was from New Jersey, had a brother on the plane, and wanted his brother not to be forgotten. He read a prepared statement but choked up.

"I was struck by how the Flight 93 tragedy was part of such a greater national tragedy," Emily recalled. "The victims just seemed to be endless. I can't remember what day victims' families started pouring into the Seven Springs Resort. Several media organizations camped out at the resort hoping to talk with some family members. It was a very controlled situation. We were kept in one room with cookies and coffee. The American Red Cross was handling the families. They told families that media were set up in one room and if they wished to speak to us they could. Only one man chose to do so. The man was ushered into the room where about twenty cameras and microphones were waiting to hear from him. He offered a brief statement about his brother whom he lost on Flight 93. Then we asked questions. By this time, family members had toured the crash site. I asked him if he would ever come back to Somerset County after such an experience. I wanted to know if the place was forever a dark spot on the map for him. He commented on how beautiful Pennsylvania was and that he and his family planned to return often. He said he looked at the site as almost holy ground. He said he chose to speak to the media because he didn't want his brother to be forgotten. In my story that night, I tried to humanize his brother and tell about his life. I wanted this man not to just be a number on a victims' roster list. This man was someone's husband, father, son, brother. I tried to illustrate that.

"I've done victims' family stories before. Sometimes I can emotionally remove myself; sometimes the story and the pain hit home more. I can't explain when or why a story will touch me deeply. I work very hard on not being a vulture. That's why I was relieved the situation was a controlled one. The last thing these families needed was a dozen reporters asking them the same kinds of questions over and over again. There is a lot of competition in the Altoona television market, but in this case all the stations had access to the same thing. The setting of the plane crash was totally controlled by the FBI and United Airlines. The news conferences were all planned. But, I imagine, if it had been a feeding frenzy, we would have all followed suit and tried to get the interview."

On Thursday, Emily had started feeling emotional when she was getting ready to interview the victims' families. Drawing on her Catholic faith, she "prayed a lot for God to just keep me going." In fact, she remembered, "I was so tired and worn, but I just kept going on automatic pilot." She also used repression as a coping mechanism. She would say to herself, "Don't think. Just do the job today. Just work."

She also frequently called her boyfriend in Altoona, to touch base. She says, "There was a lot of downtime, especially waiting for the families to arrive. Was I seeking emotional support? I guess so. I wanted to reach out and hear a familiar voice. I wanted someone to share the sadness with. Actually, this 'boyfriend' and I had broken up in March. At the time of September 11, we were talking about reconciling. September 11 really brought out a need within me to reach out to him, despite our breakup. It's like time had stopped with those horrible events of September 11, and everything was on hold, even in my personal life."

On September 11, she recalled, "It was like the world was ending. A plane was down. The newsroom was in shock watching that TV. We were thinking, 'Oh, my God, what's next?'" She wanted to go home and hug people she knew. She called up people to say, "I love you." She had called her mother, her father, her boyfriend, and her best friend, Margaret, who has family in New York.

"I also e-mailed my college best friend, Ayla, who is Pakistani and lives with her husband in Saudi Arabia. I knew even from day one, 'Here we go—our lives, our friendship will always be colored by these events.' She's Muslim; I'm American. I knew there would be a lot of fallout against the Muslim community. I was also concerned for her safety in the days ahead. I was wondering what Pakistan's role would be in the situation. Ayla and I have continued to e-mail. . . . We're both reconciled to the fact that it could be years before we see each other again. Still, she is one of my dearest friends."

Emily knew she was going to feel a wide range of emotions with this event: she was excited to cover such an enormous story, felt guilty because so many were dead, and had to be competitive to keep up with the big angles. She tried to keep all this in perspective, but when she got to her hotel room Wednesday night, after visiting the crash site, "I had a healthy cry," she said.

Managers in her newsroom have told her she's done a good job, but they have not asked her how she feels. She says she's OK and that she would have said "It's too much" if that had been true, and that her station would have helped her get help if she needed it. "Honestly, I can't see myself ever saying it was too much. I wanted to be part of the action. It's my job, after all, and the adrenaline was flowing. These are the days people in our business live for."

Emily believes the terrorists used the media to draw attention to the second plane, that "the terrorists 'played the media' with the first plane and focused everyone's attention on the second plane going in."

She added that she was prepared for a story like this by years of practice meeting constant deadlines. For this story, she was working with twenty- to thirty-minute turnarounds. She had learned about media feeding frenzies as a field producer in Washington, D.C., so she was used to that. She feels the women who covered this story did a good job, brought sensitivity to the story, and proved that they could cover such a story and cover it well. Her station has received no criticism of its coverage, just many people saying thank you for a job well done. "Viewers have told us they were 'glued to the coverage,'" she said. "I can't imagine what impact covering this will have on my career. It's too soon to tell."

24

Elizabeth Mcneil, *People* Magazine, New York City

On the morning of September 11, Elizabeth (Liz) McNeil, *People* magazine's New York deputy bureau chief, was walking to work. Overhead, she heard a plane—American Airlines Flight 11. "I'd walked about three blocks when I heard a loud buzzing sound, low and gunning, like a buzz saw. I remember thinking something bad is going to happen. A split second later, I heard the explosion. Everyone in the streets was screaming, crying, and frantically calling on their cell phones. At first, I thought it was an accident, a commuter plane."

A man on a balcony above her yelled, "Oh, my God! My wife works in that building!" "We were just looking at it, not knowing what was going on. From where I stood, fifteen blocks away, the plane looked small. We had no idea it was a jet."

Liz called her boss. "I said, 'The World Trade Center is on fire, and I'm running down there.'" She rushed back to her apartment to tell her boyfriend she was going. He advised her not to take the subway. She began running in the direction of the towers. "Swarms of people were running away in the opposite direction. Chaos is the only way I can describe it. I could see two towers on fire, and people were yelling at me not to go down. All of a sudden the sirens started, with police cars and fire trucks coming down. When I stood at Vesey Street, the street in front of the towers, there was a quiet moment, just me and another guy staring up at the towers. We could see eight to ten floors on fire."

Liz began to see people jumping out of the windows. "I saw bodies flying out. Many had on white shirts and dark pants—I remember thinking, 'A businessman's uniform.' In the tower windows, I saw people waving curtains out the window." Liz said she saw about twenty people jump out. A woman next to her was counting, and she remembers her saying, "That's twenty-seven."

"I remember wondering if the fire department had something there to catch them. I hoped they might survive, but in the back of my mind, I knew they were jumping to their deaths."

In the midst of the chaos was some order. "Before the towers' collapse, I saw people walking out of nearby buildings in a straight line. That was eerie." Police and workers from the Department of Parks and Recreation were yelling at her to "get the hell out." She started going west toward the Hudson River. "My cell phone wasn't working. I was out of touch. I saw a reporter standing outside a white van. She was from a Spanish television station. She and I huddled in her van, surrounded by sirens and yelling and people running, and tried to get through to our offices. No luck."

As she neared the Chambers Street bridge, Liz said residents of the area were everywhere. "People were screaming, 'A third plane is coming.' Then somebody yelled that the Pentagon had been hit. I thought, 'This is what a war zone must be like.'"

Liz saw various planes in the sky. "They were U.S. fighter jets, but at the time, no one knew." She said she automatically went into work mode. "I tried to get quotes, while running. Everything was happening at once. Then someone was yelling that the building was going to go. The building buckled, almost imploded down. It was so incomprehensible at the time, and yet I was watching it collapse. It is still unreal. I could see [that] where I had been just a few minutes earlier was now obscured by a moving wall of smoke."

Smoke and ash came toward her like "a huge, huge tidal wave," and she saw people covered with ash emerging from it. "I realized the rescue workers I had seen running toward the towers were probably now dead. One firefighter said that there were no words to describe what was going on down there. I tried to get some water for some of the people covered in ash. We had no sense yet of how many were dead or what was going on. I saw those floors on fire but couldn't imagine what else was going on in the building.

"There was not a lot of time between the two towers collapsing. When the second tower collapsed, there was so much debris. I was in front of it, so I was not covered in ash. I'd been pushed north and west mostly. But people were starting to walk out."

Amid the chaos, Liz and the people around her were pushed over closer to the river. "The police were screaming that the gas lines are going to explode and to get the f—— out of here. I remember thinking, 'Don't do anything stupid.' Someone had a radio. People were stunned. Some were screaming about a third plane. I was just running, trying to get quotes. After the second tower collapsed, I saw a man with a briefcase, just covered with ash, walking nearby. He looked like a zombie coming out of that cloud of debris. He told me he was a Port Authority lawyer. "I have my briefcase," he said. "But I don't know why I have it."

Liz said paper was everywhere, thousands and thousands of sheets. "It looked like ticker tape. Paper is such an odd thing to have survived. It was all matted against fences, buildings, and windows."

She found some eyewitnesses who had been in one of the buildings before the collapse. "People in the adjoining tower said it felt like an earthquake when the first tower collapsed," Liz said.

"I found a pay phone and stood in line. My boss told me to come back to the office." So Liz began the seventy-block walk. Once there, she focused on work. "That afternoon, I concentrated on typing up my information as fast as I could. We had a Tuesday deadline, and I knew I had to get it in quickly."

Managing editor Carol Wallace decided to scrap planned content and devote the entire September 24 issue to the attack. Twenty-three correspondents and twenty-five photographers were assigned to cover September 11. An eighty-seven-page account of the tragedy was assembled in less than twenty-four hours (*People*, October 1, 2001, p. 7).

Liz took a moment to call her mother to let her know she was safe. "I was getting calls and e-mails from friends asking if I was OK." The magazine staff was monitoring the news, trying to determine the number of people who might have perished and looking into who had piloted the planes.

"I edited and proofread stringers' files. I tried to find eyewitnesses. I just did whatever I was told to do. I finished at about 4 A.M. My boyfriend came up to pick me up, and we walked another reporter home since there was no public transportation." They took a car service about ten blocks, then took the subway to 34th Street, and then walked the rest of the way. "I remember seeing all those gurneys lined up outside St. Vincent's Hospital downtown. They were all empty. Then there was this horrible realization that they didn't need that many gurneys. We walked home and watched the news. It was hard to comprehend the scope and size of what we saw. I got a couple of hours of sleep."

The next day, most of the *People* staff didn't work because the magazine had gone to press, so Liz and her boyfriend went out to see what they could do to help. "We made donations. We were asked to buy cigarettes. We were told that was what the rescue workers really, really needed. We went to a memorial at Washington Square Park and lit a candle."

Liz said her neighborhood was very quiet. "We talked to police and brought them some cold drinks. We walked around through our neighborhood, checking on friends to see if everyone was OK. It's hard to describe how it felt."

The next day Liz went back to work, reporting on the death of Father Mychal Judge. She covered his funeral on Saturday. "There were thousands of firefighters in the street listening to the sermon. You could hear men sobbing, just sobbing. I remember that I wanted to go for the story, but I also wanted to go for myself. I needed to go to a memorial service."

Although Time-Life offered counseling sessions for the staff, Liz chose not to participate. "The most helpful thing to me was volunteering at Nino's Restaurant, which was open twenty-four hours a day after September 13 just to serve rescue workers. I also worked in a food tent on South Street Seaport, doling out food and wiping down counters. I felt that there was really nothing else I could do. Thousands of people died twelve blocks south of where I live. I was just doling out meatballs on a plate, but it helped me.

"I can't imagine what people went through that day," Liz said. "But there is a huge difference between being an eyewitness, being in the building, or losing someone. When I met some of the women we featured on our 9/11 moms cover, I remember fighting back tears. What can you say to them?"

Liz has been back to the site several times. "When I went, I remembered where I was when the building collapsed. I still can't comprehend the amount of death, the thousands who have lost someone they loved, the sacrifices of so many."

Liz tries to be positive. "I didn't want anybody to ask me if I'm OK. I was just doing my job. I saw brave people running into the building. I don't know if they came out. I'm afraid many did not. There is a world of difference when you can walk away."

Liz said there were many incredible stories that illustrated the randomness of who survived and who didn't. "One guy went to get an egg sandwich before work. Because of that, he wasn't in the tower when the plane hit. He lived. Some people in his office didn't.

"People watching on television had a much better sense of what was going on than we did," Liz said. "We were just looking for eyewitnesses and doing our jobs. It was really old-fashioned reporting.

"I just tried to do my job the best I could," Liz said. "Those people inside the towers went through an unspeakable act of horror. Nothing else seems significant after that. Our jobs give us something to focus on. When I was reporting on the Father Judge story, a firefighter said to me, 'Don't ever forget what you see here.' I'll never forget."

25

Fannie Weinstein, *People* Magazine, New York City

Tuesday is the day the coming week's issue of *People* is put to bed. As a result, the magazine's staff, the morning of September 11, was in the process of putting the final touches on the issue that was slated to hit newsstands on Friday, September 14. That morning, Fannie Weinstein, a staff correspondent in the magazine's New York bureau, was at her apartment in downtown Manhattan when her pager went off. The page was from New York bureau chief Maria Eftimiades. "She said a plane had hit the World Trade Center and asked if I could get down there as quickly as possible," Fannie said. Minutes later, empty notebooks and a handful of pens in hand, Fannie ran out the door.

Once outside, Fannie managed to hail a cab and asked the driver to head in the direction of the Twin Towers. The driver told her police weren't letting cars through, but Fannie insisted, offering to double his fare if he would take her as close to the World Trade Center as possible. Fannie, like other reporters who headed to the scene without the benefit of having seen any television coverage of the event, initially thought only a small plane was involved. But when she got out of the taxi fifteen blocks or so north of the World Trade Center, she realized immediately that that was not the case. What she encountered, Fannie said, was "total chaos. . . . Men and women were sitting on the curb crying. Civilians were directing traffic.

"What I remember most, though, was the sight of people standing on the street, pointing up at the sky with horrified expressions on their faces. It was like a scene from a movie." Fannie immediately began interviewing eyewitnesses. Some had seen the first plane hit, some the second plane, some both.

Although police were trying to keep people away from the World Trade Center and the area immediately surrounding it, Fannie's reportorial instincts told her to head south, toward the towers. While doing so, she zigzagged across the street, stopping every minute or so to interview people about what they had seen. "I wasn't thinking about the fact that I might get hurt," Fannie said. "All I was thinking about was talking to as many people as possible and getting as vivid quotes as possible. I was trying to get classic *People* anecdotes—anecdotes that go beyond who-what-when-why-and-where and leave readers feeling like they were there."

Because her cell phone was not working, Fannie began looking for a pay phone from which she could call Eftimiades. Shortly after 10 A.M., she finally found one—just a few blocks from Ground Zero. "I started telling Maria about the interviews I had done so far," she said. "Then all of a sudden I heard a thunderous sound. I didn't know it at the time, but what I was hearing was the sound of Tower One imploding. I was still on the phone when someone near me on the street yelled, 'We gotta get out of here!' I told Maria I had to go and quickly hung up the phone. It was at this point that I had one of those life-flashing-before-your-eyes moments. Although anyone watching the news coverage of the events knew the building had collapsed upon itself, those of us on the ground had no idea exactly what had happened.

"We had no way of knowing whether the tower had imploded or whether it had toppled onto other buildings which were then going to topple onto us. I turned to run, but after taking just a few steps, I collided with several other people who were also trying to flee the scene. I broke my fall with my hands, but within seconds, I realized my left foot was seriously injured. I tried to get up and to continue on my way, but I was unable to put any weight on my foot. Suddenly, a man—I remember only that he was bald and wearing a blue T-shirt—rushed over and told me to put my left arm around his shoulder. We hobbled together about a half a block, then ducked into the basement of a nearby building in an attempt to escape a huge cloud of dust and debris that was heading toward us.

"There were five of us in the basement: myself, another woman, the building's superintendent, and two men, one being the gentleman who had come to my aid. It felt at first as if we had found refuge. But because we were in a basement, we had no way of knowing what was going on outside. This made me feel like we were sitting ducks. After about twenty minutes, I began thinking, 'We've got to get out of here.' Realizing I was unable to walk, the superintendent found a saw and sawed a broomstick in half so I could use it as a cane. He also gave me an old tennis shoe—a men's size 12—to put on my left foot, which had swollen so much that I couldn't get my size 7 shoe back on after I had taken it off.

"Once outside, I began limping up the street. I got only a few feet, however, before a man came up to me and told me to climb on his back. I begged off, but he insisted. 'I carry my brother all the time,' he said, 'and he's bigger than me.' I let the man carry me about a block. After we parted ways, two other men approached me and helped me walk another few blocks. Eventually, we came upon a policeman who used his walkie-talkie to summon an ambulance.

"I was taken to a downtown hospital. There were a number of other patients there who I could tell had been severely injured. At the same time, I couldn't help but notice, too, that there were a lot of doctors who were standing around with seemingly nothing to do. It was at this point that I realized there were a lot fewer survivors than rescuers had initially hoped."

After an X ray confirmed a fracture, Fannie's foot was placed in a temporary splint, and she was given a shot of morphine. Still, she spent the next couple of hours interviewing other patients about what they had seen and what had happened to them.

"As the afternoon wore on, my main concern became making my way to my midtown Manhattan office so I could file the accounts I had collected. Eventually, I managed to hitch a ride on a van that was heading uptown and, at around 5 P.M., began dictating my notes to another correspondent."

Later that evening, a couple of friends drove to her office to pick her up and take her home with them. "I had my foot reexamined the following day and spent the next eight weeks relying on crutches to help me get around."

The editors of *People,* not surprisingly, decided to scrap the issue that was originally slated to close on 9/11, and the magazine's staff ended up working through the night putting together a completely new issue devoted entirely to the events of September 11. The result was an issue that, in classic *People* parlance, told the story of ordinary people doing extraordinary things. "I continue to this day to be proud of the effort," Fannie said, "and grateful as a journalist—and a New Yorker—that I had the opportunity to contribute."

III

CONCLUSION

26

Coming to Conclusions

Journalists are storytellers, observers, and recorders of events. On September 11, 2001, every woman profiled in this book embarked on a mission to tell the many individual tales within this one big and emotional story of terrorism that began with two passenger planes deliberately crashing into the World Trade Center Twin Towers, progressed to another passenger plane crashing into the Pentagon, and then climaxed with a passenger plane nose-diving into the Pennsylvania countryside. Months and likely years later, this scenario still seems incomprehensible.

Yet, on a beautiful September day, thousands of reporters, photographers, and editors began to tell the stories of firefighters and police officers, politicians and soldiers, heroes and villains, victims and survivors—all of them human beings. These storytellers have not been far from the rubble in New York City, the rebuilding of the Pentagon outside Washington, D.C., or the bravery and senseless loss in rural Pennsylvania, either personally or professionally, since September 11. This book is meant to tell the stories of a few of the very brave and professional women journalists and photographers who saw more horror than they wanted and knew more details than they could ever tell. Yet they managed, under circumstances that are usually reserved for war zones, not only to interview and photograph eyewitnesses, politicians, grieving relatives, rescue workers, firefighters, police officers, and volunteers but to do so in a way that touched an entire nation and created a historical record that will stand forever in American history. None of them thought they were brave. None of them accomplished their goals alone. But they all had one common goal: to document this momentous event in American history—to tell the story.

WHY ARE ONLY WOMEN PROFILED?

Of course, both men and women journalists and photographers covered September 11. But the authors, who have been teaching future journalists and following trends

179

in journalism for some time, were struck by the number of women reporters and photographers who were putting their lives in danger to cover this story. Would even a quarter of the number of women reporting on this story have been reporting on Pearl Harbor, the assassination of John F. Kennedy, or even the more recent Persian Gulf War? We were sure this was not the case. Had there been some trend in journalism that we missed?

Although there are more women in newsrooms these days, there is no definitive answer as to why so many were on the scene that day. At least one of the answers is that many of these women lived or worked very near Ground Zero. Some of them were at home because they anticipated working late into the night covering the city elections, were on vacation, or worked afternoon or evening hours. Coincidence or perhaps fate, then, played a large role in who got there to cover the disaster.

However, it is also true that a lot of barriers have come down. Apparently, there was no discussion in the newsrooms about whether this was an appropriate story for women to cover—discussions that certainly would have occurred in the past or that didn't take place at all because assignment editors took it for granted that women could not cover crime or war.

In this case, some of the women were asked to go, and some just went because they knew they had a job to do. Some of them subsequently went to the Middle East to cover events there, even in the face of cultural norms that denigrate women. Although debates may persist about whether women working in the mass media still face a glass ceiling, on September 11 men and women journalists stood side by side.

Actually, some of the managers we asked to facilitate participation from these women and a couple of the women profiled in this book were very suspicious of our motives for doing a book featuring only women journalists. They seemed uncomfortable with the concept because they feared that the wrong message about women would be presented. Would we insinuate that women are treated differently than men? Would women appear too soft or too weak or too emotional to be taken seriously? Or were we going to draw conclusions that women covered the story better, worse, or differently than men? Clearly, the skeptics feared that a comparison would bring up old stereotypes that they no longer feel compelled to dispel.

The authors believe the women profiled in this book speak for themselves. We wanted to let their ingenuity and professionalism shine in a spotlight they would never have sought for themselves but clearly deserve. They are simply very good at what they do. Perhaps some future journalists—both men and women—sitting in classrooms can be inspired by their bravery and can learn from their wisdom. We hope so.

THE IMPORTANCE OF EXPERIENCE

Although all the women said that nothing could have prepared them for covering the events of September 11, almost all of them did draw on some previous experiences that served them well that day. Covering previous disasters, such as plane or subway crashes, the Oklahoma City bombing, and even a hurricane helped them get through this very long day and week. They knew, for example, what information or visuals their respective news organizations would want. They knew they should go to hospitals and police captains and fire stations to get information. A big part of the job that day and night, and in the days that followed, was to separate fact from fiction and rumors from reality. But they also had to deal with a great deal of emotion—from New Yorkers who were so deeply affected by the events, and their own. Their own internal sense of ethics guided them in terms of how they dealt with victims and how they got the story.

Most were at some point tired, hungry, thirsty, dirty, and scared. The tension that can exist between journalists and police also was very evident. The women wanted in. The police wanted them out. But the journalists persevered regardless of the confrontations and discomfort because they knew they had to tell the story. Many were reminded why they have the careers they do. What they do is important. Especially on September 11, an entire nation was relying on them for information. Sometimes, they were the only reliable sources of information.

What is their advice to journalism students? Just do the job until it becomes ingrained and routine. Learn from every experience, and know that there are plenty of opportunities—internships, mentoring relationships, entry-level jobs—that provide experience that leads to jobs and then to a career.

SOMEBODY UP THERE LIKES JOURNALISTS

Although there is no answer to the question, most of the women profiled did speculate about why no journalists were killed when the towers collapsed.[1] Most of the women in New York experienced some little incident that kept them from being in or very near the buildings when they collapsed. For example, the lack of a working cell phone kept Rose Arce in an apartment with a working phone line rather than in the tower, where she had intended to go. Madge Stager is likely alive because the subway train stopped. Some hit police barricades and went east or north rather than south and west where most of the rubble landed. No matter how hard they tried, something prevented them from being too close. And when the towers collapsed, doors opened. People let them in. They survived.

Most of them believe in instincts that journalists either are born with or develop through experience. Most credit such gut feelings and luck with keeping them alive that day. Some of them are grateful to a higher power.

COVERING THE STORY THE
OLD-FASHIONED WAY

Both the failure and the marvel of technology played an important role in covering the events of September 11. Had satellites not been available, not very much coverage would have been possible from Ground Zero. Most reporters were frustrated when cell phones died or signals were gone. Laptops didn't work. A scanner failed. As a result, many reporters found themselves back in the old days of a reporter's notebook and pen, as well as the standard line "Get me rewrite" as they dictated their words rather than type them on their laptops.

Many broadcast stations also found themselves without signals when the towers collapsed, bringing down transmitters with them. They had to improvise or stay silent.

Digital cameras, on the other hand, proved to be among the marvels of technology. In spite of the pulverized concrete and dust that engulfed them, the photographers said their equipment held up well. They sometimes were able to transmit their photos over phone lines, but sometimes the more old-fashioned bicycle was employed to shuttle disks back to the office.

The question for the digital age is whether digital images will be preserved as well or better than negatives were. It's easier to dump digital images than it is to throw out negatives. Amy Sancetta said that one of her concerns is that seemingly unimportant pictures can be wiped from cameras. The big example for photographers, she said, was that picture of Monica Lewinsky hugging then-President Clinton, which was from a sequence of grip-and-grin images. "Most photographers probably shot it, too, but wiped it from their cameras. The one guy who had the picture seemed to remember the face. They went through piles and piles of slides, and they found that image. All the wire services probably shot it, but we can't save everything."

HANDLING POSTTRAUMATIC STRESS

All of the women profiled in this book—even the most seasoned veterans—experienced trauma in covering this story. Although some journalists are trained in how to interview people who are in shock or have had terrible experiences, not many are trained to deal with their own stress and trauma.

The stress involved in covering this story affected all the women to some extent. They recognized the symptoms, and they found ways to cope. For the most part, these women could recount the day in great detail, describing in very descriptive terms what they had experienced and seen. But nearly all of them also reported times of disorientation and time lapses. They knew they had been at a particular place and interviewed a particular person, but they had some difficulty in being sure of the order in which things happened or the specific time frames involved. They all had moments of total disbelief that what they were seeing was truly happening. In this way, they were no different from any other citizen of New York City or Washington, D.C.

Most Americans have experienced some degree of stress associated with September 11 that resulted in anger, fear, and anxiety. The stress was greatly magnified for the journalists reporting from the scenes of the attacks. They couldn't just sit down in front of a television set and wait for information to come to them. They had to get that information any way they could, regardless of their own physical and emotional state. In fact, those at the sites, especially in New York, had far less information than the average television viewer, simply because they could not get in contact with their own newsrooms or did not have access to numerous television networks that were scrambling to get images on the air.

There were specific symptoms that these women experienced that are common to posttraumatic stress. They had difficulty sleeping and experienced nightmares. They had extraordinary thoughts based on the visual images they had seen that day. For example, some would look at a tall building and imagine the top coming off. Some put themselves in the place of the people who jumped from the towers or who were on the hijacked airplanes. Some dreaded going over bridges or passing through tunnels. Many found themselves jumpy for weeks. A siren going off, an airplane flying too low or too fast, or any loud noise would cause a physical reaction.

For many, stress was exacerbated by the fact that they couldn't escape from it for even a moment. This has been especially true for the journalists who live in or near New York City. Part of the problem is that the Twin Towers were taken-for-granted landmarks. Many steered themselves around the city by looking to see where they were in relation to the towers. Losing a landmark is tough enough without having it ripped apart by terrorists.

There also was the terrible loss of life and the desperation of the friends and relatives who were so suddenly left behind. The almost complete lack of survivors among the rubble was a horrible thing for everyone. Although they had witnessed it, many still hoped there would be stories of survivors miraculously pulled from air pockets or vehicles. No one was prepared for the complete destruction of the towers and the people left in them.

So how did these journalists cope? Although every news organization was very supportive and quick to bring in grief counselors and trauma experts, very few of these women took advantage of group meetings, and some even found attempts to help them somewhat irritating at times. Yet they all had some way to sort and work through their feelings. Most immediately turned to family and friends. Some also formed stronger bonds with colleagues because they had gone through the experience together. Some threw themselves into work and focused on what needed to be done rather than what could not be fixed or changed. Doing things to help others and developing a stronger sense of community eased the pain for others.

Some did seek professional help, but usually with counselors or psychologists with whom they were already acquainted. In the past, journalists and others have been socialized to think that asking for help with emotional distress is a sign of weakness. Although none of the women profiled expressed this belief, they clearly preferred to grieve in private or away from the workplace. Today, the need for journalists to get trauma counseling is recognized.

Almost everyone said that at some point they had a good cry. Generally, they did not think it was wrong or detrimental for them to express their emotions and empathize with the survivors and grieving family members and friends. They allowed themselves to feel the pain and the loss and then to get it out as much as they could. Still, that reaction was mostly done in private, because they didn't want it to interfere with their ability to do their jobs.

Some experienced a strange sort of guilt, sometimes described as survivor's guilt. They were alive when so many had perished. They could go home to or call nervous relatives when so many others could not. They were very happy to be alive, but they were changed by the mere fact that they survived.

Some also had moments of regret. Some didn't get to cover the story as much as they would have liked. Others thought they could have done a better job or gotten a better picture, in spite of the wonderful work they did.

Doing their jobs on that terrible day and in the days that followed was very therapeutic for these women. Either they felt more focused, or they saw it as a way to help their country, their family, their friends—and themselves—cope with circumstances beyond the experience of most Americans. Some of them felt a new affirmation of why they are journalists and that what they do is important.

The women reporting from Ground Zero continue a long tradition of human and journalistic strength in the face of adversity—of calm, compassionate, and complete coverage in the face of unrelenting pressures and unprecedented circumstances. For all of them, the details and emotions of that day came pouring out to us. The day is engraved in their memories as if it were yesterday. Many feel grateful to have had meaningful work to do that day—"something to do that was useful to other people."

Some of those closest to Ground Zero remain troubled by what they experienced. Some have difficulty recalling the sequence of events that day, because their visual world was literally transformed by a storm of ash and debris that left once-familiar surroundings coated in a thick layer of gray "fuzz." *Newsday's* Susan Harrigan told us, "I can't 'tell' this story in the sense of giving it form—it sort of takes me over when I start. That's why stuff gets out of sequence. Talking with you was really helpful. I've realized that what something like this does is take a snapshot of one's character, for better or worse." According to WUSA's Lesli Foster, "It was actually great to communicate it all. I really haven't talked about my experience in detail." CNN's Elizabeth Cohen said, "I'm so glad it'll be in print to show my daughters someday."

For most of these women, their interviews for this book constituted the first time they had recounted the majority of their experiences that day in detail. Remarkably, all the women who were in New York when the attacks occurred have two really clear memories from September 11. One is that it was a "glorious" day with clear blue skies and warm weather that beckoned to everyone to come outside and enjoy being alive. The very beauty of that day made the attacks more surreal and more horrible in contrast.

The second clear memory is of the silence. Even the few who described the thunderous sounds that accompanied the attacks and the tower collapses also remembered the silence that followed. Somehow that silence seemed to forever memorialize the loss of life and the loss of something that was uniquely New York and uniquely American at the same time. The towers are gone, and so is American complacency.

The women agreed that it was useful for them to talk about the experience, and they were honest about how difficult and emotional it was for them. They don't consider themselves heroes, but clearly they are. At great personal risk they did what they could. They told the stories of September 11, 2001.

NOTE

1. Photojournalist William Biggart was the only journalist known to have been killed while covering the terrorist attacks. Six broadcast engineers who worked in the World Trade Center towers died when the buildings collapsed, and television commentator Barbara Olson died as a passenger on Flight 77 when it crashed into the Pentagon.

Appendix A

Biographies

Rose Arce has been a producer in the CNN New York bureau for three years. She came to CNN from CBS, where she was a planning editor. She began her television career at WCBS-TV in New York, covering the 1993 World Trade Center bombing and winning two New York Emmys for spot news and investigative reporting. Prior to that she was at New York *Newsday*, where she shared a Pulitzer Prize with colleagues for a subway crash story. She studied liberal arts and politics at Barnard College (affiliated with Columbia University).

Mika Brzezinski has been a correspondent for the *CBS Evening News* since September 5, 2001. Prior to that time, she was a host at MSNBC for sixteen months, the overnight anchor of *CBS News Up to the Minute* for three years, and an anchor/reporter at Hartford (Connecticut) station WFSB-TV for seven years. Mika earned a bachelor's degree in English at Williams College in Williamstown, Massachusetts. She was born in New York City and is the daughter of Zbigniew Brzezinski, national security adviser in the Carter administration.

Elizabeth Cohen is a medical correspondent for CNN's Health and Medical Unit. Her reports air throughout CNN news programs and on the weekly medical news show *Your Health*, which airs on the weekends on CNN/U.S. as well as CNN International. Elizabeth has received several awards for her work. In 1997, her coverage of the Phen-Fen diet drug earned her a first-place award in the American Medical Association's International Health and Medical Film Competition (now known as the FREDDIE Awards). She was a finalist in those awards in 1998 and 2000. She also is the recipient of the 1997 Russell L. Cecil Medical Journalism Award in the television category. Before coming to CNN in 1991, Elizabeth was associate producer of *Green Watch*, an environmental show on WLVI-TV in Boston. Before working in television, she was a newspaper reporter for States News Service in Washington, D.C., and for the *Times Union* in Albany, New York, where she won a

Hearst Award. A winner of the outstanding alumna award from Columbia College in New York, Elizabeth received a bachelor's degree in history in 1987. She earned a master's degree in public health from Boston University in 1992.

Ann Compton is now covering her sixth president for ABC News. In 1974, she was the first woman to be named a full-time White House correspondent by a network news organization and was one of the youngest correspondents ever to receive the assignment. Ann was also ABC News chief House of Representatives correspondent from February 1987 to January 1989. Twice Ann has been invited to serve as a panelist on the presidential campaign debates, in 1988 and 1992. During the 1980 political campaign, Ann covered the presidential campaign of independent candidate John Anderson. A White House correspondent during the 1976 election year, she was also one of ABC News's four floor reporters at the Republican and Democratic conventions. On election night, she anchored ABC News's coverage of the gubernatorial races. During her years as a White House correspondent, Ann has traveled to all fifty states and across Europe, the Middle East, South America, Africa, and Asia, with presidents, vice presidents, and first ladies.

Ann was born in Chicago. Her broadcast career began in Roanoke, Virginia, where during her junior year at Hollins College she was an intern at WDBJ-TV. She spent her first summer after graduation covering the major flooding from Hurricane Camille during the daylight hours, rushing back to the studio each night to anchor the *Eleven O'Clock Report*. After a few months' leave to pursue a journalism fellowship at the Washington Journalism Center, Ann moved to Richmond and established a state capital bureau for WDBJ-TV. In 1987, Ann chaired the Radio Television Correspondents' Association, the governing board for 2,500 broadcasters covering Washington, D.C. She was a founding member of the board of the Freedom Forum Center for Media Studies in New York City. Also that year, she received the JANUS Award for her report "Tax Shelter," which aired on *Nightline*. She won the 1987 Outstanding Mother of the Year award from the National Mother's Day Organization in New York City. In June 2001, Ann was inducted into the Hall of Fame of the Society of Professional Journalists in Washington, D.C. Ann lives in Washington, D.C., with her husband and their three sons and one daughter.

Gabrielle DeRose joined KDKA-TV, the CBS affiliate in Pittsburgh, in January 2001 as coanchor of the weekend evening newscasts. She reports during the week for the five and six o'clock news. A 1988 graduate of Penn State University, Gabrielle has a bachelor's degree in broadcast journalism and a minor in psychology. She also studied European media during the spring semester of 1987 in Manchester, England. Gabrielle began her television career in 1988 in Altoona, Pennsylvania, as an announcer and master control operator for WATM-TV, the ABC affiliate, and WWCP-TV. A year later, she moved to WTAJ-TV, the CBS affiliate in Altoona, as an anchor, reporter, and producer. She spent eleven years there, the last seven anchoring the 5, 6, and 11 P.M. news, before moving to KDKA.

Amy Eddings was the news director and morning news anchor at WFUV–New York for almost four years before she came to WNYC in 1997. She's a frequent contributor to such National Public Radio programs as *On the Media* and *Living on Earth*. Like many radio journalists in New York, Amy got her start as a general assignment reporter for the award-winning newsroom at WBAI–New York. Before venturing into radio, Amy wrote off-off-off-Broadway theater and dance reviews.

Rehema Ellis joined NBC News as a general assignment correspondent, based in New York, in December 1993. She had been a news anchor at WHDH-TV in Boston working on weekend newscasts and *Urban Update*, WHDH-TV's weekly half-hour news broadcast, since 1990. She has a graduate degree in journalism from Columbia University and a bachelor's degree from Simmons College. She worked on her neighborhood newspaper while she was in college.

Miriam Falco was born in West Berlin to a German mother and American father. She attended German-American elementary and high schools in the divided city. After high school, she moved to the United States and attended Kutztown University in Pennsylvania, just twenty miles from where her dad's family lives in Allentown, Pennsylvania. In 1988, after a full-time internship at CNN's Washington bureau during her senior year of college, Miriam moved to Atlanta, where she began her career at CNN's global headquarters as an entry-level videojournalist. After two years, and during the Persian Gulf War, she was editing videotape and line-producing for CNN's *Crossfire* and *Larry King Live* programs. Then she moved into producing newscasts. The genocide in Rwanda, the O. J. Simpson murder trial, the bombing of the Murrah Federal Building in Oklahoma City, and the death of Princess Diana—all were covered in newscasts during Miriam's tenure as a producer, executive producer, and supervising producer. At the end of 1999, Miriam switched to covering medical news as a senior producer in CNN's medical unit, primarily working with correspondent Elizabeth Cohen. Stem cell research, human cloning, cancer research, gene therapy, mad cow disease, and obesity are some of the stories covered by the Falco-Cohen team.

Beth Fertig began her journalism career as the arts editor for the *Michigan Daily*, the student newspaper at the University of Michigan. She also worked as a deejay for the student radio station and completed an internship at *Spin* magazine. She worked for a chain of suburban newspapers in Boston as a beat reporter before earning a master's degree in social sciences at the University of Chicago. An economic recession prevented a return to print journalism, so she began freelancing and volunteering for *Monitor Radio*, a public radio show produced by the *Christian Science Monitor*. She eventually moved to the *Monitor's* New York bureau and worked for a weekly newspaper. She freelanced for NPR, *Marketplace*, and WNYC's sister station, WBGO, in Newark, New Jersey. She also undertook freelance projects for WNYC Radio and began full-time employment there in 1995.

Lesli Foster joined *9 News* at WUSA-TV in Washington, D.C., in January 2001 as a reporter. She covers stories from all over the Washington, D.C., metro area during the 5 A.M., 6 A.M., and noon newscasts and became the weekend morning anchor in March 2002. Some Baltimore-area viewers may remember Lesli from WBAL-TV, where she was a reporter covering crime and other general assignments during much of 2000. Prior to her work in Baltimore, Lesli was an anchor/reporter for WEYI, the NBC affiliate in Flint, Michigan. Although Lesli grew up in Detroit, Michigan, she is very familiar with the Washington area, as she received a degree in broadcast journalism from Howard University's School of Communications.

Charlotte H. Hall is a *Newsday* vice president and managing editor, responsible for news coverage. She joined *Newsday* in 1981 and previously served as copy chief, metropolitan editor in Queens, Nassau editor, Washington news editor, and assistant managing editor for Long Island. She also spent two years as *Newsday*'s marketing director. Charlotte is on the board of directors of the American Society of Newspaper Editors (ASNE) and is a member of the Newspaper Association of America and the International Women's Media Foundation. She has served as chair of the ASNE Diversity Committee and continues to be active in diversity efforts at *Newsday* and in the newspaper industry. In recognition of her initiatives on diversity, Charlotte received the Tribune Values Award, one of the company's top two awards. She is currently serving as coeditor of *The American Editor*. Under her overall direction, *Newsday* reporters have won numerous national and regional prizes for reporting excellence, including the Pulitzer Prize for investigative reporting. She has served twice as a Pulitzer juror and has chaired the Pulitzer breaking news panel. Charlotte began her newspaper career as a reporter at the Ridgewood (N.J.) Newspapers. She subsequently held various editing posts at the *Bergen (N.J.) Record*, the *Boston Herald-American*, and the *Washington Star*. She received her B.A. from Kalamazoo College in Michigan and her M.A. in English from the University of Chicago. She serves on the Kalamazoo College Board of Trustees.

Susan Harrigan grew up in a small town—Colebrook, New Hampshire. She attended Connecticut College for Women and earned a B.A. in history in 1966. She spent her junior year at Princeton University, specializing in Russian. She worked at *Time* magazine as a researcher, went to Vietnam in 1968 and 1969 as a freelance reporter, and was a press aide for Senator Edmund Muskie when he made his run for the presidency in 1970–1972. Susan worked in TV for two years at a small station, WKBN, in Youngstown, Ohio. Then she worked at the *Akron-Beacon Journal* as a general assignment reporter and as a reporter for the *Toronto Star*. She was a Sloan Fellow in economics at Princeton, worked at the *Miami Herald*, and worked at the *Wall Street Journal* from 1978 until 1981. She then had a daughter and stopped working in newspapers for a while. She earned an M.B.A. from the State University of New York–Binghamton and began working at *Newsday* in 1986, covering banking, insurance, and Wall Street. Her family still publishes a small newspaper in New Hampshire.

Beth A. Keiser majored in psychology and mass communication at the University of Miami. An internship at the *Miami Herald* led to freelancing photography jobs for the *Herald* and the Associated Press. She began working at the *Herald* full-time in 1991, assigned to the Broward County edition. She began working for the Associated Press in the Chicago bureau in 1994 and was transferred to the New York bureau in 2000.

Emily Longnecker earned a bachelor's degree in English from Allegheny College in Meadville, Pennsylvania, and a master's degree in broadcast journalism from American University in Washington, D.C. WTAJ is her second on-air job. Her first was as a reporter and anchor in Elmira, New York, at the ABC affiliate, WENY-TV. She began working in the news business as a field producer in Washington, D.C.

Cynthia McFadden's television career combines her knowledge of broadcasting and law. Prior to joining ABC as legal affairs correspondent in 1994, Cynthia was an anchor and senior producer at the Courtroom Television Network. She holds a law degree from Columbia University School of Law and has covered hundreds of legal events, including the rape trial of William Kennedy Smith, the murder trial of Lyle and Erik Menendez, the trial of Los Angeles police officers charged with beating Rodney King, the sanity hearing of murderer Jeffrey Dahmer, the hearings on the nomination of Clarence Thomas to the Supreme Court, and the murder case against O. J. Simpson. Her reports have aired on ABC's *World News Tonight, Good Morning, America, PrimeTime Live, Nightline, Day One,* and *20/20.* Cynthia has produced and anchored special programming for Lifetime Television, PBS's *Frontline,* and Great Britain's Channel Four. She has been honored with numerous awards for programs she has produced, including the Emmy, the George Foster Peabody Award, the Ohio State Award, Silver Gavels from the American Bar Association, and the Blue Ribbon of the American Film Festival. A native of Maine, Cynthia graduated Phi Beta Kappa and summa cum laude from Bowdoin College in Brunswick, Maine.

Elizabeth McNeil is *People* magazine's New York deputy bureau chief. She has been with *People* since 1988, starting in the San Francisco bureau. She graduated from the University of California–Berkeley and started freelancing for *People*'s San Francisco office. She moved to New York, working as the newsdesk editor before becoming a correspondent in 1996.

Kerry Nolan began her career as a producer at a major rock station in Boston, where she also wrote and performed in a radio comedy troupe. A stint as a punk rock deejay convinced her that she needed to broaden her horizons, and she spent several years away from radio. The lure of the open mike and an urge to tell stories led her to WNYC Radio, where she has been local host of *Weekend All Things Considered* since 1994. She has been a correspondent for the financial news show *Marketplace* and is a regular contributor to NPR News. She is also a die-hard romantic when it comes to Manhattan. She's from New Jersey, but she's a New Yorker at heart.

Suzanne Plunkett grew up in Minneapolis, Minnesota, and studied photojournalism at Boston University. She began her photojournalism career as a photo assistant at the Associated Press in Boston, followed by staff photographer jobs at the *Lowell Sun* and the *Jersey Journal*. She was a freelancer before being hired by the Associated Press in 1999. She works in AP's New York bureau.

Susan Sachs came to the *New York Times* in 1998 and is currently a correspondent on the Metro desk. She covers immigration issues and reports extensively from the Middle East, primarily from Cairo. She previously was a reporter at *Newsday*, where she spent five years in the Middle East and three years in Russia.

Gulnara Samoilova picked up a camera when she was fifteen. In her native Russia, she was a photography teacher and specialized in fine arts photography. She earned a diploma in photography while in Russia and holds a certificate from the International Center of Photography. In the United States for ten years, she has worked for the Associated Press as a photo retoucher for eight and a half years. She continues to do her own fine arts photography projects in both Russia and the United States. She first came to the United States when her photographs were included in a traveling show of the work of fourteen young Russian photographers. She was awarded first prize in the World Press photo contest, People in the News singles division, for her photograph of survivors of the World Trade Center collapse.

Amy Sancetta graduated from Ohio State University in 1981 with a B.A. in history. She has taken pictures since she was in high school, shooting sports for her local weekly newspaper. She began freelancing for the Associated Press while in college. She first worked for the *Columbus Dispatch* and then was hired by the AP in 1983. She was based in Philadelphia until 1994, when she became the AP's national enterprise photographer. She now lives in Chagrin Fall, Ohio.

Madge Stager is a born-and-bred New Yorker who graduated from the High School of Art and Design. She has been with the Associated Press since 1972. She began with a summer job in the photo library and worked up to a management position as the Enterprise photo editor in the AP photo department.

Fannie Weinstein has worked at *People* magazine in various capacities since the Persian Gulf War. She first worked for *People* in the Detroit bureau as a stringer/freelancer until 1994, when the bureau closed. She was promoted to special correspondent and worked for the Chicago bureau, covering the Midwest (seventeen states). In 1997, she was hired as staff correspondent and moved to the Miami bureau. She joined the New York bureau in January 2000, where she is a staff correspondent. Prior to working for *People,* she was a feature staff writer at the *Detroit News* and a freelancer for a number of national magazines. Her area of expertise is crime reporting.

Judy Woodruff, an award-winning, thirty-year veteran of broadcast journalism who joined CNN in 1993, is CNN's prime anchor and senior correspondent. She anchors *Inside Politics with Judy Woodruff.* Before joining CNN, Judy was the chief Washington correspondent for *The MacNeil/Lehrer NewsHour.* From 1984 to 1990, she anchored public television's award-winning weekly documentary series *Frontline with Judy Woodruff.* Before joining the *NewsHour,* Judy was chief Washington, D.C., correspondent for NBC's *Today.* She also served as NBC News's White House correspondent from 1977 to 1982, covering both the Carter and Reagan administrations. Woodruff joined NBC News as a general assignment reporter based in Atlanta in 1975. From 1970 to 1974, she was a correspondent for WAGA-TV, the CBS affiliate in Atlanta, where she reported on the state legislature for five years and anchored the noon and evening news. She majored in political science at Duke University.

Appendix B

Dart Center for Journalism and Trauma

The Dart Center for Journalism and Trauma (www.dartcenter.org), a resource center and program developer for students, educators, journalists, and news organizations interested in the intersection of journalism and trauma issues, at the University of Washington School of Communications, has identified several forms of posttraumatic stress disorders (PtSDs).

According to the center, about one in twelve adults experiences PTSD at some time during their lifetime (women, 10.4 percent; men, 5 percent; Kessler, Sonnega, Bromet, Hughes, and Nelson 1995). Women are twice as likely as men to develop PTSD following exposure to traumatic events. Emotional, cognitive, physical, and interpersonal effects can include a combination of the following:

Emotional Effects

- Shock
- Terror
- Irritability
- Blame
- Anger
- Guilt
- Grief or sadness
- Emotional numbing
- Helplessness
- Loss of pleasure derived from familiar activities
- Difficulty feeling happy
- Difficulty feeling loved

Cognitive Effects

- Impaired concentration
- Impaired decision-making ability
- Memory impairment
- Disbelief
- Confusion
- Nightmares
- Decreased self-esteem
- Decreased self-efficacy
- Self-blame
- Intrusive thoughts, memories
- Dissociation (e.g., tunnel vision, dreamlike or "spacey" feeling)

Physical Effects

- Fatigue, exhaustion
- Insomnia
- Cardiovascular strain
- Startle response
- Hyperarousal
- Increased physical pain
- Reduced immune response
- Headaches
- Gastrointestinal upset
- Decreased appetite
- Decreased libido
- Vulnerability to illness

Interpersonal Effects

- Increased relational conflict
- Social withdrawal
- Reduced relational intimacy
- Alienation
- Impaired work performance
- Impaired school performance
- Decreased satisfaction
- Distrust
- Externalization of blame
- Externalization of vulnerability
- Feeling abandoned, rejected
- Overprotectiveness.

One specific form of posttraumatic stress that is applicable to the journalists covering the events of 9/11 is compassion stress. Charles Figley (1995) coined this term as a "nonclinical, nonpathological" way to characterize the stress of helping or wanting to help a trauma survivor. The symptoms include the following:

- Helplessness
- Confusion
- Isolation.

Figley defines another form, compassion fatigue, as "a state of exhaustion and dysfunction, biologically, physiologically, and emotionally, as a result of prolonged exposure to compassion stress" (Figley 1995, 34). Vicarious traumatization, defined by Pearlman and Saakvitne (1995), also can result when reporters are repeatedly talking with people who have undergone traumatic experiences and are exhibiting symptoms resulting from the trauma. A number of possible behavioral changes might result from vicarious traumatization:

- Becoming judgmental of others
- Tuning out
- Experiencing a reduced sense of connection with loved ones and colleagues
- Feeling cynicism, anger, loss of hope, meaning
- Engaging in rescue fantasy/overinvolvement/taking on others' problems
- Developing overly rigid, strict boundaries
- Becoming more protective, as a result of decreased sense of the safety of loved ones
- Avoiding social contact
- Avoiding work contact.

DART RESOURCES FOR REPORTERS
CONCERNING POSTTRAUMATIC STRESS

Dart Center for Journalism and Trauma
University of Washington
School of Communications
102 Communications
Box 353740
Seattle, Washington 98195-3740
Phone: (206) 616-3223
Fax: (206) 543-9285
E-mail: uwdart@u.washington.edu

Online Resources

Dart Center for Journalism and Trauma Web Site
www.dartcenter.org

International Society for Traumatic Stress Studies
www.istss.org

The Dart Award for Excellence in Reporting on Victims of Violence
www.dartcenter.org/award.html

PTSD 101, by Frank Ochberg
www.dartcenter.org/Resource/resource_ptsd101_story1.html

Role-Playing and Interactive Drama in Teaching and Learning
www.dartcenter.org/Resource/resource_UWonCue2.html

Newscoverage Unlimited
dartcenter.org/coverage_unlimited.html

National Center for PTSD
www.ncptsd.org/index.html

Books and Articles

Allen, Jon. *Coping with Trauma: A Guide to Self-Understanding.* Washington, D.C.: American Psychiatric Press, 1995.

Bloom, Sandra L. *Creating Sanctuary.* New York: Routledge, 1997.

Bloom, Sandra L., and Michael Reichert. *Bearing Witness: Violence and Collective Responsibility.* New York: Haworth, 1998.

Coté, William, and Roger Simpson. *Covering Violence: A Guide to Ethical Reporting about Victims and Trauma.* New York: Columbia University Press, 2000.

Figley, C. R., ed. *Compassion Fatigue: Coping with Secondary Traumatic Stress Disorder in Those Who Treat the Traumatized.* New York: Brunner/Mazel, 1995.

Herman, Judith. *Trauma and Recovery.* New York: Basic Books, 1992.

Kessler, R. C., A. Sonnega, E. Bromet, M. Hughes, and C. B. Nelson. *Archives of General Psychiatry* 52, no. 12 (December 1995): 1048–60.

Matsakis, Aphrodite. *I Can't Get over It: A Handbook for Trauma Survivors.* Oakland, Calif.: New Harbinger, 1982.

Pearlman, L. A., and K. W. Saakvitne. *Trauma and the Therapist: Countertransference and Vicarious Traumatization in Psychotherapy with Incest Survivors.* New York: Norton, 1995, 295–316.

Sapolsky, Robert M. *Why Zebras Don't Get Ulcers: An Updated Guide to Stress, Stress-Related Diseases and Coping.* New York: Freeman, 1998.

Shengold, Leonard. *Soul Murder: The Effects of Childhood Abuse and Deprivation.* New Haven, Conn.: Yale University Press, 1989.

Stamm, B. H., ed. *Secondary Traumatic Stress: Self-Care Issues for Clinicians, Researchers, and Educators.* Lutherville, Md.: Sidran, 1995.

van der Kolk, Bessel A., Alexander C. McFarlane, and Lars Weisaeth, eds. *Traumatic Stress: The Effects of Overwhelming Experience on Mind, Body, and Society.* New York: Guilford, 1996.

"Violence." *Nieman Reports* 50, no. 3 (Fall 1998): 4–38.

Index

ABC News, 129–39
Adschiew, Buba, 34
advice to reporters, 113, 150, 181
Afghanistan, 56, 128
Air Force One, 5, 135–39
All Things Considered, 11
Altoona, Pennsylvania, 163–67
Amanpour, Christiane, 14, 56
American Airlines: Flight 11, 3, 4, 169;
    Flight 77, 3–5; Flight 587, 28, 48
American Red Cross, 27, 46, 144, 160, 164,
    165
Andrews Air Force Base, 139
Angelucci, William (Bill), 34
anthrax threat, 15, 55, 56; ABC, 132; CNN,
    48; NBC, 39, 48
anti-Americanism, 63
Antkowiak, Jennifer, 160, 161
Aon Corporation, 13
Arce, Rose, 41–49, 181, 187
Arlington, Virginia, 5, 136, 144
Armory (family center), 132, 148, 149,
    154–58
Army Air Corps bomber, 115
Associated Press coverage, 65–107
ATF (Bureau of Alcohol, Tobacco, and Fire-
    arms), 160

Bank of New York, 117, 121
Barksdale Air Force Base (Shreveport, Loui-
    siana), 6, 136, 137

Beamer, Todd, 4
Beasley, Kevin, 17
Bedingfield, Sid, 51, 52
Bellevue Hospital, 60, 61, 129, 130, 148
Berecky, Mary, 159
Bernstein, Jim, 118
Beth Israel Hospital, 102
Binch, Devon, 129, 130
Boeing 757-200, 3, 4
Boeing 767-200, 3
Bombay, 132
bomb threats, 141, 145
Boston, Massachusetts, 3, 4
Brokaw, Tom, 33
Brooklyn Bridge, 32, 118, 123
Brzezinski, Mika, 109–13, 187
Bureau of Alcohol, Tobacco and Firearms
    (ATF), 160
Bush, George W., 4–6, 53, 135–39, 155
Bush, Laura, 5

Cambria County, 163, 165
Camp David, Maryland, 139
Canada, 6
Canadian Broadcast Company (CBC), 11
candlelight vigils, 143, 161
Cantor Fitzgerald, 13, 70, 116
Cape Cod, Massachusetts, 4
Capello, Dean, 19
Capitol Hill, 5, 6, 51–56, 141, 142

Card, Andrew (chief of staff), 135
CBC (Canadian Broadcast Company), 11
CBS News, 109–13
cell phone service, 138
Chambers Street bridge, 170
Channel 7 (NYC), 110, 111
Chase Bank, 123
Chelsea Piers, 131
Cheney, Dick (vice president), 5, 138
Chinatown, 120
City Department of Environmental Protection, 118
City Hall Park, 74
Clayson, Jane, 141
CNN, 4, 15, 147–58, 163; Judy Woodruff, 51–57; Rose Arce, 41–49
Cohen, Elizabeth, 55, 147–55, 184, 187
communication problems, 127
Compton, Ann, 135–39, 188

Dart Center for Journalism and Trauma, 195, 197, 198
Daschle, Tom, 5
debris cloud, 30–33, 44, 65–66, 75, 83, 111, 117, 170
Department of Justice, 144
DeRose, Gabrielle, 159–62, 188, 189
digital technology and photography, 105, 106
Dwyer, Jim, 61

Early Show, 112
Eddings, Amy, 23–28, 189
Edwards, Bob, 11, 12
Eftimiades, Maria, 173
Ellis, Rehema, 29–40, 189
Emergency Command Center, NYC, 19, 129
Emma E. Booker Elementary School, 4–5, 135
Empire State Building, 115
Engine 10, 95
Enterprise photo desk, 103, 104, 106
experience and reporting, 180, 181

FAA (Federal Aviation Administration), 4–6
Falco, Miriam, 147, 151–58, 189

false leads, 13
FBI (Federal Bureau of Investigation), 12, 144, 160, 164, 166
Federal Bureau of Investigation. *See* FBI
Feldman, Mike, 100–103
FEMA (Federal Emergency Management Agency), 46, 160
Fertig, Beth, 17–21, 189, 190
fighter jets, 4, 5, 136, 170
firefighters, 32, 35, 44–46, 92, 111; deaths, 38
Fleischer, Ari (press secretary), 137, 138
Force Protection Condition DELTA, 6
Foster, Lesli, 141–46, 184, 190
Four World Trade Center, 24
frame grabs, 106
Friendly, Fred, 134
Fulton Fish Market, 118, 123

Gallant, Rich, 118
Giuliani, Rudy (NYC mayor), 19, 21, 27
Glick, Jeremy, 4
Good Morning America, 131, 139
Grand Central Station, 60
Greenspan, Alan, 5
Greenwich Village, 120
Ground Zero, 7, 15, 26, 34, 46; defined, x
Gumbell, Bryant, 141

Hall, Charlotte, 125–28, 190
Harrigan, Susan, 7, 115–23, 125, 184, 190, 191
Hastert, Dennis, 5
Headline News, 149
health problems from air, 47, 86, 105, 132, 144, 150
Hevesi, Alan, 23
Heyward, Andrew, 109
hijackings, 3–5, 12
Hilan, Mark, 17, 18, 20
historic images, ix, x
Huffman, Suzanne, 205, 206
Hughes, Karen, 137
Hurricane Andrew, 95

"I Knew We Couldn't Outrun It," 122, 123
International Women's Media Foundation, 54
Isaacson, Walter, 52

Jennings, Peter, 15, 131, 133, 138, 139
Judge, Father Mychal, 171
jumpers, number of, 169

KDKA-TV (Pittsburgh), 159–62
Keiser, Beth A., 89–98, 191
Kinstle, Carol, 147, 151
Kowal, Jessica, 125, 126

Lack, Andrew, 39
Ladder 10, 95
Langley Air Force Base (Virginia), 5
Lin, Carol, 56
Little Italy, 120
Logan International Airport, 3
Long Island, 125–28
Longnecker, Emily, 163–67, 191
Los Angeles, 3, 6, 119
"The Lost," 127

Manhattan, 60
Marine One, 139
McCune, Marianne, 20
McFadden, Cynthia, 129–34, 191
McKinnon, Rebecca, 56
McNeil, Elizabeth, 169–72, 191
medical personnel, 12, 13, 44
mental health workers, 38, 39
Metropolitan United Methodist Church, 143
Mexico, 6, 132
Middle East, 63, 64
military police, 144
Millennium Hotel, 83, 93
misinformation, 13
morgues, 46, 154
Morning Edition, 11, 18
MSNBC, 31
Murrah Federal Building, 161, 162
Muslims, 166
Myers, Wayne, 142

National Guard, 96
National Public Radio. *See* NPR
NBC News, 29, 39
Newark International Airport, 4
Newark, New Jersey, 4
Newsday, 7, 41, 126, 190, 191; Charlotte Hall, 125–28; impact from tragedy on, 128; Susan Harrigan, 115–23
New York City: amount of coverage, 53; sequence of events, 3–6
New York City response, 13, 14
New York Downtown Hospital, 119
New York Federal Reserve Bank, 118, 123
New York Stock Exchange, 5, 6, 14, 119
New York Times, 59–64, 80
New York University Medical Center, 147, 153, 154
Nightline, 131
Nightly News, 33
Nikon cameras, 65, 74
Nino's Restaurant, 171
Noble, Mike, 109
Nolan, Kerry, 11–15, 191, 192
NORAD (North American Aerospace Defense Command), 4–6
north tower. *See* One World Trade Center
NPR (National Public Radio), 11–13, 20, 21, 25
NY1, 100

Office of Emergency Management, 14
Offutt Air Force Base (Nebraska), 6, 138
Oklahoma City bombing, 95, 96, 148, 152, 162
Olson, Barbara, 4, 139
Olson, Theodore (solicitor general), 4
One World Trade Center (north tower), 4, 6, 77, 91, 118
Otis Air National Guard Base, 4

Pataki, George, 15
Pearl, Daniel, 64
PEMA (Pennsylvania Emergency Management Agency), 160
Pennsylvania, 4, 52, 53, 159–67
Pennsylvania State Police, 160
Pentagon, 5, 51–53, 141–46

People magazine, 169–75
Peterson, Gordon, 141
photographers, 59, 60, 80, 82, 97. *See also* Keiser, Beth A.; Plunkett, Suzanne; Sancetta, Amy
photograph postings, 37, 79, 127
photographs, 5, 76, 84, 94; and digital technology, 105, 106
Pile, Bill, 100–102
Pitts, Byron, 111, 112
Pittsburgh, Pennsylvania, 6, 159–62
Plunkett, Suzanne, 65–71, 107, 192
pool report coverage, 137, 138
posttraumatic stress, 182–84, 195–97
Potato Chip (rubble), 91
Powell, Colin, 5
prayer services, 143, 161, 162
Press Corps. *See* White House Press Corps
PrimeTime Live, 129, 131
PS 89, 111

Rather, Dan, 111, 112
Ratner, Vic, 138
reactions to disaster, 65, 66, 112, 116, 153–55, 169
Reagan, Ronald, 53
Red Cross. *See* American Red Cross
Reeves Municipal Center, 142
reporting routine, 116
Rice, Condoleeza (National Security Advisor), 5, 135, 137, 138
Ross, Sonya, 137
Rumsfeld, Donald (Secretary of Defense), 5

Sachs, Susan, 59–64, 192
Salvation Army, 143, 149, 164
Samoilova, Gulnara, 81–87, 102–4, 107, 192
Sancetta, Amy, 73–80, 101–4, 107, 182, 192
San Francisco, 4, 6
Sarasota, Florida, 4–6, 53, 116
Schweiker, Mark (Pennsylvania governor), 161
Schmittle, John, 164
Sears Tower, 6
Senate Office Building, 55, 56

Seven Springs Mountain Resort, 165
Seven World Trade Center, 14, 35, 91, 120
Shiffman, Ken, 147
Somerset County, Pennsylvania, 6, 136, 160, 163, 165
South Tower. *See* Two World Trade Center
Space Needle, 6
Stager, Madge, 99–107, 181, 192
State Department, 141
Statter, Dave, 143
St. James Church, 119
St. Vincent's Medical Center, 131, 132, 154, 171
survivors, 13, 24, 32, 34, 171, 172
Susman, Tina, 128
Sylvester, Judith, 205

Taylor, Letta, 128
technology, role in news coverage, 181, 182
terrorists, and media, 166, 167
Time-Life, 85, 103, 171
time line of 9/11 events, 3–6
Today show, 36, 89
Toole, Mary Beth, 31
Tora Bora, 128
towers, impact from planes, 13, 43, 44, 73
Trans-America Pyramid, 6
Tribune Company, 119
Trinity Church, 123
Tuazon, Bernadette, 99–103
TWA Flight 800, 127, 152, 158
20/20, 131
Twin Towers, 4, 5, 53, 116
Two World Trade Center (south tower), 4, 6, 46, 74, 75

Union Station, 141
United Airlines, 164, 166; Flight 93, 4, 6, 159, 163; Flight 175, 3, 4
U.S. Postal Service, 55, 56
U.S. Strategic Air Command, 6, 138

Walker, Laura, 25
Wall Street, 13, 14, 121
Wallace, Carol, 171
Washington, D.C., 3, 6, 51, 141–46; Emergency Response, 142

Washington-Dulles International Airport, 3, 5

The Washington Post, 146

WCBS-TV, 41

Weekend Edition, 11

Weinstein, Fannie, 173–75, 192, 193

White House, 5, 6, 141, 142

White House Press Corps, 6, 135–39

Williams, Anthony (Washington, D.C., mayor), 142

Windows on the World, 13

WNYC Radio, 11–28

Woodruff, Judy, 51–57, 193

World News Tonight, 131

World Trade Center, 4–6, 45, 59; 1993 bombing, 41, 115

WTAJ-TV (Altoona), 159, 160, 163–67

WUSA-TV, 141–46

Yemen, 63, 64

About the Authors

Judith Sylvester is journalism area head and Huie-Dellmon professor for the Media Leaders Forum at the Manship School of Mass Communication at Louisiana State University in Baton Rouge. Born and raised in southwest Missouri, she was educated at Southwest Missouri State University (SMSU), where she received her undergraduate degree in education, and the University of Missouri (MU) School of Journalism, where she earned both her M.A. degree and Ph.D. She taught English and journalism in Missouri high schools for six years. She was the student newspaper adviser at Stephens College, a women's college in Columbia, Missouri, for a year and then spent three years as publicity coordinator in the Stephens College public relations department. She began collaborating on research projects with University of Missouri School of Journalism faculty members and eventually founded and ran the Media Research Bureau at MU for nine years. During that time, she conducted a number of research projects for media and medical institutions and was a pollster for the *St. Louis Post-Dispatch*. She joined the faculty of the Manship School of Mass Communication in 1994. Her book *Directing Health Messages toward African-Americans: Attitudes toward Healthcare and the Mass Media* was published in 1998. She has been journalism area head for six years, has taught research and mass communications courses, and has conducted research involving the civic journalism movement in the media, reaction to the O. J. Simpson murder trial, the Clinton-Lewinsky scandal, and a number of other timely issues in journalism. She also coordinates the research efforts of the Media Leaders Forum, which produces case studies for *Quill* magazine and conducts panel studies on current journalism topics. She currently has a grant to study behaviors and attitudes toward tobacco use among college students and the media messages that influence those behaviors and attitudes. She has two daughters, Jennifer and Janelle.

Suzanne Huffman is associate professor of journalism and broadcast journalism sequence head at Texas Christian University (TCU) in Fort Worth. She was born and raised in east Tennessee. A National Merit Scholar, she earned her B.A. at TCU, her M.A. from the University of Iowa, and her Ph.D. from the University of Missouri School of Journalism. She has reported, anchored, and produced news at commercial television stations in Cedar Rapids, Iowa; Santa Maria, California; and Tampa, Florida. She was reporting from the Kennedy Space Center for a network-affiliated television station when the space shuttle *Challenger* exploded soon after launch on January 28, 1986. Her academic research centers on the practice of broadcast journalism, and her research articles have been published in the *Journal of Broadcasting & Electronic Media* and other academic journals. She is coauthor with C. A. Tuggle and Forrest Carr of *Broadcast News Handbook: Writing, Reporting, and Producing* (2001) and is a contributing author to *Indelible Images: Women of Local Television* (2001).

Art Credits

Pages (209–11) are an extension of the copyright page.

Chapter 1
Photo, "The south tower begins to collapse," AP/WIDE WORLD PHOTOS. Reprinted with permission.
Map of Lower Manhattan: Philip Schwartzberg, Meridian Mapping.

Chapter 2
Photo of Kerry Nolan courtesy WYNC, New York Public Radio. Reprinted with permission.

Chapter 3
Photo of Beth Fertig courtesy WNYC, New York Public Radio. Reprinted with permission.

Chapter 4
Photo of Amy Eddings courtesy WYNC, New York Public Radio. Reprinted with permission.

Chapter 5
Photo of Rehema Ellis courtesy NBC News. Reprinted with permission.

Chapter 6
Photo of Rose Arce courtesy CNN, an AOL Time Warner company. Reprinted with permission.

Chapter 7
Photo of Judy Woodruff courtesy CNN, an AOL Time Warner company. Reprinted with permission.

Chapter 9
Photo of Suzanne Plunkett by Lonzo Cook. Reprinted with permission.

Chapter 10
Photo of Amy Sancetta courtesy Amy Sancetta. Reprinted with permission.
Photo, "New Yorkers escape the area of the collapsed World Trade Center towers,"
by Amy Sancetta, AP/WIDE WORLD PHOTOS. Reprinted with permission.

Chapter 11
Photo, self-portrait of Gulnara Samoilova, courtesy of Gulnara Samoilova.
Reprinted with permission.
Photo, "Survivors of the collapse of the World Trade Center towers make their way
amid debris," by Gulnara Samoilova, AP/WIDE WORLD PHOTOS. Reprinted
with permission.

Chapter 12
Photo of Beth A. Keiser, AP/WIDE WORLD PHOTOS. Reprinted with permission.
Photo, "A postcard of the World Trade Center towers is taped up in a damaged fire
station across the street from Ground Zero," by Beth A. Keiser, AP/WIDE
WORLD PHOTOS. Reprinted with permission.

Chapter 13
Photo of Madge Stager by Christoph Stager. Reprinted with permission.

Chapter 14
Photo of Mika Brzezinski by Craig Blankenhorn/CBS. © 2002 CBS Worldwide
Inc. All Rights Reserved.

Chapter 15
Photo of Susan Harrigan © Newsday, Inc. Reprinted with permission.

Chapter 16
Photo of Charlotte Hall © Newsday, Inc. Reprinted with permission.

Chapter 17
Photo of Cynthia McFadden by Steve Fenn. © 2002 ABC Photography. Reprinted
with permission.

Chapter 18
Photo of Ann Compton by Steve Fenn. © 2002 ABC Photography. Reprinted with
permission.

Chapter 19
Photo of Lesli Foster courtesy WUSA-TV. Reprinted with permission.

Chapter 20
Photo of Elizabeth Cohen by Kyle Christy, CNN 2002, an AOL Time Warner Company. Reprinted with permission.

Chapter 21
Photo of Miriam Falco by Kyle Christy, CNN 2002, an AOL Time Warner Company. Reprinted with permission.

Chapter 22
Photo of Gabrielle DeRose courtesy Gabrielle DeRose. Reprinted with permission.

Chapter 23
Photo of Emily Longnecker by Cecchine Photographic. Reprinted with permission.

Chapter 24
Photo of Elizabeth McNeil courtesy Elizabeth McNeil. Reprinted with permission.